Ryan Shaw expertly sets out the premise that
bilization will inspire the global church to eng
In fact, every Christian has a part in this gl
has something unique to bring to it. Shaw offers a compelling case for
rethinking global mobilization from Scripture and history, and from a
who's who of mobilizers around the world. —*Dr. Todd M. Johnson, Co-
Director, Center for the Study of Global Christianity, Gordon-Conwell
Theological Seminary*

The Church is stepping into a new landscape of global mission. This
new season demands new approaches and new perspectives in fulfilling the Great Commission. *Rethinking Global Mobilization* offers exactly
these. This is written for mission mobilizers like you and me. —*Dr.
Bambang Budijanto, General Secretary, Asia Evangelical Alliance*

With this book Ryan Shaw has done what no other writer previously
has—providing the Church with a theology of mission mobilization.
Journeying through all of Scripture, he has laid the biblical groundwork
and the justification for mission mobilization today. Shaw reminds us of
the basic truth that mission mobilization is the fuel of the mission movement itself, taking the reader a step further by explaining the importance
of mission mobilization movements. —*Dr. Marvin J. Newell, Executive
Director, Alliance for the Unreached*

Like the "men of Issachar," Ryan has discerned the times in *Rethinking
Global Mobilization* and revealed what needs to be done for the potential of the whole Church being unleashed for the great harvest. I strongly endorse *Rethinking Global Mobilization* as a tool calling the Church
to obedience and dedication in completing the Great Commission.
—*Reuben Ezemadu, Continental Coordinator, Movement for African
National Initiatives (MANI)*

You need to read this book! It's a broad-sweeping treatment of one of the most overlooked Kingdom contributions that the global body of Christ is called to live out—mission mobilization. Ryan gives this enigmatic topic the thorough treatment it deserves, and his content will help every believer and fellowship of believers become practically equipped to do their part in the essential, powerful mission mobilization movement of God on earth.—*Mark Stebbins, Mobilizer-at-large, The Navigators; Mission Advisor/Mobilization, Missio Nexus*

With the rise of the majority world mission movement, a comprehensive book on mission mobilization has finally arrived under a new missionary paradigm. *Rethinking Global Mobilization* dynamically combines biblical truth, historical analysis, missiological insights, and practical application as God's missionary people are sent and scattered into the world with the Gospel. —*David Ro, Regional Director – East Asia, Lausanne Movement*

This volume provides a thorough study of mission mobilization, bringing together conversations of the biblical foundation of mission with missionary practice through the ages. Attuned to the work of the Holy Spirit, *Rethinking Global Mobilization* presents a generation of missiological reflection on dynamic changes in the missionary movement. —*Dr. Douglas McConnell, Provost Emeritus and Senior Professor, Fuller Theological Seminary*

Ryan Shaw has written a compelling vision for mobilization out of the abundance of his calling as a global mobilizer, deep scriptural reflections, and personal fellowship with mobilizers around the world. He's pushing our boundaries of understanding mobilization, and mobilizers will find this book more than affirming and empowering as it lays the foundation for a theology of mobilization that is desperately needed for the local church. —*Sam Ngugi, Director of Mission Campaign Network*

Rethinking Global Mobilization addresses the fundamental activity of a mobilizer. It is filled with golden nuggets, helping produce healthy churches embracing God's call in mission. This is a great resource for church, seminary, and campus training programs. —*Jimmy R. Fundar, President, One Sending Body (sending arm of the Federation of Southern Baptist Conventions in the Philippines)*

Biblical, visionary, and prophetic, *Rethinking Global Mobilization* is a powerful paradigm shift for your local church. —*Rev. David P. Jacob, Director of the Center for Missionary Mobilization and Retention, Trinity Bible College and Graduation School*

Ryan Shaw is absolutely right: God is indeed birthing a focused global mission mobilization movement across the global church! There are four discipleship imperatives for the global Church: to be disciples, to make disciples, to multiply disciples, and to mobilize disciples. And *Rethinking Global Mobilization* is such a timely book in this strategic season for MOBILIZING DISCIPLES. Thanks, Ryan, for writing this important book! —*Edmund Chan, Founder and Leadership Mentor, Global Alliance of Intentional Disciplemaking Churches*

Rethinking Global Mobilization is a challenge to church and mission leaders to catch a new vision for global mission—a vision of local churches in the Christian south (Africa, Asia, Latin America, Oceania) ablaze to reach their own people groups, and the unreached within their reach. Shaw maps out strategy for making disciples and the fulfillment of the Great Commission, dependent upon the local, denominational, and even national churches catching this vision. —*Dr. Sherwood Lingenfelter, Senior Professor of Anthropology, Fuller Theological Seminary*

Rethinking Global Mobilization is a well-balanced, extensive biblical exposition and mission field exploration, taking many practical issues into consideration. Ryan Shaw provides clarity for global mobilization by correcting misrepresented truth, giving a fresh sense to terms frequently used in academic as well as mission modes. *Rethinking Global Mobilization* is a must-read for every mission and church leader. —*Dr. Wati Longkumer, General Secretary, India Missions Association (IMA); Head Chairman, Asia Missions Association (AMA)*

Mobilization, a term underprioritized precisely because it is, as Ryan makes a compelling and comprehensive case for, either misunderstood or largely ignored as foundational for the Church. Shaw's triune-rooted, historically reflective, and present-day-minded volume comes from both a personal and prophetic space. May all of us as the global Church have ears to hear. —*Scott White, Pastor of Global Outreach, Lake Avenue Church*

Rethinking Global Mobilization develops a biblical missiology of mobilization from the perspective of involving the whole Church in its priority call for local and global mission. Mission is not just for professionals, but anyone who wants to obey Jesus' call to people who do not have access to the Gospel. Very accurate and very challenging. —*Walter Pelegrina, Director, Area Training, COMIBAM International*

Nothing excites me more than to see the global church awakening to our God-given mission. Whereas we rediscovered the "priesthood" of the believer five hundred years ago in the Reformation, today God's people are embracing our "mission-hood" as message bearers. We need all hands on deck for the remaining task. Ryan Shaw has been on the leading edge of this final great wave of mission mobilization. I don't know anyone better positioned to point the way. —*Steve Richardson, President, Pioneers USA*

Rethinking Global Mobilization is a significant contribution providing deep understanding of mobilization. This is a burning issue for God and Ryan has echoed this truth well. Take this tool and blow your trumpet louder and louder, seeing hundreds of thousands of message bearer teams, from every nation, finishing the remaining task. —*Yonas Demeke, Founder and President, Ethiopian Youth Missions Movement*

Rethinking Global Mobilization provides a comprehensive look into the Bible and history on how God has mobilized His Church. It gives an excellent introduction to mobilization while providing deep insights to dive into and apply to our ministries. It's a challenge for us all to rethink global mobilization and our part in it. —*Christina Conti, Director, Let's Mobilize His Church*

Ryan Shaw is a mobilizer of mobilizers! This book is the outgrowth of a life dedicated to spurring the global Church to radical obedience and the fulfillment of the Great Commission in this generation. Prepare to have your head and heart rearranged and redirected toward the person and worldwide purposes of Jesus Christ. You've been warned! —*Steve Shadrach, Global Ambassador, Center For Mission Mobilization*

As a veteran mission mobilizer, Ryan Shaw provides a broad survey of the global mobilization movement today as well as historically. He introduces its biblical foundations, theological vision, missiological concepts, and practical strategies for the multiplication of church planting movements that will affect people movements. This book instructs and inspires readers to "launch into the deep," reaping the remaining harvest in our globalized, urbanized, and digitalized world. —*Dr. David Lim, President, Asian School of Development and Cross-cultural Studies (ASDECS)*

I have never read about mission mobilization in a way that so vividly explains it theologically, biblically, and practically. Ryan Shaw beautifully blends both the global Church and local church in God's plan and purpose for the whole world. I highly recommend this book to every missional training program in South Asia as an excellent text book. —*Dr. S. D. Ponraj, Author & Publisher – Mission Educational Books, Chennai, India*

Many are involved in mobilizing individuals to respond to the Great Commission, but rarely do we find those mobilizing the whole church to bring the whole gospel to the whole world. Ryan does this through *Rethinking Global Mobilization*, providing missiological perspective particularly essential for God's people in the majority world. I sincerely recommend this book to the body of Christ in the majority world. — *Cheuk Chung Lau, General Secretary, Hong Kong Association of Christian Missions*

Ryan Shaw has written a masterpiece. *Rethinking Global Mobilization* is a much-awaited book. As a leader from the global South, we have seen firsthand the limitations of current mission mobilization efforts, resulting in frustration. The total mobilization of the whole church has been burning in our hearts for a while and I am very grateful for this book. — *Ray Mensah, President, Ghana Evangelical Missions Association (GEMA)*

Rethinking Global Mobilization is a significant resource to mobilize the whole Church for the final era of missions. Ryan's insight of God "changing the face of global missions" is a prophetic declaration providing fresh perspective and momentum to the global Church to fulfill the mission of God. *Rethinking Global Mobilization* serves as a road map for new sending nations to develop global collaboration in missions. —*Michael Dissanayeke, President, Southern Asia Missions, World Assemblies of God Fellowship Mission Commission*

What a gift to the global mission community! Ryan Shaw has produced a compelling text that is biblically sound, intellectually stimulating, and missiologically inspiring, championing missionary ecclesiology as foundational to mission mobilization. His unreserved emphasis on the biblical mission mandate and priority of unreached peoples is a timely remedy to the Church increasingly viewing everything as mission. *Rethinking Global Mobilization* is a prophetic voice accompanied by a missiological framework of mobilization. —*Dr. Thuo Mburu, Mission Leader and Senior Pastor, Christ Is the Answer Ministries (CITAM)*

Rethinking Global Mobilization is a significant contribution. Leaders and mission mobilizers of all types will receive clarification and language for the mobilization aspects of their roles and work. Prepare to have many "Amen! That is precisely what I have been trying to say!" moments. We are making *Rethinking Global Mobilization* mandatory reading for mission mobilizers within our global movement. —*Bevin Ginder, YWAM Frontier Missions Global Elder for Mobilization*

The Holy Spirit is moving in the African Church, envisioning her to take up the baton, and *Rethinking Global Mobilization* plays a catalyzing role in the mobilization effort. *Rethinking Global Mobilization* is a tool to inspire those churches, often having little experience in mobilizing and sustaining missionaries. Readers will find insights and models for national mission strategies producing tremendous mission sending potential. —*Rev. Tilaye Daba, Director, International Mission Society, Ethiopian Evangelical Church –Mekane Yesu*

Rethinking Global Mobilization is a welcome contribution to the global body of Christ's discussion on God's mission. In my forty years of missional engagement, I haven't come across many works on mission mobilization that are so practical and detailed. *Rethinking Global Mobilization* has the potential of causing revolutionary impact in the way we engage with the mission of God and will change the mission mobilization landscape globally! —*Rev. Timothy Olonade, Pioneer Executive Secretary, Nigeria Evangelical Missions Association*

RETHINKING GLOBAL MOBILIZATION

Calling the Church to Her Core Identity

RYAN SHAW

IGNITE Media is the publishing arm of Global Mission Mobilization Initiative (GMMI), a resourcing ministry equipping the global Church for mission mobilization through practical resources, teaching, training and strategies.

100 County Rd. 263
Armstrong, MO 65230
Globalmmi.Net
info@globalmmi.net

All Scripture quotations, unless otherwise indicated, are taken from The Holy Bible, New King James Version, NKJV. Copyright 1982 by Thomas Nelson, Inc.

Cover & Interior Design by Christy Callahan (Professional Publishing Services)
Editing of Interior by IGNITE Media

ISBN (Print): 978-1-956435-16-0
ISBN (Digital): 978-1-956435-17-7

DEDICATION

To Kelly – My best friend, life partner, teammate, and co-heir with Christ. We have been directly involved in mobilization ministry together from the first day we were married. This book is as much yours as mine. You are my greatest earthly treasure.

To Noah and Emma – I am so proud of who you both are and who you are becoming. You bring such joy to my life.

CONTENTS

Foreword

Unprecedented. Has there been a word that has seen a greater increase of usage in these recent years? Most of us grow weary of its frequency, and yet it is a most fitting term for what we are seeing unfold in the area of global mission. The whole world seems to be accelerating into new crises, new opportunities, and new norms. This is equally true when it comes to matters related to reaching the world with the good news of Jesus Christ. We are in an unprecedented era of global mission.

Most of the world is not aware that for 40 years now, Christianity has been predominantly an African, Asian, and Latin American movement. With the median age of the global human population currently hovering near 31, this means that most people alive today *were born into* a world where the Christianity as "the white man's religion" is a relic of the past. Patrick Johnstone was already writing back in 2011 (in *The Future of the Global Church*) that Africa, Asia, and Latin America were already sending more people into the mission field than were the nations of the West.

One could assert that the pressing question of the past generation in mission has been, "Where to?" Courtesy of tireless, innovative research, we now possess information in response to this question that would have been unimaginable to our predecessors in its scope and granularity. The most pressing question for the next generation of mission may be twofold: "Where from?" and "How?" Coming up with answers is nonnegotiable.

Despite the encouraging growth of missionary sending from the Global South, and despite encouraging progress in engaging the seven thousand (or so) least reached ethnolinguistic peoples with the gospel, we are actually losing ground when it comes to evangelizing every person. The Center for the Study of Global Christianity estimates that from 2021 to 2025, the world's unevangelized population will have increased by 97 million. That's an increase of more than sixty thousand every single day—the unevangelized population is increasing that much faster than we are reaching them.

In light of this, new paradigms of mobilization are absolutely vital, but even these are insufficient on their own to narrow this alarming gap. New paradigms of church and of mission—new to most of us, at least—will also be essential in order to enable the surge of message bearers necessary to see the entire world effectively reached. Mobilization and sending models that are sustainable for the majority of the world's Christians must flourish, or we will certainly see the gap increase further.

Rethinking Global Mobilization drills into this challenge, addressing the reality that "mobilization from the outside" will never have the necessary impact to turn the tide or finish the task. Mission mobilization cannot remain something *done to* churches by outsiders; it needs to be a vision captured from within local churches. If we as the global Church are to have any chance of overcoming the temptations, distractions, opposition, and costs that stand between the status quo and a completed Bride of Christ, then a vision for global mission must become part of our spiritual DNA.

There are few who have a greater breadth of experience in engaging with mission mobilization globally than Ryan Shaw. He has travelled far and wide, visiting diverse cultures and contexts, encountering both the churches that form the crest of this new wave of mission and the least reached groups they are engaging. More significantly, several years ago he started a Global Mobilization Institute in Chiang Mai, Thailand to train mission mobilizers, welcoming ministry leaders from around the globe to learn and grow together in community. This training center initiated a prayer room dedicated to praying for increased mission mobilization in the global Church along with a regular monthly day of prayer for mission mobilization that many ministries and organizations participate with. There may be no one who has personally invested more of themselves into the concepts in this book than the author himself. Ryan has walked the walk.

I remember being profoundly impacted in years past by at least two horizon-expanding books. J. B. Phillips's *Your God is Too Small* greatly enlarged my understanding of God. *The Church is Bigger Than You Think* by Patrick Johnstone did the same for my understanding of the Church. It is my hope that *Rethinking Global Mobilization* will accomplish, for many, the same in the realm of mission mobilization.

Jason Mandryk
Author and Co-Director of Operation World

Introduction

Several years ago, while driving near my home in Chiang Mai, Thailand, the Lord spoke through what some call the "inner, audible" voice of God. It came with authority, stunning me, accompanied with peace. *I am changing the face of global mission.* I discerned God intended to change the basic expression of the mission movement (see glossary) and understanding of mission mobilization (see glossary), aligning them with His scriptural standards. I became aware this would mean a change in the fundamental expression of Christianity, resulting in shifts in mission and mobilization. Over the last decade this direction has been confirmed by ministry leaders and missiologists alike.[1]

The statement was staggering, with layers of meaning, relating to the who, what and how of global mission itself, while broadening the global Church's understanding of mission mobilization. The Lord wants His people in step with the Spirit, advancing in mission and mobilization through the progressive revelation of Jesus. History reveals as the world and society changes, the expression of the Church adapts as well.[2] This is also true in the understanding of the mission of that adapting Church, and how she engages in mobilization. We are in such a time right now.

The statement implied shaking. Such drastic change does not come easy and is often painful. We take comfort in the way things have been. Sometimes, to help us embrace change, God puts us in circumstances we would never choose. But in His eternal wisdom align us with where He is leading. To varying degrees, the body of Christ has entertained false outlooks about mission and mobilization, creating a lag in emphasis in historically sending nations while failing to take root in emerging sending nations. Overcoming these outlooks, conforming His people to His biblical and Spirit-led plans, is part of the unfolding change in global mission.

I believe God is birthing a focused **global mission mobilization movement** (see glossary)—not merely a few people becoming engaged with cross-cultural mission to the unreached but the body of Christ as a whole prioritizing seeing the earth filled with the glory of God. The growing number of ministries, organizations, national associations, courses, and conferences devoted to mission mobilization are reasons for encouragement. The burgeoning global mission mobilization movement is not orchestrated by any one organization, ministry, or association, but directly by the Spirit Himself. We are in a changing world—where a globalized Church is positioned as never before to reach a globalized world through globalized mission mobilization producing globalized cross-cultural mission.

This book aims to bring a measure of definition and strategy to this developing move of God, broken into four distinct parts.

- Part 1, we lay foundations for rethinking global mobilization. What is mission mobilization? Has our understanding been too limited? Where is God leading global mobilization? What are the messages of mobilization? What are core aspects of mobilization needing emphasis? We also seek to broaden the concept of mission mobilizers. Who are they? What are their characteristics, their message?

- Part 2, our focus turns to the biblical background of the Great Commission itself. Looking at Jesus' four primary Great Commission passages while emphasizing that storyline has an end—the fulfillment of the Great Commission. What does that end look like? Where is redemptive history headed? We consider the biblical view of the identity of God's chosen vehicle—the global Church, while highlighting what a local expression (a local ministry) is in the eyes of God. This background helps us correctly internalize mission mobilization as a core of local ministries.

- Part 3, we analyze mission, mobilization, and revival history from AD 30 to the present, considering three major historical eras, with most time spent on the last 500 years. Providing an analytical grid, we explore trends and principles in God's progressive revelation in mission and mobilization, helping discern what the Spirit is saying today.

- Part 4, we answer the common question, "What do we mobilize the Church to do?" With many diverging and random activities under "global mission," articulating a biblically based, strategic framework is necessary. We consider a comprehensive, four-point progressive strategy of biblical, Holy Spirit-inspired processes and how they affect mission mobilization. This big-picture, progressive strategy brings focus to mission mobilization.

Each distinct part will help us understand global mobilization more clearly, discerning the shifts God is bringing. The book reveals changes Jesus is inviting His global Church to align with as He brings clarity to global mobilization. Revealing what Jesus intends His global Church to become, it includes theology, theory, and practice. Little of the content is brand-new. Yet the way it is brought together, formulating a strategic framework for global mobilization, may be new. It is necessary periodically to refresh ourselves with core principles and practices of how the Kingdom of God advances that may fall by the wayside. We see them in a new light, seeing how the various pieces of the puzzle fit together. I trust this is part of the progressive revelation God uses to advance His Kingdom among all peoples.

The in-depth study of mission mobilization has been a neglected subject in missiology (the study of global mission), primarily because we tend to define mobilization in a limited, rather than comprehensive way—calling the global Church to embrace her core God-given identity. Mission mobilization, from this larger perspective, needs dedicated study. Global leaders like Steve Hawthorne, David Lim, Randy Mitchell, Timothy Olonade, Max Chismon, Jay Matenga, Steve Shadrach, David Jacob, Mike Adegbile, Mark Stebbins, Bruce Koch, David Ruiz, Paul Borthwick and others are encouraging this needed dialogue. This book encourages the conversation, shedding light on mission mobilization in the global Church, while considering biblical, Spirit-led processes to advance the global Church toward the culmination of the age.

Our generation stands on the shoulders of giants in mission study and practice who have gone before us. When a giant passes, we are often guilty of failing to continue applying the insights they left. Many before us have planted and watered, and we can now see an amazing harvest by applying mobilization principles to the current missiological context in a globalized world.

Personally, as a graduate of Fuller Theological Seminary's School of Intercultural Studies in Pasadena, California, I enjoy the enduring legacies of Dr. Donald McGavran (first dean from 1965–1980), Dr. Ralph Winter (professor from 1966–1976 who subsequently founded the US Center For World Mission—Now Frontier Ventures), Dr. J. Edwin Orr, Dr. Peter Wagner, Dr. Arthur Glasser, Dr. Paul Pierson, Dr. Dudley Woodberry, and more (including my father, Dr. R. Daniel Shaw – professor of Anthropology and Bible Translation). These giants of mission thought, study, and practice over the last 50 years have marked my own missiological convictions. It is vital to not allow core principles they taught to be overlooked today, but instead build on them.

I have been involved in global mobilization for 20 years, traveling to over 65 nations in a mobilization capacity, primarily in the global South. I pray this writing opens the way for greater emphasis on comprehensive, overarching mission mobilization across the global body of Jesus Christ.

Part 1

Foundations of Mission Mobilization

1

Why Mission Mobilization?

I sat down to pray early one morning with God's Word open before me. The Holy Spirit put a word in my spirit. Luke 5:4 jumped off the page. I immediately sensed it had broad implications for the direction the Lord wanted to take His global Church: *Launch out into the deep and let down your nets for a catch!* It was a startling word. What could it mean?

The context of Luke 5:4 is Jesus relating with Peter, James, and John, who would later become the inner core among His disciples. They already had a few interactions with Jesus. He had healed Peter's mother-in-law. They had watched Him heal all the sick brought to Him the day before (Luke 4). They knew Jesus was different, special. On this particular day, Jesus got into Peter's boat, asking him to push off shore so He could speak to the multitudes from the boat. Peter complied and listened to Jesus' teaching. When Jesus stopped speaking, He looked at Peter and said to him, "Launch out into the deep and let down your nets for a catch" (v. 4). Peter was reluctant as he had just been out all night fishing, catching nothing. Yet because he recognized the uniqueness of Jesus, Peter wisely obeyed (v. 5). The result was a catch of fish Peter had never seen before, so much the boat began to sink (vv. 6-7). Experiencing Jesus' authority on display, Peter surrendered to Jesus as a disciple (v. 11).

A generally accepted interpretation relates to the lost being caught in the net. This is true, yet another aspect caught my attention. "Let down your nets for a catch" referred to **local ministries** (see glossary) around the world (no matter how big or small) developing an environment where every believer is regularly confronted with Jesus' redemptive storyline, plans, and purposes for the nations. In essence, local ministries engaged in mobilization within their own fellowships. As a result, the nets among remaining ethnic peoples became filled to overflowing through Jesus' body internationally becoming activated in mobilization—local ministry by local ministry. The verse is a call globally for local ministries and church network ministry structures to give focused attention to wholehearted love for God overflowing into widespread mobilization.

Often, local ministries are engaged in various forms of global mission, catching little, frustrated as Peter was (v. 5). Jesus gave Peter a different strategy and immediately a great catch was pulled in. The application is that if we approach mission mobilization within each local ministry,[1] a great catch among **unreached people groups** (see glossary) will correspondingly take place. It seems the Holy Spirit is calling the global Church to a new dimension in mobilization, deliberately positioning her for greater influence among the unreached ethnic peoples of the world. It is a call beyond the status quo of mobilization, meditating on the promises of God to His Church for the nations and responding in a fresh way.

I am convinced the global Church is about to give way to a "great catch" across every nation and people group. Yet we must access it God's way, laying down some "sacred cows." This requires a comprehensive mission mobilization plan. This is what this book is about. As my friend Reuben Kachala says, "to see a great sending movement to the nations requires a corresponding great mobilization movement among the 'unsent' across the global Church"[2]—implementing mobilization principles within communities of believers and calling the body of Christ to her core identity (see glossary) as God's ever-expanding, multiplying, missionary people in this age. This means new perspectives, strategies, and workforce in mobilization, beyond the small number of believers involved in what we traditionally call "mobilization."

What does "launch out into the deep and let down your nets for a catch" (Luke 5:4) look like? Local ministries implementing core principles of Mission

Mobilization Movements[3] into their communities. A village house church in rural Bangladesh; a church of forty members in Chiang Rai, Thailand; a campus fellowship of twenty-five students in Istanbul, Turkey; a church of eighty members on a rooftop in Karachi, Pakistan; a denomination of a hundred plus local churches in Cape Town, South Africa; a megachurch of two thousand in Sao Paulo, Brazil; and countless other ministry possibilities.

Mahesh De Mel, mission director of the National Christian Evangelical Alliance Sri Lanka (NCEASL), shared with me a detailed national church planting strategy.[4] The plan is to plant a church in every village across Sri Lanka (38,000 villages). The next part grabbed my mobilization attention. The country is broken into 44 districts with each district having an interdenominational pastor's fellowship. Through these fellowships' pastors are envisioned to commence a mobilization effort within local ministries, enabling their members (lay people and lay leaders) to be trained in the strategy of planting churches in every village of Sri Lanka. The only way to see a national church planting strategy achieved is through an equally large-scale mobilization effort among the individual local ministries. That is where the battle is won or lost.

"Launch out into the deep and let down your nets for a catch" represents individual local ministries going beyond the comfortable and convenient with fresh obedience—renewing enthusiasm for a global movement mobilizing the Church, compelled outward. Like Paul, our corporate calling is toward "obedience to the faith among all nations for His name"(Romans 1:5). Jesus appears to be inviting the global Church to increase faith, pursuing the mandate set before her with revived zeal. It is common to get sluggish in any work after a while. In mobilization it is necessary to renew vision and single-mindedness, staying the course.

CAPTURED BY A VISION

"The evangelization of the world in this generation!" This powerful catch-phrase was the cornerstone motto of the Student Volunteer Movement for Foreign Missions in the US, Canada, and United Kingdom between 1886 and 1940. According to David Howard, this statement was more than a motto, catalyzing over 20,000 new cross-cultural workers to the ends of the earth in that generation.[5] It was a vision statement, bringing focus to the efforts of global mission in that era. Their goal was to mobilize a generation in the Western world to take up God's mantle, engaging with His big picture purpose. They had the end of this present age in mind, believing it possible. As their catchphrase was taught, prayed, and believed across campus ministries and churches of that day, it galvanized a generation to see themselves as part of the global, redemptive storyline of God, in turn surrendering their lives for Jesus' glory on the earth.

Many years ago, this catchphrase first caught my attention. I was an Intercultural Studies student at Fuller Theological Seminary in Pasadena, California, taking mission history classes from renowned mission historian Dr. Paul Pierson. Studying the development of the modern mission movement over the last three hundred years, I stumbled upon the Student Volunteer Movement (SVM) and its compelling catchphrase. I was fascinated by the processes God worked in modern history to raise up His global mission enterprise. I was particularly struck by SVM's all-encompassing catchphrase and the vision and clarity it produced.

Following seminary, becoming involved in global mobilization myself, I periodically heard a similar concept in some mission circles. It modernized the "evangelization of the world in this generation" catchphrase, reflecting the current cultural, historical, and theological landscape. Similarly, it clarified the biblical, Spirit-led culmination of history in this age, calling for urgency, intentionality, and sacrificial focus among the people of God: "The Fulfillment of the Great Commission in This Generation."

I was captivated, seeing from Scripture the realistic possibility of the literal fulfillment of Jesus' Great Commission. Not in human strength and effort, but through the presence of the Spirit accelerating this emphasis within His global Church. Not a pipe dream, but attainable through the victory of Jesus and spiritual resources available through His New Covenant. Not merely a pep rally cheer, the phrase represented the core purpose of the global Church in this age, inaugurated through Abraham himself (Genesis 12:3). It represented the completeness God intended to do in and through His Church, preparing the way for the return of Jesus.

Historically, the potential of the Great Commission being fulfilled has been unlikely. According to mission historian Kenneth Scott Latourette, the harvest force during the years of the SVM (1886–1940) only came from a few

Western nations, with Africa and Asia being almost entirely unreached at the time.[6] Fulfilling the Great Commission was logistically impossible due to the small percentage of the body of Christ compared to the overwhelming numbers of unreached peoples globally. Today, the global Church exists in some form in all 196 countries of the world.[7] The move of the Spirit over the last 100 years has dynamically prepared the global Church for realizing the fulfillment of the Great Commission[8] —but only as she is deliberately mobilized and equipped to emphasize her primary calling.

The phrase "the Fulfillment of the Great Commission in this Generation" drastically reordered my life. It became ingrained in my personal life purpose statement[9] and my wife's and my marriage mission statement.[10] My prayer life shifted as the phrase became a centerpiece of strategic intercession. I have prayed for the fulfillment of the Great Commission and interrelated points thousands of times. It is the focal prayer emphasis of the GMMI Global Harvest Prayer Room in Chiang Mai, Thailand, with a sign on the wall declaring, "The Fulfillment of the Great Commission in this Generation."

Life and daily decisions became directly related to how they would either enhance or detract my participation in realizing this fulfillment. How I used time, energy, and money became bound up in this purpose. I read as many global mission, spiritual life, and mission and revival history books as I could, broadening my understanding, while enjoying relationships with godly mentors, friends, and colleagues who shaped my perspectives and convictions. I saw throughout Scripture this focal point consistently showing up, the Lord rooting my Great Commission vision in His Word. I have taught this phrase more than any other subject over the last twenty years, calling others to teach it, pray, and pursue it as well.

I have always sought to do ministry in light of the big picture realization of this phrase. This first led me to become involved in mobilization. I began to see the primary way God would accomplish this phrase. Through biblical, Spirit-led, and anointed mission mobilization becoming emphasized corporately across the global Church. The Church embracing her core identity as Jesus' multiplying, reproducing, "missionary" community among near and distant cultural peoples. Effective or inadequate mobilization is a significant factor in the global Church either progressing or being hindered in cross-cultural mission. One might naturally ask, "How does God mobilize His people and ministries for direct partnership in the Great Commission?" This key question enables effective mobilization and is at the heart of this book.

Is This Motivation Effective?

While some argue a motivation of fulfilling the Great Commission is not effective,[11] the facts don't necessarily back this up. Followers of Jesus are wired by God to give themselves wholeheartedly to God's purposes. We may cover it with other things, rationalize it away, or minimize its importance. Yet lingering in the background it is in our DNA. We are meant to multiply. God spoke to Adam and Eve in Genesis 1:28: "Be fruitful and multiply, fill the earth and subdue it." He affirmed our DNA with Noah after the flood: "And as for you, be fruitful and multiply, bring forth abundantly in the earth" (Genesis 9:7). This signified a twofold emphasis on physical and spiritual multiplication: multiplying spiritual understanding, wholehearted love for Jesus, faithfulness, and obedience, as well as multiplying disciples and spiritually alive, Bible-believing, communities of faith all over the earth is core to our DNA. Recognizing Jesus' global purpose, we want to obey, participating in His unfolding story. I am convinced it is not finishing the task itself that is resisted. Instead, the message has become diluted and misrepresented, understood through a traditional lens, failing to grab the imagination of believers.

Others critique the "goal" orientation as being Western. It is worth noting this is usually from Westerners themselves as Africans, Asians, and Latin Americans are often motivated by a variety of forward-looking goals. For example, the AD2000 and Beyond Movement, championed by Argentinian mission leader Luis Bush, had as a goal "a church for every people and the Gospel for every person by the year 2000," primarily adopted by non-Western believers and churches.[12] Goals themselves are not cultural, yet the means by which Western or majority world cultures approach goals are often different. Westerners tend to be more task oriented in pursuing goals, while majority world cultures may have similar goals, yet engage them through a predominantly relational approach.

Biblical hope is meant to characterize the body of Christ, even when scriptural promises appear impossible. Hope, by definition, clings to what is future, believing it will happen according to God's words. Forward-looking hope anticipates the tremendous global harvest God has envisioned since Genesis 12:3, partnering with Him in its fruition.

Jesus, our perfect example, is characterized by hope and faith. Possessing perfect faith in God, humanity, and the future promises of the Father. As G. Campbell Morgan relates, "first, Jesus' unceasing obedience to the will of God. Second, Jesus' faith in the possibility of the recovery of human beings from our corruption. Third, His unqualified faith in the future of God's plans. We never find a hint of anticipation of ultimate failure in Jesus."[13] Jesus knew where history was going, teaching disciples to pray, "Your Kingdom come, Your will be done" (Matthew 6:10), looking with certainty to the days when His will among all peoples would be fulfilled. This same forward-looking faith is ours as well. The writer of Hebrews declared, "But the word which they heard did not profit them, not being mixed with faith in those who heard it" (Hebrews 4:2), revealing the necessity of faith being mixed with the certainty of the work of God being fulfilled.

Jesus revealed in John 4:34, "My food is to do the will of Him who sent me, and to finish His work." Morgan suggests, "The food Jesus refers to is the fulfillment of His mission in relation to its impact on the harvest among all peoples."[14] Jesus' death and resurrection paved the way for the New Covenant to be experienced by all peoples. Our food too includes realizing the ripeness of the harvest among the nations, giving ourselves directly to the "finishing" of Jesus' work in the world. Our hearts long for Jesus to receive the glory and honor He deserves among all peoples. Yet apart from "lifting our eyes and looking at the fields" (John 4:35) we remain with stunted tunnel vision.

Paul reinforced this hope in Romans 15:13: "Now may the God of hope fill you with all joy and peace in believing, that you may abound in hope by the power of the Holy Spirit." He added in Romans 5:5, "Now hope does not disappoint because the love of God has been poured out in our hearts by the Holy Spirit who was given to us." It is life-giving to orient local ministries toward a hope of global harvest among all people groups. Hebrews 11:1 affirms, "Faith is the evidence (confidence) of things not seen." We haven't yet seen the fulfillment of the Great Commission.[15] Yet we have certainty of it taking place because of Jesus' promise. The writer of Hebrews continues, "Without faith (confidence) it is impossible to please God" (v. 6). Pleasing God includes growing confidence of what Jesus promised is coming, whether it seems possible to our finite minds. Peter asked in 2 Peter 3:11–12, "What manner of persons ought you to be in holy conduct and godliness, looking for and hastening the coming of the day of God?," implying the importance of forward-looking hope to the end of the age.

Can It Be Done?

Sometimes people ask if I really believe we could see the fulfillment of the Great Commission. It is an understandable question in light of how large the task is and the great challenges in the way: the exploding world population, hostile governments, militant Buddhism, Hinduism and Islam, global hardheartedness, growing injustices, and more.[16] The response of Joshua and Caleb in Numbers 13–14 while spying out the promised land is a picture of correct faith in the face of obstacles. Ten other spies (people of God too) deemed it impossible to take the land, citing considerable barriers and obstacles: "We saw the giants and we were like grasshoppers in our own sight." Conversely, Joshua and Caleb reported, "Let us at once go up and take possession. For we are well able to overcome it" (Numbers 13:30). The ten saw the natural circumstances around them, always producing fear. Joshua and Caleb saw the God who promised to give the land in the first place.[17]

Joshua and Caleb's account inspires faith in the God of the seemingly impossible—a desperately needed quality in global mission. God loves to show Himself strong when everything looks impossible. This is a principle of God's advancing Kingdom. In the modern global Church with its sophisticated organizations, we have tended to make the Great Commission overly complex. But Jesus' vision requires only simplicity, common sense, and actively responding to the Spirit. God appears to be orchestrating circumstances globally, preparing the optimal environment for mission mobilization across His Church to be prioritized like no other time since the early Church. Jesus' certain goal of the fulfillment of the Great Commission will be reached.

Rethinking an Often-Misrepresented Theological Truth

While fulfilling the Great Commission is God's work, He has set up His Kingdom in partnership with weak, empty vessels (2 Corinthians 12:9).

Believers whom God fills with the treasure of Himself (2 Corinthians 4:7). Obviously, God could do it alone through His sovereignty. Yet He has deliberately chosen not to. The Great Commission is a mutual partnership between the Lord of the harvest and His Church. We cannot do God's part for Him, and He won't do our part for us. Yet the global Church's response has generally been slow.

A partial reason is a basic theological misunderstanding. It is a common, orthodox position to state God doesn't need His Church. While technically true, it misrepresents a larger truth more accurately revealing His heart. As Mike Adegbile affirms, "mission is not first what the Church does, it starts from who the Church is."[18] Mission has its root in her nature. The Church's nature and her different functions are conceived in view of her missionary calling. The missionary calling of the Church predates her existence, having its root in the call of Abraham (Genesis 12:1–3). God's eternal purpose was to extend His redemptive blessings to all the families of the earth through the descendants of Abraham. Sadly, many local ministries have deviated from God's conception of the Church, thereby ignoring the big burden in the heart of God and despising the essence of their existence."[19]

While no believer would argue God is not sovereign and all-powerful, it is technically incorrect to say He can do whatever He wants. God has purposefully bound Himself according to His all-wise plans. Scripture reveals that though He "can," Jesus has chosen to work in partnership with His global Church, though she is weak and finite. This scriptural theme must be restored in the global Church to correctly embrace her core identity.

From the days of Adam, God set up His Kingdom in partnership with humanity, stating in Genesis 1:26, "Let us make man in our image, after our likeness. And let them have dominion over the fish of the sea and over the birds of the heavens and over the livestock and over all the earth and over every creeping thing that creeps on the earth." David prayed in Psalm 8:6, "You have given him (humankind) dominion over the works of Your hands; you have put all things under his feet." The writer of Hebrews reiterates in Hebrews 2:8, "You have put all things in subjection under his (humankind's) feet. For in that He put all in subjection under Him, He left nothing that is not put under him (humankind)." It is often assumed "him" in the Psalms and Hebrews passages is Christ, yet a closer look reveals it is humanity, supporting the original Genesis 1:26 passage.

Jesus, fully God, became "Word made flesh" (John 1:14) identifying with humanity in all things, except sin. Through the cross redeeming what was lost by Adam in the garden of Eden. Jesus, as last Adam (1 Corinthians 15:22, 45, 47), restored humanity to accomplish God's purposes of justice and reaching all ethnic peoples. Jesus' redemption empowers the global Church as His hands, feet, and mouthpiece to this generation all around the world.

Therefore, it is necessary for the global Church to self-evaluate. Are we being obedient to our core identity and the expressed will of God? Have we shrugged off who we truly are, opting for lesser priorities? Maybe we think it costs too much, is seemingly impossible, or is simply for someone else. It only costs too much to those looking at what they may lose (in worldly matters) instead of what is gained through obedience to the will of God. It is only impossible to those trusting in humanity's ability more than God's power to accomplish His will. It is only for someone else for those who have surrendered their responsibility in the will of God, misunderstanding His intent.

Why Still So Much to Be Done?

Roughly one-third of the world's population is still in the category of unreached people groups, having too small of an indigenous church to adequately reach their own people.[20] Usually where 2 percent or less of the ethnic group population are followers of Jesus.[21] Steve Shadrach asks this question: "Since 1974, most mission agencies have placed a priority on unreached people groups, and missiologists have spent decades studying every country, language, and culture to break down the remaining task into bitesize pieces. The assignment is clearly set before us, so why isn't the global Church finished with world evangelization yet?"[22] It is common to ascribe reasons for this as the difficulty of the peoples themselves, opposition to the gospel, lack of finance, and more. Yet there is much more to why still so many people remain unreached.

The premise of this book is a primary reason is the way the global Church has approached the Great Commission, failing to see it as her core identity. Coupled with the general neglect of engaging its own (mission mobilization), relegating mission to a professional few. We will never achieve Jesus' purpose until we align with God's ways in Scripture. As a result, never has a clear mobilization vision and strategy been more necessary across the global Church—a strategy rooted squarely in biblical revelation.

A TRANSITION TIME

The global Church is in a transition time of significant change—a paradigm shift—progressing us from what "has been" to what "is coming." It is Jeremiah 1:10 on display in the Church, "To root out and to pull down, to destroy and to throw down, to build and to plant." It is necessary to think differently, asking new questions, responding to the Lord's invitation in Jeremiah 33:3: "Call to Me, and I will answer you, and show you..." Though we often think we have a handle on mission mobilization, in reality we have barely scratched the surface. There are new models and patterns of ministry, new understanding to discern, emphasizing mobilizing local ministries for reaching unreached people groups.

On the surface the mission movement looks a bit stale. Numbers of long-term workers from traditional sending nations continue to dwindle[23] while emerging sending nations seem unsure how to effectively become involved. Discipling all ethnic groups, multiplying culturally relevant simple churches, millions reconciled to God in Christ, the global Church coming into faith and obedience—in essence the whole Great Commission mandate—stands at a crossroads.[24] Will the global Church continue with business as usual or embrace paradigm shifts to reap the global harvest?

At such an important time the global Church needs clarity—clarity bringing alignment with the Spirit. Alignment means seeing mobilization differently. We need different approaches to sending **message bearers**[25] (see glossary) to the mobilization message, to who the Church is becoming spiritually, to prayer and intercession, and more. Yet generally we find confusion of what global mission and mobilization are, both interpreted however it suits the person using them. Global mission tends to include all the good works the global Church does (with little evaluation of how these actually serve God's big-picture goals among the nations) to anybody who is unsaved (with little strategic consideration of the access these might have to the gospel). While mobilization has generally been reduced to individual recruitment of international workers or a person speaking to a group about global mission.

Embracing Core Identity

A primary transition is God rooting His people in core identity. Identity is fundamental to the human race. Every individual finds identity in something, often shifting throughout a lifetime. Whether a job, role, family, socioeconomic level, home, or education level, identity defines how we view ourselves and think others view us.[26] Emotional ups and downs are often connected to measuring up to an identity. In many cultures, identity revolves around a particular group. Yet these all fall short of God's identity for us. God wills His people to lay down false identities, growing in His *core identity*. Every follower of Jesus possesses the same core identity, whether we know it or not. Embracing core identity enables believers and local ministries to walk in the will of God—living for His glory on earth.

So, what is the global Church's core corporate identity? We are children of God, bought with the blood of Jesus, grafted into His global family, bondservants of the King as He works out His Kingdom purposes. Mike Adegbile affirms we are God's "missionary people," His channel for multiplying biblical, Spirit-led, spiritually vibrant communities of disciples among all least reached peoples, seeing the Kingdom of God rooted among them, diffusing His righteousness and justice among the nations.[27] Not just for believers wanting this identity, but the very identity God has marked on all who are in Christ. The people of God aligning with their core corporate identity is the significant purpose of mission mobilization and what God is increasing throughout His global Church.

Following His death and resurrection, Jesus gave His **Great Commission** (see glossary) to all disciples. This was a reinterpretation by Jesus of the age-old promise of God to Abraham (Genesis 12:3) years before.[28] Disciples take His gospel, in words and demonstration of power (1 Corinthians 2:4), to the ends of the earth, discipling all ethnic peoples. But how? The original disciples would have been confused by this commissioning. What was the vehicle to accomplish this? Were they to do it through Jewish Israel? No, the disciples had heard Jesus tell the Jewish leaders the Kingdom was being taken from them (Matthew 21:43).

The only instruction Jesus gave was to go back to Jerusalem (the lion's den where their master had been crucified forty days before) and wait for the gift of God (Acts 1:3–8). They obediently did so. What transpired next was the coming of the Spirit and what G. Campbell Morgan calls the birthing of the vehicle God intended to spread the glory of Jesus throughout the whole earth.[29] The brand-new entity, the "Church," came into being that day. For what? To produce a people empowered by God cooperating with His age-old purpose of redeeming fallen humanity. The "Church" was created as "God's missionary people," **scattering** (see glossary) among all ethnic peoples, incarnating the gospel of the Kingdom, reaping a great global harvest. This core identity has never changed.

Global Mission—Our Core Identity

It is possible to read the whole Bible from the viewpoint of the global mission of God, as Christopher J. H. Wright reveals.[30] Doing so enables the people of God to find their core identity. This is at the center of the global Church's calling in mission mobilization. All the portions and doctrines of the Bible, from the Old and New Testaments, come together around God and His glorious purpose—filling the earth with His glory. God's global mission, realized through the delegated mission of His people, binds the Bible together from beginning to end.

By rooting ourselves and local ministries in the purpose of God's Word, we recognize the singular truth, suggested by David J. Bosch, that global mission is not merely an activity of the global Church, but an attribute of God Himself.[31] God is a missionary God, Jesus a missionary Messiah, and the Spirit a missionary Spirit. Therefore, mission mobilization starts with God Himself, who is on global mission, aligning His body with the priority purpose on His heart. We do not mobilize the Church to merely good works, but to come into alignment with the heartbeat of God.

As such, according to Charles Van Engen, global mission is the global Church's primary task, not one of many.[32] It is common to lump mission together as one of a handful of "projects" the Church or individual believers care about. In doing so we make something out of global mission God never intended. Abraham is one of the most important figures in God's biblical narrative of mission. In Paul's own ministry, it was Abraham's calling as a "blessing to all the nations of the earth" (Genesis 12:3) that motivated him. In fact, Paul's life mission statement is summed up in Romans 1:5: "for obedience to the faith among all nations for His name." His words similarly describe

God's promise to Abraham. For Paul, Abraham revealed God's agenda for redeeming the whole world, extending the scope of impact to every nation, producing children as stars from all ethnic peoples.[33] This is why mission mobilization matters—helping the global Church become rooted in her core identity.

The Gospel Includes Responsibilities, Not Only Blessings

A common mistake is proclaiming the gospel in a way that believers see their salvation as primarily about them. It is true God redeems His people for Himself, restoring relationship, free from the curse of sin. God blesses us with "every spiritual blessing in heavenly places" (Ephesians 1:2), laying hold of His blessings, privileges, and benefits in experiential ways. Yet discipleship goes beyond the purchased blessings through Jesus' redemption. The gospel includes often overlooked responsibilities.[34] The faith of Abraham receives the blessings of the gospel, while recognizing it lays responsibility upon the people of God. Responsibilities don't earn salvation, but are love responses for all God has done through redemption. We joyfully take up these responsibilities of the Kingdom, motivated by love, as Paul declared: "The love of Christ compels me" (2 Corinthians 5:14–15).

Contending for an Explosion of Mission Mobilization

The global Church appears positioned as never before for a strong push in mission mobilization. She has never had a larger number of believers in almost every country, never had such volume of teaching and training, never so much light on biblical strategies, and never so many resources. With all God has generously provided the global Church through His redemption, there is no excuse for not reaching all the unreached frontier ethnic peoples in this generation. Some may object, citing statistics of cross-cultural mission engagement declining in recent years. Yet it can be argued that while "traditional" mission concern is trending downward, this creates a vacuum for a broader, more comprehensive outlook on global mobilization to emerge. May the "traditional" give way to the Spirt-led, biblical understanding of mobilization across the global Church.

I believe the global Church is on the cusp of an explosion of focused mobilization across denominations, organizations, and individual local ministries. More mobilization-focused ministries, courses, tools, and trainings have sprung up globally in the last decade than ever before in history.[35] An emphasis on mobilization appears to be accelerating globally and will culminate with time in the global Church walking in her core identity as God's missionary people. This requires redefining and rethinking mission mobilization beyond the status quo to the broad, comprehensive, wholistic intent on God's heart.

Comprehensive mobilization acceleration is not limited to Western nations. In 1800 the Church globally was primarily located in Europe and North and South America.[36] By contrast, by the 1990s the body of Christ had expanded to almost every country on earth.[37] This means local ministries today in Pakistan, India, Malawi, Ethiopia, South Sudan, Malaysia, Indonesia, and many more traditionally receiving nations are empowered now as mission senders. Today's global Church has been entrusted with stewarding the fulfillment of the Great Commission. This requires the Church in every nation doing their part, mobilizing, and equipping their own. More organization and money are not what is needed. But empowering every believer and local ministry released to do what is already in their hearts by compulsion of love for Christ, resulting in a widespread global mobilization movement becoming realized.

Overcoming Challenges

The COVID-19 pandemic has brought unprecedented challenges to the global Church.[38] She has been shaken, yet is emerging as a purified body, tried and proven, pruned for greater fruitfulness in the coming decades. I am confident the global Church is growing in experiential knowledge of God, developed through embracing God in the midst of challenges. This follows an important spiritual pattern. Resurrection always follows death. Victory often comes through apparent defeat. Challenges embraced are the foundation for breakthrough and overcoming. We gain strength when forced to use the spiritual muscles of faith. Instead of looking upon the global situation as a setback, we arise in faith, trusting the Lord to bring victory, light, spiritual progression through it, preparing the global Church for greater influence in the coming decades.

My prayer is that God uses this global struggle to realign His people with what matters most. The pandemic has been an opportunity for the global Church to pause, take stock, prioritize what is truly important in cross-cultural mission. The way global mission has been done, the strategies used, the focal points, the work force itself—all need rethinking.[39] As we look back, the year 2020 will be a dividing line, a time when things before were done in a particular way, while after the global Church will have undergone massive paradigm shifts in how it does cross-cultural mission among the unreached as well as mission mobilization.

***

Now that we have seen a bit of God's intent to call His Church to engage in mobilization, let's proceed to better understand what we mean by mission mobilization. What is the multifaceted work of "mobilization" really about? Let's take a closer look.

2

What Is Mission Mobilization?

Several years ago, I spoke to a large campus ministry fellowship at Kenyatta University in Nairobi, Kenya. Challenging the group with the mission heart of God, I invited them to consider if God was calling them as "missionaries." Hundreds of Kenyan students stared back at me as if I was speaking a foreign language. After the meeting I asked one of the ministry leaders why it appeared the students were completely missing what I was saying. He said, "You kept using the word *missionary*. For most of them a missionary is the stereotypical 'white person' they see occasionally around Nairobi. They could never see themselves as a 'missionary,' because they have never been shown that God's mission is for them."

This was an eye-opening experience on two foundational levels. First, it revealed the word *missionary* is full of hindering baggage. When used globally, it can conjure up angry emotions related to colonialism, imperialism, and painful injustices. It wrongly stereotypes, to the one hearing it, those serving God among the nations as being white.

Later that day I met a small group of the same students I spoke to in the larger group. I asked for alternative terms than *missionary* for those crossing cultural barriers to unreached peoples with the gospel of the Kingdom. The one that struck me was "message bearer." They could see themselves using this term to describe Kenyans taking the gospel across cultures. For me the term has stuck ever since. I rarely use the word *missionary* anymore, referring instead to *message bearers* among unreached ethnic peoples. This seems to be a necessary terminology shift. Throughout the rest of the book, I use the term *message bearer* to replace the traditional term *missionary*.

Secondly, the experience revealed the need for enculturated mission mobilization. The students' failing to engage with mission had nothing to do with understanding the heart of God, but with the poor packaging of the message into their own cultural outlook. Mission may be periodically mentioned in their ministry but not in a practical way, failing to impress them with the vision of Jesus in and through His Great Commission. And surely not leading them to consider themselves in such a capacity. Global mission was presented as peripheral, not central to what the Church is about. Maybe an outside conference or retreat, but not integrated into the regular flow of their local ministry. This made it difficult to gain traction over time. I saw mobilization had to be more than recruiting or a one-time event, instead becoming a regular part of every believer's development as a disciple. Mobilization includes the process of educating, inspiring, and activating an entire local ministry to integrate mission into the core of their ministry identity, not just the periphery.

THE WESTERN INFLUENCE ON MOBILIZATION

Because much of global mission and mobilization efforts have historically derived from Western cultures, the individual recruitment emphasis has become normalized. Western cultures generally see the world through individualistic lenses while majority-world cultures see the world through a communal, group-centered lens.[1] Western cultures compartmentalize an individual's job, role, position. Many believers see global mission as only for those special few with a clear-cut calling (as a profession) in mission, but not for them. Mobilization has generally bought into this compartmentalization approach instead of empowering the whole global Church (no matter what profession believers have) with a wholistic (not individualistic), communal mission mobilization approach, engaging individual local ministries and the whole global Church toward living for Jesus' glory on earth.

Defining Mission Mobilization

To accurately grasp mission mobilization, we need to define our terms. Often, we use terms we assume everyone understands through the same lens. In reality every person, culture, and even theological stream come to these terms with different worldviews. Because we believe the Lord is inspiring a surge in mobilization across His global Church, it is vital to have shared understanding of what we mean by these words.

A starting point is clarifying what we mean by "mission" itself? Then we can proceed to define *mobilization* as serving that overall mission. Max Chismon, international director of Simply Mobilizing, provides a helpful understanding of *mission*:

> Reaching unreached people groups is the start of God's greater mission agenda. This first phase of mission is the establishing of a "beachhead" of the gospel for the growth of an indigenous church that is then capable of impacting its own people with the gospel through church planting and disciple making. Outsiders do the first phase as no indigenous church yet exists. The second phase of mass church planting and disciple making is done primarily by the people belonging to the now reached people group. There is yet a third mission phase and that is putting Christ's Kingdom on display through the transformed lives of God's people. This is where metaphors such as, city on a hill, light of the world, living epistles etc., come into their true significance. Once this third phase of Christ's kingdom, becoming a "witness" in all people groups (nations), then Jesus said, "the end will come" (Matthew 24:14)—Great Commission accomplished.[2]

How then can we define *mission mobilization*? Let's use a few definitions as building blocks to progress toward a comprehensive whole. Fred Markert, YWAM Network For Strategic Initiatives leader says, "Mobilization is the process of envisioning and educating God's people about His strategic plans for the world. And it is the means of keeping them involved and moving forward until they find their specific place and role in world evangelization."[3] Larry Reesor adds to this mobilization outlook by asserting, "Mobilization is teaching believers in a local church to understand God's global plan, motivating them to a loving response to God's word, and providing opportunities for them to use their gifts, abilities and resources individually and corporately to accomplish His global plan."[4] In addition, Steve Shadrach helps us cast attention to what he calls the "unsent" suggesting, "The 'unsent' are the hundreds of millions of us Bible-believing Jesus followers around the world who have little or no mission vision."[5] These are in nations all over Africa, Latin America, and Asia where the numbers of Jesus followers are significant, even more than 50 percent of total national populations. The "unsent" are the key to the premise of this book as we rethink global mobilization.

Building on each of these helpful definitions we can thus define mission mobilization from a global perspective in two separate ways: from a macro level (the big-picture, body of Christ-wide perspective) as well as from a micro level (the individual local ministry). Both emphasize mission mobilization as calling the Church to her core identity.

At a macro level, mission mobilization is the strategic process through which the global body of Christ is empowered by the Spirit of God to emphasize the message, vision, and strategies of the Great Commission, within local ministries in every nation, activating every member in their assigned roles, toward the fulfillment of the Great Commission.

At a grassroots, or micro level, it is the strategic process of an individual community of believers moving along the journey of being educated, inspired, and activated in the Great Commission, every disciple engaged and fulfilling their assigned roles in the Great Commission.

Seeing mobilization in this light requires taking off some blinders. It can seem a bit far-fetched and unrealistic. If so, a reason is because the global Church has tended to minimize the biblical emphasis of the Great Commission, overlooking our core identity. The global Church's view of mission has generally been lowered from the New Testament's. It is necessary to regain a high view of God's plan of redemption history and call others to it in our spheres of influence. Greg Parsons, Director of Global Connections at Frontier Ventures, asserts, "Mission mobilization is a strategic new category that churches are increasingly recognizing as key to their global outreach. It is becoming more and more understood by alert mission thinkers and strategizers."[6]

Steve Hawthorne suggests, "While it is the nature of the Church to be moving out with God in mission, it is rarely, if ever, automatic that believers move into costly mission endeavor without the teaching, counsel and encouragement of other followers of Jesus."[7] When believers are exposed to others within their local ministry becoming mobilized, their own lives are touched. There is a contagious nature of grassroots mobilization, a chain reaction from small group to small group within the local church, eventually influencing the whole. The pattern of the Spirit is taking sinners, making them disciples, forming Christ within, growing them in intimate fellowship with Jesus, equipping them with spiritual power, preparing for their specific role in the Great Commission, and thrusting them out into this. This is the process mobilizer God has set up to accomplish His redemptive purposes.

Hawthorne continues, "Those engaged in mission mobilization see themselves contributing to how believers and local ministries mature to become and do all Christ is calling them."[8] Some aspects of mobilization call disciples to grow in their spiritual being, while others focus on areas of direct mission engagement. Mobilization answers the questions "who we are" (identity of the global Church) and "why we are here" (glorifying Jesus among all the peoples) as Christopher J. H. Wright has helped us grasp.[9]

Dr. Ralph Winter, founder of the US Center for World Mission (now Frontier Ventures), has said, "The greatest mobilization effort in history is now gaining momentum, moving ahead with a quickening pace, and with more and more goals that are concrete, measurable, and feasible." Emphasizing the importance of **mission mobilizers** (see glossary), he continues, "The number one priority is for more mission mobilizers. Anyone who can help 100 missionaries to the field is more important than one missionary on the field. In fact, mission mobilization activity is more crucial than field missionary activity."[10] I remember hearing Dr. Winter's statement when I was in my early twenties and being skeptical. Wasn't a frontline, pioneer message bearer among the unreached the most strategic role in mission? Since then I have come to wholeheartedly agree with Dr. Winter's assessment. Winter was a pioneer in helping to think of mobilization as a separate entity from global mission itself.

Mission mobilization then, from the big-picture perspective, centers on helping local ministries in every nation become educated, inspired, and activated in Jesus' Great Commission—the core identity of the Church. This includes grasping theological, theoretical and practical aspects of the plans, purpose, and actions of God in "blessing all families of the earth" (Genesis 12:3) and the role of individual local fellowships in carrying this out. I am confident the Holy Spirit is orchestrating present circumstances so that denominations, independent church networks, associations, and campus ministry organizations in the coming years, experience the profound effects of mobilization—seeing mobilization movements multiplied among them.[11] At present widespread, grassroots, mobilization within local ministries is far from common.

The Role of the First Two Beatitudes

The first and second beatitudes in Matthew 5:3–4 are instructive as a core paradigm of mobilization and subsequently fulfilling the Great Commission.[12] Global mobilization can become full of human strength and ingenuity, instead of offering ourselves to Him who is all in all. We set our hearts to grow in these two beatitudes, resisting the natural tendency to do mobilization ministry in human strength and effort.

Jesus says, "Blessed are the poor in spirit, for theirs is the kingdom of heaven. Blessed are those who mourn, for they shall be comforted." Though appearing to have nothing to do with our topic, they are central to approaching mobilization correctly. Jesus' first beatitude is not dealing with physical poverty, instead getting at a spiritual issue. The Old Testament concept of poverty reflects the humble and helpless putting their trust in God. The "poor" admit spiritual bankruptcy. The "poor" are sinners, under holy wrath, deserving judgment and death. The "poor" have nothing to offer God, nor can they buy favor from heaven. They are thoroughly dependent on God's work through Christ in every aspect of their lives. The "poor in spirit" renounce self-effort, abilities, capacities, and natural strength before God, embracing nothingness in and of ourselves. Poverty of Spirit looks to God to fill the global Church with Himself as the foundation to accomplish the Great Commission.

Jesus goes on to describe God's Kingdom citizens as those who "mourn" (v. 4). Jesus is referring to embracing the painful gulf between what He has made available and what the global Church is actually experiencing in God. When studying Scripture, we marvel at the promises of what God has made available to human beings. But when honestly evaluating our lives, we see how much we come up short. Our low spiritual state hinders the Church from being who God intends. This has a direct correlation with the often casual, complacent response to the Great Commission.

When honest, we see how little influence, authority, and power we possess (in ourselves) as God's servants. We love Jesus, wanting to serve Him and impact others. Whether they be families, friends, co-workers, colleagues, or the unreached globally, we want others to encounter God. It quickly becomes clear that in our strength and natural abilities we cannot influence others in any eternal sense. Personalities and human persuasion impact naturally, yet not in an eternal, spiritual way, bringing change to the heart. We often overlook this, relying on strengths and even gifts, instead of God. Admitting inability to influence another in a truly spiritual sense is a key application of "poverty of spirit." We look to the One possessing all power to influence another in an eternal, spiritual way.

Jesus put these two beatitudes together because our hearts become saturated with true "poverty of spirit" as we rightly "mourn." The Lord is ready (and more fervent about this than we are) to increase spiritual breakthrough to emphasize and prioritize the Great Commission across the global Church. The way forward is embracing total dependence upon Jesus, mourning our general neglect to walk in all that has been made freely available.

MOBILIZATION IN SCRIPTURE

It is common to hear it said the words *mobilization* or *mobilizer* are never used in the Bible. This is true, corresponding with a variety of words in modern Christian vocabulary not found in the Bible.[13] For example, the word *Trinity* never occurs in the Bible. Yet the doctrine of the Trinity is affirmed throughout. *Mobilization* and *mobilizer* are the same, consistently implied throughout Scripture. In fact, a premise of this book is that redemptive history comprises the "mobilizer God" calling the total extent of His covenant people into being in this age. Consistently mobilizing us to align with His purpose—

revealing His glory and plans to all the "families of the earth" (Genesis 12:3), ushering in the fullness of His Kingdom at His second coming. Mobilization awakens and disciples the Church to the vision of God's glory being realized among all peoples.

God—The Ultimate Mobilizer

The nature of God is to consistently invite every believer and local ministry into agreement with His will. Dean Gilliland, professor of Intercultural Studies at Fuller Seminary, writes, "Global mission can be said to be founded on the self-revelation of God."[14] There is no God besides Him. He alone is Father, Creator of all things and for whom we live (1 Corinthians 8:5-6). If there is One God, then He is God of all peoples. He desires every believer to recognize the universal nature of the gospel, not merely individualizing it for themselves, so common in the global Church. Redemptive history at its core could be considered a mission mobilization effort among God's people.

Starting with mobilizing Abraham, God set in motion His plan to create a covenant people (Israel) as a community of blessing to the nations. When Israel multiplied in the land of Egypt and Pharaoh enslaved them, God set up circumstances enabling them to flee Egypt, "mobilizing" the Covenant people into the promised land. Though it took longer than planned, Israel eventually conquered the peoples, taking the land, a picture of the global Church mobilized to reach the unreached peoples of the world.

At each stage of Israel's development throughout the Old Testament (from Moses to the judges to the kings to the prophets), there was a mobilization process of key individual leaders implementing timely Kingdom processes. Always toward the end of progressing His global, redemptive purpose. God is seen mobilizing the prophets who themselves became mobilizers, calling Israel to align with the heart of God in their generation. Like many mobilizers today, the Old Testament prophets faced great rejection from Israel. Yet God's mobilization plan continued to progress.

Jesus as Mobilizer

Jesus came on the scene implementing His own mobilization plan with a different angle. Jesus' three-year ministry was characterized by sacrificial servanthood, compassion, love, miracles, truth, authority, and power. Arthur Glasser asserts Jesus perfectly fulfilled the well-defined Old Testament role of a messenger sent by God—prophet, priest, king, and servant. In addition, Jesus took on key New Testament mission roles—evangelist, apostle, and teacher.[15] Jesus' supreme authority as rightful King was demonstrated by healing disease, raising people from the dead, delivering from spirit oppression, and embracing the most outcast and rejected of society. These were signs to all that the Kingdom of God had come near (Luke 10:9). By leaving what was comfortable to redeem humanity Jesus modeled incarnation to the global Church. He is our perfect example as we engage with the world.[16]

Jesus' calling of the twelve disciples was foundational mobilization. He poured into and trained them over a three-year process for leading the Church forward in the Great Commission upon Jesus' ascension. Jesus was training the apostolic leaders who would "turn the world upside down" (Acts 17:6), spreading the Gospel far and wide in the first century. Jesus was preparing for the future expansion of His Kingdom by teaching, coaching, modeling the Kingdom in perpetual motion. His earthly ministry was primarily focused on teaching the gospel of the Kingdom, paving the way for His followers to take His multidimensional message, accompanied by its power to transform lives, to all the nations upon His ascension and the coming of the Holy Spirit. This is a core principle in mobilization.

Greg Parsons highlights some of the things Jesus did not focus on. "He didn't focus on planting churches, on evangelism, or theological training. Rather, His ministry concentrated more on the big picture than anyone."[17] Steve Shadrach adds, "In Matthew 9:36–38, Jesus exhorted us to pray earnestly for the Lord to send out laborers into His harvest. Have we overlooked the key Jesus was giving us in Matthew 9 to reaching the whole world? Could it be the Master was trying to show us focusing on the saved will ultimately result in winning the lost? Jesus first saw the great need (v. 36), but then concentrated His ministry on equipping more laborers."[18]

Paul's Mobilization Calling

Paul too had the primary calling of a mobilizer, also possessing the conviction that God was One, therefore the God of all peoples—laying on the Church the inescapable obligation to mission.[19] Paul firmly believed the Church was built on the foundation that all peoples are one in Christ. The global community of faith exists to express the will of God, providing continuous expression of God's incarnation in and through Christ. Paul was so committed to God's saving power being experienced by all humanity that he exuberantly proclaimed, "The gospel is the power of God unto salvation for all who believe, first to the Jew and then to the Gentile"(Romans 1:16).

Paul was adamant that "God through Christ reconciled us to Himself and gave us the ministry of reconciliation…God was in the world reconciling the world to Himself…so we are ambassadors for Christ, God making His appeal through us" (2 Corinthians 5:18–20). For Paul, because God had taken initiative in humanity's redemption by reconciling us to Himself, those reconciled in turn become His message bearers of grace to those not yet understanding His redeeming work.[20] He was mobilizing the churches with the vision of God's glory among all nations.

All Paul did was focused on planting communities of believers in many cities that would multiply themselves outward in concentric circles. Paul instilled spiritual depth within the life of every church, who they were in Jesus and their practical outworking as a missionary community. His apostolic teaching had mission mobilization at its core. Paul encouraged the churches to follow his own example, going where other believers were not. He was constantly pushing the boundaries of where the Kingdom was already known, looking beyond to the "unreached" of his day (2 Corinthians 10:16). And his followers and churches did so as well. This is why it could be said in Acts 19:10 that within two years the Kingdom had spread all over Asia Minor—not through Paul himself, but through the Great Commission oriented churches he planted. These believers grew into maturity by experiential knowledge of God, spreading the Gospel beyond the parameters of where it had previously gone. Paul revealed the nature of the Church, expanding the experiential realities of the Kingdom of God among all peoples.

Mobilization is prioritizing the focal points of God's redemptive narrative in Scripture. Calling the global Church to the sum total of all God meant local ministries to become in His Kingdom—embracing core identity. God's pattern—aligning with His two highest priorities—is quite simple: growing in the Great Commandment (Matthew 22:37-38), which always overflows into active engagement in the Great Commission (Matthew 22:39; Matthew

28:18-20). These are foundational cornerstones as God mobilizes a global people joyfully, faithfully, and obediently partnering with Him in this age.

AN EMPHASIZED MESSAGE

It is not difficult to biblically discern that before the return of Jesus the Holy Spirit will prioritize the message of the Great Commission in individual local ministries across His global body. I am confident the global Church will be engaged in faithful mobilization at every local ministry level, mobilizing God's people outward in Jesus' mission. We exist to experientially know God in increasing measures, while proclaiming His Kingdom among all ethnic peoples, both near and distant. Yet the Great Commission message has never been emphasized in the Church in history to the extent on the Lord's heart. Generally, it is sidelined as a department or committee, on the periphery of a local ministry—not its core identity. Of course, the message of the Great Commission has grown throughout history, with significant forward momentum beginning in the mid-1700s through the "modern mission movement."[21] But generally, its focus is not front and center in the lives of believers nor local ministries.

Limitations of Common Mobilization Understanding

Over time, I have come to see how limited mobilization actually is in the global Church. It is the overlooked core of the mission movement. Without it, mission itself cannot become all God intends. Of course, it is given lip service across denominations, organizations, and church networks, cited in mission and vision statements. Maybe a ministry has a conference every few years, a periodic mission speaker, an outreach to a neighboring village, a prayer session for the nations every once in a while. Many leaders, including mission mobilizers themselves, talk about mobilization in these limited ways.

Yet a holistic, comprehensive vision of mobilization remains wanting. Local ministries talk enough about mission to make believers aware it exists, while neglecting to go deep enough for active engagement. Barna Research Group indicates only 17 percent of believers can even describe what Jesus' Great Commission is,[22] while over 50 percent say they have never even heard about the Great Commission in their churches. This travesty reveals a lack of adequately understanding the gospel across the global Church. These statistics call into question how the modern, global Church is defining discipleship, confirming the need for comprehensive, wholistic, biblically based mobilization.

The Laborers Are in the Harvest

A favorite verse among mission mobilizers is Matthew 9:37–38: "Then He said to His disciples, 'the harvest truly is plentiful, but the laborers are few. Therefore, pray the Lord of the harvest to send out laborers into His harvest.'" Jesus was busy in effective ministry, going city to city, teaching the Gospel of the Kingdom and healing every disease among them. No matter how many cities Jesus visited, He knew He was but one man, unable to be everywhere at once (in His flesh). Jesus looked on the multitudes (v. 36), moved with longing as they had no one to shepherd them into the Kingdom. Jesus knew He would soon go to the cross, rise from the dead, commissioning the disciples to reproduce Himself among every ethnic people in every village, town, and city across every nation.

Yet there was a problem—the laborers were few. Had Jesus only called a few? Jesus was not saying there should be few but stating the present situation, resulting in a call to action—pray. In truth, God's will is for the laborers to be many.[23] As we proceed toward the end of the age, this will be realized. But while laborers are still few, "pray the Lord of the Harvest to send out (thrust out forcefully) laborers into His harvest" (v. 38).

Where do these multitudes of laborers come from? Over the last 50 years there has been an unprecedented move of the Holy Spirit globally, thrusting millions of people into the Kingdom of God. According to Todd Johnson, director of the Center for the Study of Global Christianity, a majority of these are in majority-world countries throughout Asia, Africa, and Latin America.[24] So much so that Johnson affirms, "Christians can be found today in every nation of the world."[25] A friend once told me, "The laborers are already in the harvest." What he meant was these significant "harvests" (coming to Christ within present unreached peoples and nations) in time produce Kingdom laborers who themselves become "scattered," crossing cultural barriers, among remaining unreached peoples within their own countries (near culture) and beyond (distant culture). The vast majority of newly scattered message bearer teams are part of previous "harvests" bringing them into the Kingdom. This process relies on effective mobilization implemented within the local ministries planted through the present "harvests" across our nations coming to Jesus.

Mobilization directly empowers local indigenous ministries, full of these harvested laborers. This massive harvest force, from all nations, is made ready to be "thrust out" primarily among **near culture peoples** (see glossary). They are mostly lay leaders, lay people—regular, normal disciples, growing in experiential knowledge of God, empowered, and anointed by the Spirit, acting as conduits among every unreached community, seeing transformation impacting the spiritual, societal, ecological, relational, and physical realms through the Kingdom of God. Some just a few years ago.

Spiritual Warfare in Mission Mobilization

No ministry emphasis stirs the backlash of the enemy like mobilizing the Church to embrace her core identity. Unfortunately, spiritual warfare often unknowingly comes through leadership in the global Church. Many pastors and ministry leaders are stuck in traditional ideas of mission, ignoring it altogether while some have ulterior motives. Friends in a Latin American nation had their calling in mission rejected, belittled as unimportant by church leaders. The pastors sought to manipulate this couple's vast ministry giftings for their own church instead of releasing them to bless the nations. Mission proved secondary to keeping the best people for the home ministry. In my own journey in mission, I once had a pastor tell me, "Why would you want to hide yourself in obscurity among unreached peoples when you could really be something in ministry here?"

This mindset reveals the tremendous spiritual battle to keep pastors and leadership teams from an outward focus on unreached peoples. God is seeking to pull down these strongholds of the mind (2 Corinthians 10:4). Strongholds biblically refer to ideas, thoughts, concepts in the mind keeping people from right thinking about something. Mobilization is not easy work, yet one which the Lord pledges, "I am with you until the end of the age"(Matthew 28:20). Jesus' presence and redemptive work through the cross and resurrection are enough to defeat the schemes of the evil one against the progressing global Church in mobilization. God has promised to establish the work of His hands through our obedience (Psalms 90:17). Satan's defeat through Jesus' death and resurrection must be applied by His praying people across the global Church for mobilization to move forward according to the Lord's intent.

***

So far in this part of the book, we've considered why an emphasis on mobilization is necessary and defined what we mean by mobilization. Let's proceed to now consider a host of core aspects involved in mobilization. These are elements that need to be incorporated into our entire mobilization message and process.

3

Core Aspects of Mission Mobilization

At the core of mission mobilization is the Holy Spirit calling the global Church into agreement with Jesus and His Kingdom ways—the Father's supreme plan to fill the earth with the glory of His Son. This requires overcoming tunnel vision agendas and distractions, embracing His big-picture purpose among the nations. The global Church's tendency is to react much as Martha did when Jesus told her, "Martha, Martha, you are worried and troubled about many things. But one thing is needed…" (Luke 10:41) It is common to be distracted by many "good" things in church life. Yet neglect our core identity as lovers of God prioritizing Jesus' glory among the nations.

There are many practical elements, slices of the pie, that God wants to impart to His global Church through mobilization. These go beyond periodically waving the flag of 'global mission' as generally understood. Empowering local ministries to "launch out into the deep and let you're your nets for a catch" (Luke 5:4) means mentoring, teaching, and coaching them to engage with God's heart for the nations as well as aspects of true discipleship. Growth in these areas is a major factor in whether or not local ministries effectively partner with Jesus in fulfilling the Great Commission. Some practical elements of mobilization focus on discipleship while others bring attention to specifics of mission. Let's consider some of these.

We will start with areas specific to discipleship, progressing to areas focused on mission understanding. Are you a pastor, elder, mission pastor, bishop, denominational executive, campus ministry leader or area overseer or another ministry leadership role? Corporately, each ministry leader's dedication to mission mobilization in their local ministry realm, contributes to the sum total of where God is taking mission mobilization. Millions of dedicated leaders across the global Church, emphasizing mission mobilization, creates a turning of the tide. Each local ministry creating an environment where the following points of emphasis can be regularly highlighted in creative ways.

MISSION MOBILIZATION IS CALLING THE GLOBAL CHURCH...

The following elements are only an introduction. Much more could be said about each one and the reader is encouraged to let these items be a starting point, seeking out more understanding related to each one.

To Cooperate with the Two Great Purposes of Redemptive History

Scripture clarifies two great purposes on the heart of God for His global Church: One revolves around who we are becoming inwardly and the other who we are becoming outwardly. They are two sides of the same coin as we cannot spiritually influence outwardly if failing to grow in spiritual maturity inwardly.

First, the spiritual maturing of the body of Christ. Another way to put it is growing in Jesus' "Great Commandment" (Matthew 22:37)—loving God with all our being and our neighbors as ourselves. Progressing from spiritual immaturity to maturity (Matthew 5:48); from the introductory elements of salvation to the meat of the Kingdom (Hebrews 6:1); from being hearers of the Word to doers (James 1:22); from carnal Christianity to walking in the Spirit (Galatians 5:16–18); from passive faith to true, wholehearted discipleship; from lukewarm Christianity to vibrant, vital relationship with Jesus (Revelation 3:14–22). True faith is a journey of consistently progressing in fellowship, dependence, and obedience to Jesus (Philippians 3:12–14). The Holy Spirit graciously takes these growing spiritual dynamics, empowering us as witnesses among unreached peoples, both locally and globally.

Paul affirms this ultimate purpose in Ephesians 4:13: "Till we all come to the unity of the faith and of the knowledge of the Son of God, to a perfect man, to the measure of the stature of the fullness of Christ." Jesus communicates the same concept with slightly different terminology in the pinnacle verse of the Sermon on the Mount: "Therefore you shall be perfect, just as your Father in heaven is perfect" (Matthew 5:48). A more accurate translation of *perfect* is "mature." A high standard indeed, but how? By living according to Jesus' definition of righteousness revealed in the Sermon on the Mount related to six particular areas common to humanity—anger, lust, marriage, speaking without care, not taking revenge, and loving your enemies (Matthew 5:21–28)—we grow in maturity. The rest of the Sermon on the Mount reveals seven Kingdom activities Jesus calls disciples to grow in: good deeds, prayer, fasting, pursuing true treasure, overcoming worry and anxiety, pure relationships, and guarding your way (Matthew 6:1–7:12). Each activity helps us grow in spiritual maturity, conformed to the image of Christ.

The second great purpose of redemptive history is the bringing in a massive, complete harvest among every ethnic people group through the activated global body of Christ. This is the greatest justice movement humanity will ever experience, rooted in true biblical justice. This process is anchored in seeing those who are different from myself (culturally, ethnically, linguistically, religiously) as valuable, choosing to love them instead of being repulsed and suspicious of them. Achieving the second purpose flows from faithfulness to the first. The second cannot happen apart from the first, while the first has its expression in the second. One without the other is a misapplication of biblical Christianity. Empowering local ministries to embrace both big-picture purposes of redemptive history is a key element of mobilization.

To Grasp the Depth of Spiritual Life Needed in Mission

The New Testament reveals the Holy Spirit's standard for message bearers isn't age, but spiritual depth. Growing in spiritual maturity, they possess experiential understanding of Christ, His Word, and ways. Their spiritual lives are dynamic, marked with love for God's Word, encountering Him through worship and prayer, discerning His "still small voice" (1 Kings 19:12). They have been tested, overcoming challenges of the normal Christian life, being the fragrance of Christ.[1] They are discerning schemes and tactics of the evil one, resisting "fiery darts" (Ephesians 6:16). They have some cross-cultural ministry experience in the home community. Mobilization is calling local ministries to pursue the highest standards of true discipleship, scattering disciples of the highest spiritual quality, whom the Holy Spirit separates to cross cultural barriers to unreached peoples, both near and far.

To Proclaim the Full Message of the Gospel of the Kingdom

"What is the gospel?" As followers of Jesus, experiencing the new birth, we ought to have a solid grasp of the fundamentals of our message. Yet often we hear a hodgepodge of parts of the gospel yet rarely the biblical whole. The gospel is commonly reduced in its scope, appearing vague. A common thread usually heard as "the gospel" is an emphasis on eternal salvation. However, many limit the message to eternal life alone. The gospel is much more comprehensive and exhaustive, covering the fullness of what God intends for all humanity, both in this life and throughout eternity.

We are often guilty of presenting a slanted gospel, providing a few points of truth while neglecting entire core elements and processes of the whole. Salvation is obviously the introduction, yet Jesus calls His body to equip all peoples of the world with so much more. The gospel of the Kingdom revealed throughout the New Testament is a comprehensive message.[2] It starts by providing background information necessary for unreached groups like Muslims, Buddhists, Hindus to grasp what Creator God is like. What He did through creation, how Adam and Eve disobeyed, passing a sinful nature to all humanity. The gospel reveals how God became a man, suffered, yet overcame death to universally redeem lost humanity who believe in Him. The gospel details how to be born again, becoming citizens of the Kingdom of God, progressing to reveal the seemingly limitless benefits, privileges, and blessings of life in this Kingdom while clarifying the joyful responsibilities as well. The gospel invites us to partner with Him in proclaiming His Kingdom authority among all the ethnic peoples. Finally, the gospel of the Kingdom provides a forward-looking vision of the future, how redemptive history unfolds and what to expect in the lead-up to the second coming of Jesus and the transition from this age to the age to come, the fullness of the Kingdom of God.

To Be Rooted in God's Word

Disciples of Jesus embrace the Bible as God's perfect and authoritative revelation to all humanity. Believers are meant to grow in experiential knowledge of the Bible throughout their lifetimes. Yet, a concerning trend is believers generally becoming less biblically literate, not growing in reading, studying, and meditating on the Word.[3] This is further impacted by growing attack and skepticism on the authority of the Bible itself. As John Stott has said, "whenever Christians lose their confidence in the Bible, they also lose their zeal for evangelism and mission. Conversely, when they are convinced about the Bible, then they are more determined about evangelism and mission."[4]

A significant aspect of mission mobilization is calling local ministries to dedicated growth in Scripture, fascinated, discerning God's leading, strengthened by it. Truths of Scripture are not merely memorized, but applied to everyday life circumstances, made real through experience. It is God's will all believers embrace a lifestyle as a vibrant student of God's word. Not merely pastors and Christian leaders. Local ministries weak in rootedness in Scripture are unable to press forward effectively in the Great Commission.

Feeding, meditating, and praying God's Word is not merely a good idea. It is the primary way the Spirit releases spiritual strength among believers to stand for God and His Kingdom. Believers neglecting the privilege of going deep with God through His Word are forgoing a key way God's people live in victory. Rooting ourselves in God's Word empowers believers against temptation while discerning His voice, walking according to His will. A helpful development in the life of a believer is a Bible Study Action Plan—a personal plan to help daily grow as a student of God's Word.[5]

To Walk in the Will of God

Mobilization empowers believers and local ministries to discern the will of God. In Colossians 1:9 Paul prayed for the believers "to be filled with the knowledge of His will."[6] Paul was suggesting believers not only can know the will of God, but ought to know the will of God. To Paul, the will of God has at least a threefold reference: (1) daily living according to principles of life pleasing to Jesus; (2) the general, big-picture ways, plans, and purposes of God that He has called every member of His body to participate in at some level; (3) the specific work and ministry assignment He assigns us to do in the world. God wills every believer to be filled with a clear-cut vision of His general and specific purpose.

The big-picture purpose of God in this age is the fulfillment of the Great Commission. This is the general will of God that all salvation history is progressing toward. Salvation history refers to understanding the personal redemptive activity of God within human history effecting His eternal saving intent of humanity.[7] Accordingly, the particular assignments of each individual believer contribute to that overarching general will of God in some way. Mobilization helps believers discern God's assignment for their individual lives as they feed into His overarching, grand plan. The legitimacy of life callings ought to be measured by whether they agree with God's big picture, general will in the earth. God's will for individuals will always serve His bigger picture will on the earth. The common separation of these two is a reason why more believers are not engaging in some way with God in global cross-cultural mission.

To Be Rooted in a Right View of God

It is common across the global Church to buy into a shallow, weak view of God, unaware we've succumbed to it. A. W. Tozer once said, "What comes to our mind when we think about God is the most important thing about us."[8] A low vision of God produces skewed perspectives, and a corporate faith never intended. This contributes to believers conjuring up a creation of their own imagination when considering God, instead of the supreme vision of God revealed in His Word and by the Spirit.

The greatest attacks of Satan always surround the deity of Christ and the Bible being the authoritative Word of God. It is common to find believers who once were committed, yet today have succumbed to the societal line that Jesus is a great model figure, but not God. Or the growing belief that the Bible is important, with lots to teach, but not the final word from God for humanity. We find people saying, "I love God in my own way." Yet there is only one way to love God, according to His prescribed ways detailed in Scripture. These truths never change, no matter how the culture shifts and need to be reiterated in relevant ways.

To Grow in Seeing Ourselves Correctly

The book of Revelation calls Satan the "accuser of our brethren" (12:10). Seeking to undermine believers to see themselves according to the world's standards instead of God's, Satan sows deception in their minds and hearts. Satan wants believers buying into a false narrative about who they are. God spoke to Samuel about this same issue in 1 Samuel 16:7: "Do not look at his appearance or at his physical stature, because I have refused him, for the Lord does not see as man sees; for man looks at the outward appearance, but the Lord looks at the heart."

Human beings measure by a completely different standard than God. God looks at the heart, the inner desire to love and please Him, though we are weak, finite, prone to inconsistencies. God doesn't look at externals—what family we are from, ethnic heritage or caste, level of education or literacy, birth order or gender, socioeconomic level, how well we communicate, the size of our ministry, or a hundred other areas we falsely measure ourselves by.

It is necessary to deliberately cultivate God's viewpoint, letting His truth wash over us, rooting out inadequacy, insecurity, and fear—along with the pointed attacks that we are unworthy, unspiritual, hypocrites, unholy, causing us to forget we have an advocate with God who has washed us in His blood, making us righteous. Mobilization includes enabling the people of God to overcome self-rejection. Often based in failure to distinguish the accusations of the evil one from the convicting work of the Spirit. Many believers disqualify themselves. Instead, the blood of Christ applied to repentant hearts qualifies us as His ambassadors. God is absolutely for us, seeing believers as cleansed in the blood of the Lamb, washed as white as snow, though still prone to weakness.

To Focused Engagement in Mission

It is common today to refer to everything the Church does in outreach as mission. *When Everything Is Missions* is a helpful book righting some of the wrongs related to how believers understand mission.[9] Effective mobilization empowers local ministries to develop clear, biblical goals, measuring all we do in global mission in light of these constant points of focus. Mission history reveals ways the Church has struggled with focus in global mission. Two examples were an emphasis on education (developing schools) and medicine (developing hospitals). Taking the place of the primary objective of mission, the secondary goal displaced the central heart of mission. While the hoped-for end was always reaching people for Christ, the outcome was institutionalization. Time, personnel, and money were put toward keeping the schools and hospitals operating, while the number of unreached peoples coming to Christ, gathering into churches ceased.[10] The primary goal must always motivate mission activities.

Important humanitarian needs (education, medicine, development, anti-trafficking, social justice) have often preoccupied global mission from the primary emphasis of proclaiming Jesus' redeeming gospel—gathering new believers into reproducible, multiplying churches. A historically proven trend is that starting with the humanitarian, intending to progress to the gospel, rarely gets us there. Yet when starting with the gospel and planting churches, important humanitarian areas get taken care of as well. True Christianity always influences the whole, bringing transformation—but the order has to be in place.

Mobilization calls the global Church to cross cultural barriers (both near and distant cultures) with the focal mission goal of multiplying **church planting movements (CPMs)** (see glossary) toward igniting **people movements to Christ** (see glossary) within a particular responsive village, neighborhood, and family. Through which, over time, a responsive subculture of an ethnic people group is discipled. Every mission activity should be measured against whether or not it enables local ministries to proactively pursue these goals.

To Overcome Negative Stereotypes of Mission

Mission mobilization helps educate believers and local ministries to understand cross-cultural, global ministry. With many viewpoints swirling, it is necessary to discern what is biblical and of the Spirit. This means becoming aware of the viewpoints, wrestling and applying biblical truth to them. Only then can we help those around us throw off tainted viewpoints, embracing biblical perspectives.

This core aspect includes an honest recognition of previous generations of "missionaries," particularly related to colonialism and imperialism. While many sincere, culturally sensitive "missionaries" appropriately utilized the open door of colonialism for the advance of the Kingdom among unreached peoples, some abused it, seeking to "civilize" and change the cultures of the people. Some of that negative legacy is still reaping problems today in nations where believers could never see themselves as "missionaries" because of this baggage.

What are tainted viewpoints needing biblical and missiological correction? While not the purview of this writing to provide corrections to these viewpoints, we do want to identify some of them toward encouraging reflection in the mind of each reader, developing biblically based, informed missiological responses. Spend time wrestling with each, searching out what the Word of God says. A goal of mobilization is enabling believers and local ministries to overcome these viewpoints by knowing and experiencing truth related to each one.

Common misunderstandings about global mission include:

- There is so much need here. God has called us to our "Jerusalem" first.
- Global mission equals physical poverty and suffering.
- Global mission tries to make the people like the home culture, destroying local culture.
- Hasn't the Great Commission already been fulfilled? There are Christians now in almost every country?
- If we mobilize our people for mission, we will lose our best Christians and leaders.
- There is no direct profit to my local ministry if we send workers to the nations.
- Global mission is for white people.
- Africans and Asians are receivers of "missionaries" and cannot be senders.
- There are just a few who are called into global mission, while the

rest are just meant to sit back home.

- A "missionary" should not be employed. Employment of any kind is secular and can absorb the calling. "Missionaries" must be in full-time ministry and not bivocational ministry, helping earn an income.
- Global mission is for Christians in wealthy countries who serve people in poor countries.
- "Missionaries" are often fringe people who don't get along well with others and who cannot get a "real" job in their home country.
- Global mission is the same as denominational reproduction in a country.
- Global mission is one-time village evangelism or weekend crusades.

To Take Responsibility for Their Portion of the Wall

Several years ago, the Lord provided a glimpse of His plan for mobilization through Nehemiah 1–3. The book opens with Nehemiah receiving devastating news about his people and city. The walls around Jerusalem had been destroyed, the gates burned with fire—exposing the people to attack from surrounding enemies. Nehemiah seeks God and God reveals His plan. He sends Nehemiah back to Jerusalem, where he views the damage for himself. Next, Nehemiah gathers the Jewish leaders, challenging them with a God-given vision of rebuilding the wall. The plan included each family working side by side, repairing and rebuilding the particular portion of the wall near their home. Each family both worked on the wall while protecting themselves against outside attack. By all the families working together, they were able to do the unimagi-nable—complete the rebuilding of the wall in a miraculous 52 days!

It is not difficult to see the parallels with mobilization. The "building" imagery often used in the exile and post-exile historical and prophetic writings (Ezra, Nehemiah, Jeremiah, Ezekiel, Haggai, Zechariah) can be applied in the New Covenant as the expansion of the Kingdom of God in this age through the global Church. The families working side by side represent the myriad of denominations and church networks (ministry structures) globally. What would happen if each ministry structure across the nations possessed a vibrant vision of mobilization for the Great Commission? What if they implemented a deliberate strategy to systematically mobilize and equip their grassroots local churches for mission, scattering multitudes of message bearer teams to the unreached? Such a widespread multiplication of this process could produce a massive grassroots mission mobilization movement across networks and denominations, accelerating each local ministry taking up responsibility of contributing to the fulfillment of the Great Commission.

To Emphasize the Remainder of the Task

Mobilization prioritizes subcultures of ethnic people groups having least opportunity to reach their own people. It is necessary to distinguish between reached and unreached peoples. Yes, there are many unbelievers around the world. Yet not all unbelievers are "unreached" peoples. An unreached or least-reached people is a people group (sharing similar culture—beliefs, values, and behaviors, language, religion, ancestry, or other character-istic that is often handed down from one generation to the next) where the indigenous community of believing Christians is too small (usually 2 percent or less of their total indigenous population) to sufficiently evan-gelize and plant churches among their own indigenous people. They need outside help.[11]

Applying this measuring stick, we see how lopsided much global mission ministry is—focused on those already reached. In fact, statistics of current global mission sending reveals about 77 percent of all "missionaries" are serving among already reached peoples,[12] while 6 percent are serving among unreached Muslim peoples, 2 percent among unreached Hindu peoples, and 4 percent among unreached Buddhist peoples with the remaining 11 percent spread out among animist, atheist, Taoist, and other traditional religious backgrounds. These statistics reveal a general failure to prioritize unreached peoples. Mobilization empowers believers and local churches to be spiritually strategic in sending, emphasizing ethnic peoples with little to no believers already among them.

Additionally, mobilization enables believers and local ministries to cate-gorize particular unreached people groups. Unreached people groups are diverse, having multitudes of subcultures. Evangelism and church planting strategies target specific subcultures sharing common age, socioeconomic level, values, interests, experiences, and traditions. These may be in an urban city center or a rural village. Focusing on distinct, likeminded subcultures is a key strategy for seeing potential people movements to Christ as people tend to come to faith together with others like them.

To Two Overarching Principles of Mission

Mobilization includes training local ministries to know where to begin related to engaging a particular unreached people group in mission, both locally and globally. There are two primary areas local ministries consider before the Lord. These are applied after discerning a specific unreached ethnic people group and subculture to target. These two are held in constant tension. We do both of them.

First, message bearer teams sow seed widely within a subculture of an unreached people group, through acts of love, looking for receptivity to the gospel.[13] A new wave of vibrant, focused evangelism is necessary among every unreached people group and subculture therein. The key is the target people hearing and seeing a demonstration of the Spirit and power (1 Corinthians 2:4) as the gospel of the Kingdom is revealed in a culturally relevant way. Nothing enhances the gospel moving swiftly like on fire disciples, motivated by love, gossiping the gospel in a myriad of culturally relevant ways.

Second, faithfully reaping a ripe harvest prepared by the Spirit. Jesus taught His disciples to give priority to responsive, receptive people. The ministry of reaping is equally important as sowing, requiring a different skill set altogether. The fulfillment of the Great Commission will not happen through the ministry of sowing the gospel alone, but through effective reaping as peoples sown among become receptive.[14] Many factors play into a people's responsiveness, including crises, exposure to outside ideas, disillusionment with the status quo, and more. When responsive peoples and subcultures are identified, focused attention should be made on winning whole sections of that group to Jesus. Without the global Church effectively reaping, this ripened harvest will not be brought into the Kingdom. Mission mobilization emphasizes reaping a great harvest among receptive unreached peoples, not merely sowing.

To Focus on Both Near and Distant Cultures

Mission mobilization educates believers and local ministries that global mission isn't only going long distances, crossing continents and oceans, to an entirely different people. Of course, more of these message bearer teams are desperately needed, yet they are not the only types. The world today is full of migration, causing mixtures in every nation of a wide range of ethnicities, cultural characteristics, religious blocks, heart languages, some in rural and other in urban settings. God is propelling His global Church into cross-cultural mission in a fresh way, reaching every subculture, both near and distant cultures from our own, within every nation. This may mean directly engaging while never leaving one's hometown.

The numbers of those whom God intends as message bearer teams in the coming decades is staggering. This is a significant part of the change the Lord is bringing in global mission. Progressing from the "few" of traditional mission sending to the multitudes of biblical, Spirit-led scattering. What if His will was for around 20 percent of members of any local church (whether that church has 40, 400, or 4,000 members) to be scattered as cross-cultural message bearers among receptive unreached peoples? Will they all cross the world? Likely not.

We will consider this strategy in detail in chapter 16. For now, it will suffice to introduce the concepts. Around 15 percent of local church members go to what missiologists call **near culture unreached peoples** (see glossary). Ralph Winter describes this as E-2 evangelism in his E-scale approach to the types of evangelism among different groups.[15] This means they likely don't cross national borders, instead targeting a subculture of an unreached ethnic people group within their own nation. A different culture, yet sharing many similarities to their own. Most will not go further than a 200-mile radius with many remaining in the same city as the sending church. The remaining 5 percent are scattered from a particular local ministry to **distant culture unreached peoples** (see glossary), or what Winter refers to E-3 evangelism.[16] This refers to going to another country, to a people of vastly different culture, language, worldview, and more. Unreached nations, with the vast majority of their ethnic people groups having 2 percent or less born-again believers, need an infusion of these type of message bearer teams settling for at least three to five years. Both the 15 percent to near cultures and the 5 percent to distant cultures are essential for the fulfillment of the Great Commission. The distinguishing feature among these two types of evangelism is culture, not geography.

To the Three Primary Activities of Mobilization

The global Church needs to be educated, inspired, and activated in global mission understanding. First, intellectual understanding related to what the Great Commission is and is not, grasping its biblical foundations, what biblical strategies God has ordained to bring the greatest fruit, where unreached people groups are, what they believe, how they live and much more. Believers and local ministries will not be mobilized in a vacuum. They need consistent instruction.

Second, experiential understanding, inspiring God's people. Inspiration comes in many ways. Through diligently seeking His face for the nations and His will being done among them. When we stand in the gap for the unreached, God inspires our hearts. Through the distribution of information. When we provide relevant information about the status of the Great Commission, details related to what God is doing among unreached peoples, stories of triumph and challenges, faithfulness and obedience, inspiration flourishes. When believers see global mission through new lenses, perspectives, providing quotes, statistics, testimonies, teaching, inspiration happens. Believers need to see the breakdown of societies in smaller categories of peoples, inspiring them to dream, burdened with God's heart for each subgroup and culture.

Lastly, helping every disciple identify and become activated in their assigned role(s) in the Great Commission. Every believer has a role, a particular assignment contributing to the big-picture purpose of the fulfillment of the Great Commission. A primary reason for the present status of the Great Commission is the lack of every believer taking personal responsibility in some form. Mobilization is not merely recruiting a few workers, but helping every disciple, whether or not they will ever meet an unreached person, become activated in the specific role God has ordained for them. At least six roles have been identified.[17] This is the beauty of the Great Commission. No one has a more important role than another. The Lord has set up His

Kingdom so that we need "all hands on deck"—, every believer faithful in their divine assignments.

***

In this chapter we have caught a glimpse of many core aspects involved in mobilization. Implementing these specific aspects will progress the global Church in her core identity in significant ways. We now want to take a focused look at the all-important role of the mission mobilizer. Apart from individual leaders taking up their assignment to blow the trumpet and emphasize mobilization, the fulfillment of the Great Commission is just a pipe dream.

4

Types of Mission Mobilizers

In October 1998, I had a profound experience with the Lord. During an extended time seeking His face, the Lord impressed me with clear words and mental images, followed by peace. The impressions correlated with international events, disasters that had taken place earlier that year. *I will raise up a hundred thousand people who will flood the nations, even as floods have devastated much land throughout the earth this year.* Initially, I had no idea how to interpret this. Since then I have come to understand these are 100,000 mission mobilizers—leaders empowered by the Holy Spirit, within many nations, igniting the global Church with mission emphasis and activation. Their influence is not sporadic, but like a flood deeply saturating land. The flood imagery is key to understanding this guidance, revealing the extent the Lord will go to make mobilization a focal point.

WHAT IS A MISSION MOBILIZER?

What comes to mind when you think of a mission mobilizer? This role is generally understood through a one-dimensional lens (primarily an organizational recruiter), instead of a multifaceted role in God's global purposes. It is common to understand being a mobilizer for a short season of ministry, while rare to find mobilizers remaining faithful decade after decade. A major reason is a lack of comprehensive understanding of a mobilizer. Calling the global Church to grow in her core identity as a multiplying, reproducing, missionary community requires multitudes of mobilizers being identified, trained, and empowered.

A mission mobilizer is a disciple whose heart has been moved and aligned with Jesus' redemptive purpose among all ethnic peoples. They understand His heartbeat for the world, awakening other disciples and entire local ministries to be educated, inspired, and activated in the Great Commission. Mobilizers sound the rallying call, blowing the trumpet, within individual local ministries and across umbrella denominations, church structures and networks. Mobilizers are leaders embodying the exhortation of 2 Timothy 2:2: "And the things that you have heard from me among many witnesses, commit these to faithful men who will be able to teach others also."

A Misunderstood Role

The Church will not mature apart from thousands of mobilizers arising across ministry structures (denominations, independent churches, church networks, organizations, Bible/ministry training schools) with the single-minded purpose of empowering the people of God in their core identity in global mission. It is due to the present lack of mobilizers understanding their role that the global Church conversely misunderstands the Great Commission and what God is calling her to do.

Mission mobilizers are a misunderstood role in Christian ministry. We understand a pastor, mission pastor, worship leader, children's ministry leader, etc. But a mission mobilizer—who is that and what do they do? Ministry in a local church is generally understood as are those directly involved in global evangelism, yet the person bridging this gap is minimized. This appears to be beginning to shift as the Spirit emphasizes mobilization, raising "voices" (Isaiah 40:3) preparing the way of the Lord. These are growing in confidence, though still misunderstood.

Mission mobilizers are in every local church, denomination, and para-church ministry, often not knowing they have this role. God has sovereignly placed them within His people already. They are pastors, teachers, evangelists, while others are lay leaders and lay people within a community of believers. Each one emphasizing God's redemptive storyline and how every believer can be involved. Many are leaders within denominational structures or church networks, marked by the Lord as His voice to mobilize and equip within these ministry structures.

Mission mobilizers presently tend to be perceived as outsiders. They are often misinterpreted by leaders of local ministries. Yet what if a majority of mobilization was done within a local ministry or the wider ministry structure that ministry is associated with? What if mobilizers were part of their denominations and church networks, already known by the ministry structure they are mobilizing and equipping? The implementation of proven mobilization strategies within that structure cannot be done by outsiders. To go to the next level of mobilization, multitudes of mobilizers will lead from within these entities. I am confident this will produce lasting and sustainable mobilization from the inside, not merely from the outside.[1]

God Is Raising Isaiah 40 "Voices"

Over 2,500 years ago, the Spirit spoke a prophecy through Isaiah directly applying to the body of Christ today. Isaiah 40:3–5 declares, "The voice of one crying in the wilderness: prepare the way of the Lord; make straight in the desert a highway for our God. Every valley shall be exalted and every mountain and hill be brought low; the crooked places shall be made straight and the rough places smooth; the glory of the Lord shall be revealed, and all flesh shall see it together; for the mouth of the Lord has spoken." Isaiah reveals a foundational call of the people of God—voices in every generation calling God's people to their core identity: *preparing the way of the Lord.*

John the Baptist embodied this calling, preceding the coming of Jesus in the first century. John's forerunner ministry laid groundwork so Jesus' purpose could be accomplished. John proclaims in John 1:23, "I am 'the voice of one crying in the wilderness; make straight the way of the Lord.'" With simplicity, courage, and humility, John became a "voice" of God in his generation, preparing for Jesus' first coming. Yet John's ministry was not the culmination of the Isaiah 40 prophecy. Verse 5 reveals, "The glory of the Lord shall be revealed and all flesh shall see it together." This did not happen during John's ministry. John's voice was a key partial fulfillment, yet not the ultimate fulfillment of Isaiah's prophecy. His was the first fruits of millions of "voices:

God intends to use. The Holy Spirit is searching for similar voices today to "prepare the way of the Lord."

The fulfillment of Isaiah's prophecy will not be complete until this "Isaiah 40" generation comes to maturity, corporately mobilizing the global Church for the fulfillment of the Great Commission. The Holy Spirit is searching for "voices" in local ministries, small groups, campus ministry fellowships, Bible schools, and more. May we, like John the Baptist of old, discern our calling as "the voice of one crying in the wilderness, make straight the way of the Lord," responding in faith and courage.

TYPES OF MOBILIZERS

Mission mobilization is a large, complex, multifaceted entity, with many types of leaders. We have generally lacked awareness of how many are in the category of "mission mobilizer." It is necessary to identify the wide variety of mobilizer roles. Not all are the same. Some focus on particular functions while other mobilizer types are involved in other areas altogether. Each is necessary, functioning at a high level, to see the global Church become all God intends in mobilization.

In Ephesians 4:11, Paul reveals five core leadership functions Jesus established to equip local ministries. This passage is in context to empowering the global Church to accomplish its calling. These particular gifts are roles serving the global Church. This verse gives a glimpse into the organization and administrative structure of the early Church.[2] There were three types of leader functions in the early Church. Some whose authority was recognized across the whole church (apostles). Some who travelled across many ministries (prophets, evangelists, teachers) and those focused on one local ministry in one place (local church pastors).

According to Paul (4:12), each of the five leadership functions' ultimate purpose is to equip churches and ministries to grow into mature disciples, discipling ethnic people groups themselves. Thus, we can say the five leadership offices each have an aspect of a mission mobilizer. They can be understood as five different types of mobilizers. As we've established, it is possible to view God's big-picture redemptive storyline through the lens of God, Jesus, and Paul as mobilizers (see chapter 2). We can go a step further and understand the same about these five leadership functions in Ephesians 4:11.

Ministry leadership (when correctly focused on what the Bible and redemptive history are focused on) is for the distinct purpose of equipping God's communities of believers to be mobilized—educated, inspired, and activated in the Great Commission.

The global Church has fallen into a dangerous practice never intended in Scripture—leaders doing all the work of ministry themselves. Many believers in local ministries are bored, unable to express the gifts God has given, because those in public ministry have often misunderstood their function, crossing into the purview of each believer in the local churches.

According to John Stott, this leads to either one of three models of a local church. The traditional, pyramid model where the pastor is at the point of the pyramid, while members are within the pyramid in levels of inferiority. This model is foreign to the New Testament. Scripture reveals a pastor figure in a shepherding role with every member contributing to the ministry using their gifts. Another model is a bus. The pastor is driving the bus while the congregation are the passengers, nodding off as they drive to their destination. Different from either of these is the correct biblical model of a local ministry made up of members each possessing a particular function or role.[3] We see this in Ephesians 5:19–21 where each member is instructed to bring a psalm, hymn, or spiritual song to the meeting.

Let's consider these five Ephesians 4:11 mobilizer leaders in the body of Christ, defining what they do, who they serve, and how they function.

Pastor-Mobilizer

This type of mobilizer is a pastor or ministry leader overseeing a church or ministry group. This could be a local church, campus ministry fellowship, or Bible study leader. The Latin word for "pastor" is *shepherd*. God is seeking to raise shepherd mobilizers seeing their primary function in church leadership as mobilizing the flock to be God's true missionary community, both locally (near cultures) and globally (distant cultures). They mobilize using the platform of their ministry function. This goes beyond recruiting laborers to the macro view of mission mobilization—guiding their ministry on the journey of being mobilized and equipped. Through their leadership, they encourage growth and understanding in mission across the whole group. Without pastors deliberately functioning in this way, it will be difficult to see those under their leadership engaged in their roles in the Great Commission effectively. Well-known contemporary and historical Pastor-Mobilizers include John Piper, David Platt, Francis Chan, A. T. Pierson (1837–1911), and A. J. Gordon (1836–1895).

Apostle-Mobilizer

This leader is usually appointed to oversee a denomination, church network, campus ministry organization, or an area or district of such a ministry structure (overseeing multiple local ministries). They keep the big-picture purpose of their ministry structure's function in the mission movement at the forefront. As the Greek word *apostle* refers to a "sent one," they see themselves as dynamically involved in educating, inspiring, and activating their whole ministry structure in cross-cultural ministry (both within near cultures and distant cultures). God has placed them within a leadership context to equip the local ministries under their leadership to flourish as individual Great Commission ministries. Providing mobilization tools, courses, and resources to the local ministries under their direction, they work to see local ministries educated, inspired, and activated in Great Commission understanding. They see to it that pastors and leadership teams of local ministries are trained to mobilize and equip their ministries. It is rare today to find this type of apostle-mobilizer, yet God is calling many along these lines. Historic examples include Nicolaus Von Zinzendorf (1700–1760), Charles Simeon (1759–1836), A. B. Simpson (1843–1919), John R. Mott (1865–1955) while contemporary examples include Reuben Ezemadu (Nigeria), Daniel Bianchi (Argentina), Luis Bush (Argentina) and Rick Warren (USA).

Prophet-Mobilizer

This is a leader God reveals specific guidance about particular strategies and insights in mobilization. They speak with authority as ones hearing from God related to pathways forward. Their main task is equipping others to grasp insights related to the plans, purposes, and ways of God in mission. They fellowship deeply with the heart of Jesus, discerning His ways and communicate these with clarity to the churches. They help churches, often bogged down with tunnel vision, to remain focused on the will of God, who they are as Great Commission ministries. It is easy for local ministries to get sidetracked, losing their identity as God's missionary community. Examples include Ralph Winter (1924–2009), Donald McGavran (1897–1990), Roland Allen (1868–1947), Loren Cunningham (USA), and Thuo Mburu (Kenya).

Evangelist-Mobilizer

Many scholars understand an evangelist as the person gifted to do the work of evangelism. Keeping in mind our Ephesians 4:12 passage, leaders equip the saints to do the work of ministry. Evangelist-mobilizers, then, equip churches in local and cross-cultural evangelism and mission. They have been specifically trained by God to effectively evangelize and in turn train churches in outreach. They equip members to be "scattered" to multiply new churches. The evangelist-mobilizer is intensely practical, revealing the "how" of reaping a harvest among a targeted people group, either locally (near culture) or globally (distant culture). Historical evangelist-mobilizers have included John Nevius (1829–1893), David Livingstone (1813–1873), and Jonathon Goforth (1859–1936), while in contemporary circles David Garrison (USA), David Watson (USA), and David Lim (Philippines) fall into this category.

Teacher-Mobilizer

This may be a local leader within one local church or who travels to teach a grouping of churches in a geographic area. Their role is opening the Word of God, revealing the will and plan of God from Scripture. Rooting believers in discipleship, declaring, and applying the whole message of the gospel of the Kingdom. Teacher-mobilizers practically reveal the multifaceted roles for every believer within the mission movement. Teacher-mobilizers anchor the churches in the overall theme of Scripture—the mobilizer God aligning His global Church with His redemptive purposes in the earth. They connect the dots for believers to see their lives as directly part of God's story in the earth. This is a crucial role as teachers reveal the redemptive purpose of God in and through salvation history, applying it to our Great Commission context today. Examples include Hudson Taylor (1832–1905), Ajith Fernando (Sri Lanka), Max Chismon (New Zealand), Steve Hawthorne (USA), and Christopher J. H. Wright (USA).

FURTHER MOBILIZER CATEGORIES

Beyond these five leadership-mobilizer functions in Ephesians 4:11, there are other categories of mobilizers as well.[4] These influence less through a position within a ministry structure, but through relationships. Both are necessary to effectively advance the body of Christ. Mobilization is a process whereby God uses many different people at different times to nudge His people forward in His grand purposes.

Recruiter-Mobilizer

This is the category we are most familiar with in mobilization circles. They serve with a particular mission sending organization, denomination, or ministry, recruiting workers through their structure. They often recruit among the younger generation, spending much time on college campuses, recruiting for short-term experiences, or the like. It is usually the case that believers are prepared to respond to a recruiter-mobilizer because of the effectiveness of each of the other types earlier on in their journey.

Trainer-Mobilizer

These types of mobilizers provide training through Bible schools, seminaries, conferences, seminars, and mission education courses. These may be formal, nonformal, or informal training, exposing believers to what mission is about, why it's important, training a wide variety of focal points related to global mission. Trainer-mobilizers have experience in mission, engaging other believers primarily through information exchanges. They help believers wrestle with the possibilities of how God may be calling them.

Discipler-Mobilizer

Personal, one on one influence, is a most effective form of individual mobilization. This refers to a relationship a person has with typically an older, more experienced believer where spiritual influence, direction, and encouragement are transferred from one to another. Mission emphasis is also made as the discipler-mobilizer connects the believer with resources, tools, books, information, trainings, examples, further relationships, and more. These mobilizers deliberately put God's mission heartbeat at the center of discipleship.

They also serve as a model to the believer, demonstrating the kind of life they want to live.

Motivational-Mobilizer

These mobilizers are voice's a believer hears or reads, inspiring them to grow in global mission. They are motivators, often a one-off type connection that stays with the person for a long time, impacting in a dynamic way. They may be speakers at churches, conferences, Christian colleges—yet are not limited to this. They can also write a biography or teaching book, inspiring the believer in mission at just the right time.

Divine Contact-Mobilizer

This usually is a one-off situation where God provides timely divine guidance through a person related to a specific role in mission that an individual is meant to have. This connection can often be supernatural in nature, speaking through a person who may have little idea of how God used them in the interaction.

Historical-Mobilizer

This is most often a further step in the mobilization process. It involves reading the lives and books of those engaged in mission, potentially from generations ago, being propelled into similar action ourselves. Historic voices come alive through books, mobilizing today's generation to come into God's fullness.

Intercessor-Mobilizer

This refers to a mobilizer praying for others. Through their prayers, God directly influences believers with a heart for their individual Great Commission roles. Prayer, and its accompanying experience of the presence of God, is a powerful mobilizer. When mobilizers pray for believers to become engaged in mission, a powerful inner strength arises within the lives of believers to pursue those particular roles.

MOBILIZER SPHERES OF INFLUENCE

In addition to the five leadership-mobilizer roles in the global Church (Ephesians 4:11) and seven types of mobilizer categories looked at, there are also varying spheres of influence mobilizers may possess. It is helpful to discern and identify the sphere of influence the Lord has assigned to us. Not all mobilizers have the same influence. One sphere is not more important than another and should not be understood as what we aspire after. Instead, in humility, we embrace the sphere the Lord has gifted us to mobilize in, faithfully doing our part in that sphere. This does not refer necessarily to a mobilizer having an assigned role or title along these lines. They may have a position yet often do not, using spiritual authority without a particular position. Here are six potential spheres God may assign a mission mobilizer.

One-on-One Mobilizer

This refers to an individual relationship where a mobilizer influences another regarding the Great Commission. These may be one or more of the above seven mobilizer types. This may be in one's family, workplace, campus, church, or some other relationship. This is the base level where every follower of Jesus should be mobilizing other believers they have a relationship with.

Local Ministry Mobilizer

This refers to a mobilizer helping their local church or campus ministry fellowship to progress along the journey of being educated, inspired, and activated in mission. They are not necessarily the leader(s) of the local ministry itself, though they may be. Often local ministry mobilizers influence the group from the periphery. Such a local ministry may be 50, 500, or 1,000 people. Their sphere of influence in mobilization is at the local ministry level, using a variety of tools and means to influence that local ministry with core principles of mobilization.

Church Network or Denomination Mobilizer

This is a mobilizer working across a particular like-minded ministry structure, whether large or small. Their influence may reach across the whole of the organization or a region or area. Their role or position may have nothing to do with mobilization. Yet they influence using their position. Having access to local ministries within their structure, they mobilize by being known and trusted, having credibility, within the organization or denomination. They implement core principles of mobilization, enabling local ministries to mobilize and equip their own.

Itinerant Mobilizers

Many mobilizers are called to influence beyond their particular organization, church network, or denomination. God empowers them to network across these wider lines, bringing leaders together to develop and implement mobilization strategies.

Area or National Mobilizer

This could refer to a mobilizer hosting mobilization courses in a geographical area or national level. Or a mobilizer who travels to local ministries motivating and mobilizing in a particular area of a nation or nationally.

Regional Mobilizer

This mobilizer sphere of influence builds on the previous one. Not merely mobilizing in an area or nation, but across several nations—a global region. These mobilizers implement a mobilization strategy to empower churches, networks, and organizations within that region, influencing them with mission mobilization. Through teaching and training, gathering people together, they influence at a wide level for mission mobilization.

Global Mobilizer

This is the highest sphere of influence, on a global scale. These mobilizers may be within a particular ministry structure or across many. Yet their mobilization impact is global. Their influence is felt in mission mobilization in many ways. Through promoting global initiatives, mobilization strategies, teaching and training, convening of key leaders, strategic consultations, prayer, and more.

***

The global Church needs multitudes of effective mobilizers in each sphere of influence. All function as Isaiah 40 voices, emphasizing her core identity of the Great Commission and biblical, Spirit-led strategies to accomplish it. It is necessary to seek the Lord to know the specific sphere He has assigned each mobilizer. Again, one is not greater or more important than another, all are essential in mobilization, needed parts of the proverbial "body."

Now that we've grasped who mobilizers are and what they do, let's consider a crucial part of their overall message.

5

Mission Mobilizers: Rebuilding Ancient Ruins

Commonly, mission mobilizers are understood as raising the flag of "global mission," the "unreached," or the like. This is true, as we have seen, yet incomplete. Mobilizers influence believers and local ministries to grow in love for Jesus, and from the overflow of that love, obey Jesus' commands, including the Great Commission. Mobilizers, then, disciple according to Jesus' definitions of discipleship, through which believers align with how their lives can be maximized for Jesus' glory in the earth. One of the greatest short-comings in the global Church today is often weak, incomplete discipleship, influenced by prevailing culture more than Kingdom culture. The Kingdom of God impacts society, first transforming people then transforming systems and segments of society through transformed people. A crucial element of mobilizers then, has little to do with talking about "global mission," but spiritual depth. This is a necessary factor to empower local ministries to "launch out in the deep and let down your nets for a catch" (Luke 5:4).

REBUILDING ANCIENT RUINS IN THE
THE OLD TESTAMENT

Biblical prophecy is multilayered. There are usually at least three primary references to any single biblical prophecy, with many lesser references at various historic points that can also be applied. This holds true of many, if not most, Old Testament and New Testament prophecies, while there are obvious exceptions. Misunderstanding this principle is where many mistakes are made in discerning the meaning of biblical prophecy.

First, an initial layer of reference is to an immediate historic event, usually within the lifetime of the prophet—a partial fulfillment of the prophecy. Second, that same biblical prophecy refers to circumstances taking place far in the future, usually near the end of the age, before Jesus' second coming— representing the ultimate fulfillment. The historic event (first layer) is a partial fulfillment meant to be studied, providing a glimpse of a similar type of circumstance that will happen further in the future as the ultimate fulfillment (second layer). Between these two references are often many similar, yet lesser historical occurrences that also have direct connection to the original prophecy. Third, all Scripture can be personalized to an individual while being useful to illustrate certain situations the people of God corporately may find themselves in (2 Timothy 3:16–17).

Rebuilding Ancient Ruins in Jeremiah and Ezekiel

In the last two weeks of May 2014, I had a unique experience with the Lord. God strung together application of two specific passages He had impressed on me sixteen years previous, in 1998. In 1998, I had spent an extended season in prayer. During that time, these two passages were impressed on me so strongly that I have never forgotten them. I knew there was significant application in these passages, but in 1998 I didn't know what it was. In the two weeks during May 2014, sixteen years later, I began to discern their application.

The two passages were in Jeremiah and Ezekiel:

> "Behold, I will bring it [Israel] health and healing; I will heal them and
> reveal to them the abundance of peace and truth. And I will cause the

captives of Judah and the captives of Israel to return, and will rebuild those places as at the first. I will cleanse them from all their iniquity by which they have sinned against Me, and I will pardon all their iniquities by which they have sinned and by which they have transgressed against Me. Then it shall be to Me a name of joy, a praise, and an honor before all nations of the earth, who shall hear all the good that I do to them, they shall fear and tremble for all the goodness and all the prosperity that I provide for it." (Jeremiah 33:6–9)

"Thus says the Lord God: 'On the day that I cleanse you from all your iniquities, I will also enable you to dwell in the cities and the ruins shall be rebuilt. The desolate land shall be tilled instead of lying desolate in the sight of all who pass by. So they will say, 'This land that was desolate has become like the Garden of Eden, and the wasted, desolate and ruined cities are now fortified and inhabited.' Then the nations which are left all around you shall know that I, the Lord, have rebuilt the ruined places and planted what was desolate. I, the Lord, have spoken it and I will do it." (Ezekiel 36:33–36)

The context of both passages is Israel having been conquered, her people carried away to Babylon in slavery, and her land and cities made desolate. Israel's captivity in Babylon took place over the 70 years from 608–538 BC. The state of Israel during her captivity can be paralleled with the state of the global Church at present. Both passages refer to the process following the Babylonian exile itself (538 BC), when Israel's barren places would be rebuilt, using similar language. Both are core prophetic utterances forming summaries of the overall contents of each book. That means their message is significant and should be paid attention to.

Both Jeremiah and Ezekiel prophesied during Israel's 70-year captivity in Babylon (608–538 BC), a horrible time in Israel's history. Because of ongoing, determined, rebellious disobedience and idolatry, God raised the dreaded Babylonian empire to destroy Jerusalem and the temple. Babylonians killed many Israelites while taking the elite captive to Babylon. Leaving the poor to fend for themselves in a destroyed land, ultimately dying of starvation. This event ended the Israelite monarchy, the line of kings stemming from David, appearing to bring the covenanted promises of God to an end.[1]

Yet during the 70-year captivity, Jeremiah and Ezekiel encouraged the people. Though presently captive because of transgressions, that wasn't the end of their story. There was a big-picture plan God was orchestrating. In time, God would cleanse and forgive them the former iniquity that drove them into exile. God would restore health and healing where there had been spiritual brokenness and barrenness. The 70-year captivity would end. Then God would send them back to the promised land, full of spiritual vitality and wholeness, to rebuild the temple and city walls around Jerusalem (see the books of Nehemiah, Ezra, Haggai, Zechariah). God would restore, revive the "desolate" and "barren." So much that outsiders see the transformation among them and through their spiritual influence bring transformation among others. This spiritually parallels the global Church today regaining her spiritual inheritance and intended glory and purpose, resulting in the world seeing Jesus in a dramatic way—revealed through the increased light shining through His corporate people.

The Davidic line of kings would not be reinstated, as Israel hoped. Yet the way would be prepared for the coming of the true King issuing forth a new spiritual community, the Church, to shine His light among all peoples. The Church would be a praise and honor unto the King, living out the gospel before the nations. The spiritual intent of the Lord from the beginning would come to fruition among His people: "The wasted, desolate and ruined cities are now fortified and inhabited" (Ezekiel 36:35). The nations would "hear" of God's goodness in spiritually reviving, rescuing His people, in turn seeking God in fear and trembling.

These two passages reveal a stunning reversal—desolate and barren ruins turning into tilled and fortified cities in plain view of the world. So much so that outsiders call the global Church the "Garden of Eden" and want whatever we have. This message of ultimate restoration is a regular theme of the Old Testament prophets. Throughout their history, Israel needed encouragement that God had a plan (with many layers of fulfillment leading to ultimate restoration at the end of the age). Yet the message of restoration is also for us today, speaking directly into the themes of this book, and where God is apparently taking His global Church in mobilization.

In the Jeremiah and Ezekiel prophecies, the immediate historic event (partial fulfillment) was the end of the exile, the return to Jerusalem and surrounding cities, and the spiritual restoration of the Jews (working to rebuild the temple). Yet, many details in both passages did not come to pass in the years following the exile. The further future, ultimate fulfillment refers to the few years before the second coming of Jesus, when natural Israel (Jews alive during that time period) will endure another painful period (not unlike the Babylonian exile, but mercifully shorter) where the global forces of darkness will seek to obliterate them. Following the devastation of that period, in context to the literal return of Christ in the sky, the surviving Jews will be ultimately restored (as promised in myriads of Old Testament prophecies), come to saving faith in Jesus as Messiah, returning to Jerusalem to rule and reign with Him throughout the millennial Kingdom (1,000-year period). All the details in both passages will be seen at that time.

The spiritual reference of these prophecies refers to the global Church spiritually becoming all God intends, through the cleansing blood of Christ, leading to the fulfillment of the Great Commission and subsequent second coming of Christ. Each detail in these two passages lived out in ways beyond what is presently experienced in and through the global Church. Because of God progressively maturing the global Church spiritually, she will become the attractive light, drawing multitudes of subcultures within unreached peoples to the Lord in significant numbers before the return of Jesus. The promise of global harvest cannot happen apart from the global Church spiritually rebuilding of ancient ruins," the core truth of these two prophecies.

In May 2014 the Lord applied these two passages as promises of the extent He would go in transforming the global Church spiritually. And through renewal of the global Church, reaching the nations. These passages are an invitation to contend for the promises of God to be fulfilled, enabling the Church to become a wholehearted people after God's own heart. Proclaiming this message is a key function of a mission mobilizer. The promises in both passages speak of spiritual awakening in the global Church producing the highest spiritual quality of laborers scattered among all ethnic peoples. This is where the mission movement is going and why it is so important to grasp. Let's unpack what "rebuilding of ancient ruins" means.

Rebuilding Ancient Ruins in Haggai

During the same period in May 2014, I studied the book of Haggai and discovered further pieces of the rebuilding ancient ruins tapestry. In Haggai, Israelites returning to Jerusalem from exile in Babylon, following the 70-year captivity, had begun rebuilding the temple. The temple was the dwelling place of God, the centerpiece of worship in the ancient world. The people of God could not worship or sacrifice apart from its restoration. In Haggai, about 15 years had passed since returning from the Babylonian exile. They had given up their building project, necessary to reinstitute Mosaic worship. Haggai was instructed by God to call the Israelites back to their mandate of "rebuilding the temple"—purposefully building the spiritual life of the Israelite community. The book of Haggai is a spiritual parallel of the global Church today. We need to spiritually grow into the fullness of our spiritual inheritance (continue building the temple) toward the end of reengaging with God's big-picture purpose of reaching all the peoples.

"Rebuilding the temple" correlates with building the spiritual life of the people of God, enabling His people to become the light He intended among all ethnic peoples. "Rebuilding" spiritually is a primary purpose of God in history, resulting in the great harvest among every ethnic people into His Kingdom. This is the big-picture promise of Haggai 2:7: "And I will shake all nations, and they shall come to the desire of all nations, and I will fill this temple with glory." Referring to both a partial fulfillment through a particular historical event and its complete, ultimate fulfilment at the end of the age. This promise has a direct correlation with full restoration of the spiritual community. The one cannot happen without the other. The spiritual community becoming all God intended and the fulfillment of the Great Commission are dynamically related. The restoration of deep spiritual life in the global Church is the precursor, and primary mechanism, resulting in the coming great harvest.

REBUILDING ANCIENT RUINS IN THE NEW TESTAMENT

How do we understand God's "temple" purpose in the New Testament? The presence of God no longer dwells in a building, but in the lives of disciples.

"Rebuilding ancient ruins" refers to developing the spiritual life of the people of God, restoring the means (global Church) God intended to accomplish this. The spiritual life of the global Church is often in ruins today, little resembling the authentic faith revealed in the New Testament. God's definition of biblical Christianity is what Jesus described in the Gospels, what the early Church in the book of Acts was like and what the apostles taught in the Epistles. We often find a hybrid of discipleship today, which is not discipleship at all.

"Rebuilding ancient ruins" refers to embracing the standards of Scripture, choosing the fear of the Lord, obeying His commands. Turning from distractions, complacency, compromise, lukewarmness, restored to vibrant New Testament faith. It includes repentance, confession, and receiving Jesus' empowering grace, becoming what we cannot in our own strength. The Bible reveals Jesus is returning for a prepared, purified Bride. It is this same Bride, shining Jesus' light across the nations, that attracts multitudes to Jesus among unreached frontier peoples.

There are presently about one billion Christians affiliating with Protestant, evangelical churches globally.[2] Of this number, multitudes are caught in myriad areas of compromise. Whether addiction to pornography and immorality, drunkenness, materialism, pride, covetousness, anger, envy and jealousy, or other chains, the global Church is not yet what she ought to be. Yet God has a plan to transform this, referred to biblically as "rebuilding ancient ruins," rescuing the global Church from the Laodicean spirit (Revelation 3:14–22). God is working to restore the ancient ruins of relationships, economies, finances, health, marriages, friendships. He will see to it that a dynamic reversal transpires, cleansing and delivering His people, rescuing her from her past, enabling her to shine His light among all the ethnic peoples.

Rebuilding Ancient Ruins in Acts 15

Acts 15:16–17 is another piece of the "rebuilding ancient ruins" tapestry. The apostle James references another Old Testament prophet, Amos 9:11–12, to justify the plan of God for the gospel being made available to Gentiles, not just Jews. The first steps of the history-spanning global mission movement, culminating at the end of the age, was just under way. James reveals the "tabernacle of David" being rebuilt, leading to humanity becoming motivated to call on the name of the Lord. This is a yet future promise in direct correlation with "rebuilding ancient ruins." The early Church experienced a partial fulfillment of these restorations, yet the ultimate fulfillment will come in and through the fulfillment of the Great Commission as the body of Christ is spiritually restored to her true inheritance in Jesus.

"Rebuilding ancient ruins" is a return to authentic New Testament faith, laying hold of all God has laid hold of His Church through Jesus' death and resurrection (Philippians 3:12): embracing the cross, denying self, forgiving others, and much more. Jesus purchased so much through the cross. Much it seems we are hardly walking in today. "Rebuilding" is a call to become all Christ intended for His global Church and is inextricably linked to the results in the Jeremiah 33, Ezekiel 36, Haggai 2, and Acts 15 passages—harvest among presently "desolate" peoples of the world and the fulfillment of the Great Commission in this generation.

Rebuilding Ancient Ruins in Mission and Discipleship

While the global Church is expending much energy in mission today, much is done in human strength. To operate instead in God's strength, we deliberately "rebuild ancient ruins." The two go hand in hand. Mission mobilizers help individuals, local ministries, denominations, and networks "rebuild ancient ruins," becoming a dwelling place of the powerful presence of God, walking in His ways, embracing Kingdom life.

The Spirit is calling the innumerable company John saw in Revelation 7:9 from unreached peoples of the world. Mission mobilizers historically have promoted the global mission side, while the Spirit today is raising up mobilizers prioritizing both. Discipleship includes the responsibilities of the Kingdom, not only enjoying its benefits. God has orchestrated His Kingdom that disciples follow hard after this King out of love, taking up Kingdom responsibilities Jesus sets before us. Thus, mobilization as "rebuilding ancient ruins" includes calling believers and communities to return to their first love, obeying Jesus according to Scripture.

***

The truths of this chapter are proven throughout church and mission history. A recurring historical trend is the direct correlation between renewal and subsequent mission thrusts among that same people. Historic revivals preceded all the major advancements of the mission and mobilization movements of the past, including that which launched the Church and mission movement in the book of Acts—Pentecost.[3] This crucial factor cannot be overlooked. Jesus is calling a wholehearted global Church to reach all unreached peoples, not the often self-absorbed, lethargic, spiritually bored Church we tend to see today. It is time to spiritually "rebuild ancient ruins" with thousands of mission mobilizers proclaiming this message as a core part of mobilization.

Having considered foundations of what mission mobilization is in part 1, let us proceed to root our understanding of the Great Commission in Scripture. This helps us grasp that mobilization is calling the global Church to her core identity. Part 2 focuses on a variety of core elements of the Great Commission and the global Church's role, many of them misunderstood today.

Part 2

Biblical Background of The Great Commission

6

Jesus' Fourfold Commission

A significant piece of mission mobilization is helping local ministries and believers internalize what God has set before the global Church as His corporate destiny. Believers commonly have little understanding of the Great Commission. The phrase is often used assuming all believers know its biblical meaning. This is true among pastors and ministry leaders as well as lay people. Going to Bible school is not a qualification for correctly grasping Jesus' Great Commission. For this reason, it is necessary to consider the biblical meaning of what Jesus called us to prioritize in this age. Doing so helps local ministries engage in the ministry emphases Jesus laid out, overcoming well-meaning distractions in mission. It is because we are somewhat unaware of what Jesus actually taught in the Commission passages that confusion in mission mobilization has transpired.

THE FOUR COMMISSION PASSAGES CREATE A COHESIVE WHOLE

The "Great Commission" passages in the four gospels create a cohesive whole. Often, we focus primarily on Matthew's words in our understanding of Jesus' calling for His Church. However, Matthew's recording of Jesus' commission does not give the whole picture. We also must take into account what Mark,

Luke, and John include as the recorded words of Jesus related to our commission. In this way, we find unity of vision in our commission, yet with particular emphases from each.

Jesus did not give us four of the same commission—just using different words. They are actually four distinct "commissions" forming the entirety of Jesus' "Great Commission" and portraying the priority of the body of Christ between the time of Jesus' first and second comings. These four commission passages then provide us a comprehensive picture of the various focal ministry points Jesus intends the global Church to prioritize in global mission.[1]

Jesus' Commission in Matthew

> And Jesus came and spoke to them, saying, "All authority has been given to Me in heaven and on earth. Go therefore and make disciples of all the nations, baptizing them in the name of the Father and of the Son and of the Holy Spirit, teaching them to observe all things that I have commanded you; and lo, I am with you always, even to the end of the age." (Matthew 28:18–20)

The broad purpose of Matthew's gospel is revealing the Kingdom of God has come, manifested through the life of the King. The book introduces the nature of the Kingdom of God, its demands on followers and its ultimate fulfillment through the return of Christ. Jesus is revealed as King, rejected by those He came to love, yet returning to rule in power and majesty. The centerpiece of Matthew is the King's authority to rule and reign. His authority includes every right of a King—setting in motion new laws, ways of living (the Sermon on the Mount), and bringing about victory (revealed in the cross and resurrection). Jesus is the embodiment of a true King in every way.

In Matthew, Jesus' commission is that of the ultimate King and lawgiver. Based on His absolute authority, His body is consistently moving outward, discipling (this includes more than making individual disciples) the nations (all ethnic groups in every nation), baptizing those submitting to the King, and teaching them to live according to a new moral standard. The entire commission is clothed with Jesus' rule and reign as authoritative King. The King Himself sending us to proclaim His Kingdom and Kingship among all peoples. This commission confronts humanity in its first area of need—

being void of true authority. The world needs authority on issues of moral and ethical standards. It has always been lawless, tolerant, deceived about the nature and existence of sin. A primary way conviction comes is through being provided a moral standard based on true authority.

Who Is Responsible for the Commission?

Jesus' commission is given to every follower of Jesus. It is often mistaken as being for "mission professionals," or some specific few most of us do not feel we qualify for. Instead, it is given to everyone calling upon the Lord, believing Jesus died for their sin—those loving, obeying, and living according to the will of the Father. Every disciple has a God-ordained role in helping every ethnic people group recognize the supreme place of authority given to Jesus as eternal King. You may never leave your home city, yet through engaging with your God-ordained role you can impact millions for the sake of the Gospel. No disciple is exempt from the Great Commission.

Reasons Jesus Declared the Extent of His Authority (v. 18)

"All authority has been given unto Me!" The disciples needed to hear this for several reasons. First, helping them overcome the offense of the cross. Jesus' death was still a mystery to them. They were shocked by the events forty days before. How could things have spiraled out of control so quickly? How could Messiah be killed? The cross taught voluntary suffering as one of the greatest forms of power. Jesus' suffering and resurrection achieved absolute authority, eternal rule, and reign for Jesus.

Second, Jesus was emboldening disciples in the commission He was about to give. They needed to see their commission was substantiated by His own hand, backed by absolute spiritual authority. Because of His resurrection, defeating death, providing assurance of His authority, disciples and churches proceed with confidence in the Great Commission. They are not left to their own devices.

"As you are going..." (v. 19)

There are a few translation issues to clarify in this commission. First, the word *go* has been simplified from the original language. The best rendering is, *"As you are going..."* Jesus assumed all disciples would be "going" in some form. The implication is something is wrong if disciples are not moving outward in obedience to His commission. He expected disciples would be surrendered to His rule and reign, choosing to live in neighborhoods, towns, villages, cities, and nations with little recognition of Jesus as supreme authority. This does not refer only to traditional "missionaries." It includes every disciple prayerfully considering where the Holy Spirit is planting them with professions, families, etc., for the distinct purpose of revealing Jesus as supreme King over all. Many jobs can be done in a variety of unreached countries and cities—doctors, lawyers, engineers, teachers, farmers, accountants, and more. Instead of considering a home location for such a job, ask the Lord where He is leading you to do that job, while simultaneously helping others recognize Jesus' supreme right as King over all.

"Disciple the nations" (v. 19)

The next translation problem is, "Make disciples of all the nations." The original language translates best as, "Disciple all ethnic groups." From the former, we approach the gospel in an individualistic way, "making disciples." This is good and right as there is a clear individual element to "discipling nations." Yet the tendency is overemphasizing individual discipling at the expense of "discipling all ethnic groups." The commission is to disciple ethnic peoples (and every subculture within that overarching group) as a whole—influencing them in their entirety, toward the King's standards and ideals.

But how? By living, teaching, and providing examples of the Kingdom of God in their midst, targeting particular like-minded subcultures. We influence the ungodly elements of culture by exposing ethnic groups to a thoroughly different, countercultural way of living—the Kingdom of God. Jesus' message bearers declare the fact of His Lordship, announcing within that people group that He is King—calling for a supreme standard of life according to the created order. Disciples declare the King's moral standards and ideals, revealing the greatest intellectual height is growing in the knowledge of God and our emotional ideals being realized in loving God and neighbors. We live and work among unreached ethnic people groups, simultaneously declaring His authority based upon the proof of His resurrection.

"Baptizing them in the name of..." (v. 19)

Obviously, individuals make up ethnic groups and respond by changing allegiance from sin and idolatry to Jesus and His Kingdom ways, becoming new creations in Christ. At the same time, there are many within the ethnic group (subculture) who do not respond. As some respond, Jesus instructs us with two specific responsibilities. The first is baptizing those who have identified with Jesus in His death and resurrection. Jesus emphasizes baptism, and the early Church in the book of Acts followed suit. Baptism doesn't save us but symbolizes dying to the sinful nature, being raised from enslavement to sin. It is an outward expression of an inward transaction—becoming dead to sin and alive to God. It is a scriptural command we align with according to Jesus' intention. Some discard baptism, not wanting to be legalistic about salvation. This is understandable as there has been some abuse surrounding baptism. Yet if we believe Jesus is the epitome of wisdom, we yield to His supreme ways, trusting those who are truly His are obeying for the right reasons.

"Teaching them all I have commanded you" (v. 20)

The next responsibility Jesus gives as we "disciple ethnic groups" is to "teach them to observe all things I have commanded you." The highest calling of a believer is to hear and apply the truth and teaching of Jesus in the context of a loving, intimate relationship. Every disciple is to make His ways, will, desires, and promises the centerpiece and rule of their lives. Disciples no longer have a say over how they live. We are joyful bond slaves to Him who has known us and bought us by His own blood. His goodness, love, and mercy draw us to offer ourselves at the feet of this worthy One. We long to know what pleases Him, receiving His gracious enabling to obediently walk this out. Our hearts cry out, "Lord, teach me to live before You!" The only way a person can do this is through taking the Word of God and applying it within their own culture and life experience. This is helped by others who have experienced a measure of that Kingdom life in their own life, helping them consider what it means in their own cultural environment.

But where do we start? The Sermon on the Mount (Matthew 5–7) is the focal point. The Sermon on the Mount encapsulates the overall teaching of the four gospels. It is then expanded and expressed in different ways throughout the New Testament. It is not a stretch to conclude the Sermon on the Mount is what Jesus referred to when he states, "Teach them to observe all I have commanded you." It is the description of true life in the Kingdom of God, practically revealing the standards of that life.

"I am with you always" (v. 20)

Jesus doesn't merely give us this commission and leave us to our own devices. He provides the empowering necessary to faithfully fulfill His Great Commission by declaring, "And lo, I am with you always, even to the end of the age." This is the greatest promise any disciple could receive. Jesus Himself promises to be with us as we dedicate our lives to knowing Him, loving Him, and obediently responding to His commission. It is the promise of His abiding presence with us. The measure of how much we experience His being "with us" is dependent upon our willingness to engage and relate with Him. It is this inner abiding presence of Jesus, through the indwelling Holy Spirit, that empowers and emboldens disciples to press on in obeying this commission.

Jesus' Commission in Mark

"Go into all the world and preach the gospel to every creature. He who believes and is baptized will be saved; but He who does not believe will be condemned. And these signs will follow those who believe; in My name they will cast out demons; they will speak with new tongues; they will take up serpents and if they drink anything deadly it will by no means hurt them; they will lay hands on the sick and they will recover." (Mark 16:15–18)

The gospel of Mark reveals Jesus as the miracle-working servant of God. After declaring Jesus is God, the book proceeds to reveal Him as servant of God and humanity. Mark's gospel emphasizes the service and works of Jesus, meant to inspire faith in God. Jesus' work is accomplished in victorious power. He is not perceived as King, but a servant willingly getting dirty among the people. His work is multifaceted. First, destroying the work of the deceiver, delivering from demons, and overcoming every disease and second, transforming these same human lives. Overall in Mark, Jesus is doing His work so that humanity, and all she has dominion over, might be restored. Toward this end, He is healing creation itself, ridding people of what destroys, and in the process transforming their lives into His own likeness.

"Preach the gospel to all creation" (v. 15)

The original language best renders "preach the gospel to every creature" as "to all creation." Jesus has a big-picture focus in mind when He communicates to *all creation*. This is different than preaching to "every creature." Jesus fully recognized all creation needed His restorative truth to become what it was created for. This is what God created in perfection in Genesis. He then placed humanity in authority over all creation. While man lived in unhindered fellowship with God, obeying His laws and living according to His prescribed ways, all creation experienced the tranquility it was meant for. Sin then entered the picture, bringing devastation to Adam's descendants (all humanity) as well as creation itself. God has entrusted humanity with dominion of the earth, but in our sinful state, we have only brought destruction. However, as new creations in Christ, living in the victory and power of His resurrection, the destruction can be reversed.

Renewal for Individuals (v. 16)

Through disciples obeying Jesus' command, identifying with the suffering and brokenness of corrupt humanity, people are given a choice. Will they believe or reject this offer of transformation, healing, and renewal? For those who receive it, they believe in Him and His transformative power. They further identify with Him through baptism. We understand baptism as twofold:

First, identifying with Jesus' death and resurrection through immersing in water, representing an internal transformation that has begun.

Second, the indwelling Holy Spirit being given to a new believer as a down payment of the age to come, to which they now belong. The individual is now saved and receives the renewing, healing power to walk in freedom from the variety of corrupt practices they had formerly lived in. This same victorious power, if applied, produces the resulting transformation of creation/society itself. The one who hears and does not believe remains in the power of the evil one and his demonic hordes. They remain in bondage to every form of human corruption standing defiantly against the knowledge of God. They are still under the destructive power of forces harming humanity and creation itself. Overcoming the destructive nature of these operative forces is possible only for saved human beings, regenerated through the resurrection life of Jesus.

Transforming All Creation

Mark's Great Commission passage is only possible through a life transformed by the resurrection of Christ, consistently living under its authority. It is for those being filled with the Holy Spirit and cultivating deep fellowship with Him. Living in and releasing Jesus' power upon broken humanity is reliant upon an ongoing obedience to the revealed Word of God and His will. We cannot expect God's power to be present and available if we are living contrary to His ways revealed in Scripture. That obedience also applies to obeying the commission itself. By deliberately placing ourselves in contact with broken, hurting humanity, power is released for individuals to be transformed, thus renewing society as a whole.

"And these signs shall follow..." (vv. 17–18)

Those who hear and believe receive Jesus' power released through the Holy Spirit. The specific signs mentioned in verses 17–18 are for all true disciples to operate in for the glory of Jesus, not merely pastors or professional missionaries. It is sometimes understood they are signs of God's equipping for a particular ministry. This is not the biblical understanding. Instead, they are proof of the power that Jesus' resurrection provides those who believe in Him.

As we proceed toward the fulfillment of the Great Commission, these signs testifying of the superiority of Jesus over created order will be increasing. Scripture reveals the body of Christ reaping the great harvest, prior to the second coming of Christ, will demonstrate tremendous spiritual authority, breaking down walls of deception holding hundreds of millions enslaved and captive. They will know that Jesus is who He says He is because of seeing His power demonstrated before their eyes.

Overcoming Destructive Forces in Creation

Through His resurrection, Jesus overcame the destructive, harmful, sinful forces in creation itself. These forces have corrupted humanity, destroying relationships, breaking down bodies, corrupting the whole creation. Because of humanity's sinful, broken, self-centered inheritance, society itself has fallen from the glory God originally intended. In the Great Commission, Jesus is setting before the global Church the privilege of participating with Jesus'

84

power to heal creation itself. This is primarily done through identifying with His resurrection, embracing His spiritual authority, and becoming filled with the indwelling Spirit on a daily basis. Through victory over every destructive power, Jesus can give disciples empowering strength to live in victory over hindering forces. This helps free humanity from its corruption and in so doing see creation itself becoming restored to God's purpose.

In the Steps of Jesus' Own Ministry

Spiritual authority is the result of faith in the power of Jesus, confirming truth that is being proclaimed. It validates Jesus' authority, superior over all others. Jesus promises that, for all who believe in Him, aligning with His will to restore creation, spiritual power is available. From the housewife to the marketplace worker to the evangelist. Jesus is revealing a crucial truth in these verses—most cultures do not respond to the gospel through a verbal proclamation alone, needing a demonstration of spiritual power confirming what is communicated. Most cultures possess a supernatural worldview, the same paradigm of the early Church. Jesus preached the gospel in a threefold manner: declaring truth, healing the sick, and delivering the oppressed. Two-thirds of Jesus' own ministry included demonstrations of power over illness, disease, and oppressive spirits. As His hands and feet, the extension of His ministry on earth, we too are meant to walk in His authority.

The Essence of the Commission

Matthew's commission focused on the proclamation of the Kingship of Jesus. Mark's commission calls us to embody and proclaim the risen Christ as the restorer and transformer of the whole creation. That embodying and proclaiming is accomplished by identifying with broken, confused, corrupt humanity by sacrificial service. Being saved doesn't mean we have entered into the healing of the creation. It is only when we, through living fellowship with Jesus, are pouring out our lives among the suffering, broken, abused. The body of Christ is called to put ourselves into the suffering of humanity, share in their brokenness, and release transforming power through Christ upon them.

Jesus' Commission in Luke

> Then He said to them, "Thus it is written, and thus it was necessary for the Christ to suffer and to rise from the dead the third day, and that repentance and remission of sins should be preached in His name to all nations, beginning at Jerusalem. And you are witnesses of these things. Behold, I send the Promise of My Father upon you; but tarry in the city of Jerusalem until you are endued with power from on high." (Luke 24:46–49)

The writer of the Gospel of Luke was Greek. The influence of Greek culture upon civilization has been significant. Greek philosophy possessed a drive toward the perfection of the individual. Luke, as a Greek, was profoundly influenced by his cultural background. He found in Jesus the perfect human realization the Greeks aspired after. The entire gospel is full of examples of Jesus as the perfect embodiment of God's purpose for humanity. We see Jesus' physical, mental, and spiritual development as He proceeds in life and ministry. Luke reveals Jesus' temptations and how they helped prepare Him for what was to come. Luke views Jesus' resurrection as empowering sinful humanity with His own human perfection. Jesus makes it possible for broken human beings to be conformed into His own image. Luke indicates in his resurrection account Jesus progressed from a natural body to His eternal, resurrected body. He went beyond all limitations experienced in His flesh and was now experiencing things only possible in His resurrected form.

"You are witnesses of these things" (v. 48)

In Jesus' commission, Luke emphasizes the body of Christ revealing to the world the glories of Jesus as the perfect embodiment of a human being. Through His death and resurrection, Jesus makes possible the transformation of human beings into the same image of glory He possesses. "You are witnesses of these things." We reveal the perfections of Jesus to the world as His witnesses, seeing His image reproduced in the lives of those taking Him at His word.

Jesus stated, "You are witnesses of these things!" What things?

1. **Witnesses to the fulfillment of prophecy.** First, in verse 44, Jesus states, "That all things must be fulfilled which were written in the

law of Moses and the Prophets and the Psalms concerning me" (the preceding words in the commission and just prior). Jesus is claiming His ministry summed up the whole content of the Old Testament Scriptures and is thus the fulfillment of the Old Covenant. These three reveal the will of God for humanity (law of Moses), correction for failure to obey the will of God (the Prophets), and longing after the will of God (put to songs) in Psalms.

2. **Witnesses of his suffering and resurrection.** The second area of "these things" is found in verse 46. We are witnesses of the facts of Jesus' suffering and subsequent glory through resurrection. Through these events, Jesus not only fulfills the past but inaugurates a brand-new era of the Kingdom of God. His death and resurrection transition from the Old to the New Covenant Kingdom of God. The old was represented by the ideals of the law of Moses, the corrections of the Prophets and the inspired longing of the Psalms, while the new is accessed through "repentance and remission of sins." His suffering and glory, anguish and victory, death and resurrection provide the shift from the Old to the New Covenant. Jesus' witnesses unfold the facts of these to the world. Revealing to every ethnic group the suffering Christ while subsequently stressing the victory of His resurrection. This is the entryway to walking in the likeness of Christ.

Whole-Life Transformation

Jesus is seeking whole-life transformation for humanity through His words, "repentance and remission of sins." Transformation begins through repentance, the longing within humanity for renewal and restoration. Without repentance, no individual can be saved or renewed. There can be no remission of sins except there first be repentance. Genuine repentance, expressed in faith, always produces remission of sins. Repentance comes as we see the beauty, goodness, and mercy of God through Jesus. When the light of His perfect life shines on ours, we are moved with brokenness—undone because of how far from His standard we really are. The body of Christ's commission, then, is to be witnesses among unreached people group of the glory, purity, and holiness of Jesus, moving them to repentance.

The Extent of the "Remission of Sins"

"Remission of sins" is more than forgiveness, including breaking the desire for sin and overcoming its poison. This is a significant act of mercy as God reverses the curse over our lives. Sin loses its power to bind and hold us captive. The body of Christ is commissioned to *"witness"* among every ethnic group to the fact of God's "remission of sins" revealed through our own lives being delivered from sins' power.

A Witness Is More Than Words

It is common to reduce "being a witness" to what we say about Jesus: "We witness to somebody." Yet, it is surely much more than this. A witness is a believer dying to sin, self, and all contrary to the heart of God. A witness reveals Jesus' resurrection through a life experiencing victory. Our lives are as much a witness as the words we utter. Jesus intends our words align with experiencing the crucified and victorious life as true witnesses. A witness is the result of a human life produced by the death and resurrection of Christ. Jesus' death and resurrection have been made real in a witness's life. Through such a disciple, Jesus' grace is revealed to the world. This is the New Testament concept of a "witness."

Embracing the Impossibility of the Commission

These ideas cut to the heart as we realize just how far we are from such a standard. We are failures, inadequate for the task. If the commission ended with these words, anxiety would plague us. Thankfully, Jesus promises the necessary power to faithfully obey the commission: "Behold, I send the promise of My Father upon you; but tarry in the city of Jerusalem until you are endued with power from on high!" Only through the power of the Spirit is it possible to embody this high calling, walking it out. Being filled with the Spirit is to experience "these things" in and through our own lives. This doesn't happen through intellectual understanding alone or through imitating another but through experiencing these things as we share Jesus' own life through the indwelling Spirit.

Trusting in the Power of the Spirit

In Luke's commission, the body of Christ are "witnesses" who "declare" experiential truth of Jesus. Declaring is never reduced to speaking well or winning a debate. Natural abilities are of little value in Kingdom endeavors. The degree "declaring" is in the power of the Spirit determines its true impact. It is common to rely on human abilities, strengths, and personality to impact for Christ. The Lord never intended trust in these things. They aid us yet are not the foundation of "witnessing." We surrender them, receiving Jesus' true power, letting this be the foundation we proceed from in God's work. Human strengths can be the hindrance to operating in the power of the Spirit. "Witnessing" is impossible apart from dependence on the Holy Spirit.

Jesus' Commission in John

So Jesus said to them again, "Peace to you! As the Father has sent Me, I also send you." And when He had said this, He breathed on them, and said to them, "Receive the Holy Spirit. If you forgive the sins of any, they are forgiven them; if you retain the sins of any, they are retained." (John 20:21–23)

John's resurrection and commission accounts were taken as an eyewitness. Though Mark and Luke likely did not personally experience what they reported, John did. John had a close, intimate relationship with Jesus, different from the other disciples, known as the "beloved disciple" (John 20:2). John's gospel reveals Jesus as manifesting the mission of God. Jesus is Word made Flesh, revealing the Father, equal with Him in every way.

"Peace be to you!" (v. 19)

The commission begins with Jesus stating an initial time to the disciples, "Peace be to you!" (v. 19). He is calming their fears, revealing He is the same one they had known for three years. Jesus shows them His hands and side (v. 20) revealing they have nothing to fear. In verse 21, Jesus repeats, "Peace to you." The second time for a different purpose, preparing them for the commission He is about to give. Jesus is appointing them for the work to come. The commission would produce much trouble, yet Jesus' peace would prevail. Several scriptural instances reveal God giving a commission using the words,

"Peace be unto you," including Gideon in Judges 6:23. God's preparation of "peace" enables the body of Christ to respond in obedience.

"As the Father has sent Me, so I send you!" (v. 21)

John's gospel reveals Jesus as the sent One manifesting the Father to the world. Subsequently revealing the responsibility of those sent by the Son to the world. We continue the work Jesus began through His earthly ministry. Not as mediators of reconciliation with God but those proclaiming it. Jesus was sent to show the world what the Father is like. Human nature longs to "see" the Father. Much heartache this longing—seeking fulfillment outside the glory and love of the Father, expressed through Jesus, "He that has seen Me has seen the Father." In a similar manner, believers are sent into the world to reveal the beauty, holiness, and attractiveness of Jesus. When the world relates with believers, there ought to be a realization they have seen Christ. This fact brings a measure of shame as we are not yet what we ought to be. Revealing the Father and Son moves people to a choice: responding to what they have seen or continuing in their own ways.

"Receive the Holy Spirit" (v. 22)

Jesus then provides the empowering necessary to reveal the Father and Son. Of ourselves, we cannot accomplish this calling. Jesus' breathing on the disciples with the promise, "Receive the Holy Spirit," revealed two points. First, the Spirit could only come upon them through Jesus. Second, the only way to fulfill the commission was doing so in the power of the Spirit.

Jesus was reminding the disciples how He revealed the Father—through the empowering of the Spirit. Though fully God, Jesus laid down the rights of His divinity to accomplish His work on earth (Philippians 2:6–7). Instead, He relied on the Spirit working through Him. Jesus modeled the only way we also could be faithful to God. The entire ministry of Jesus was one of fellowshipping with the Holy Spirit, fully in tune with Him. We are sent as Jesus' ambassadors with the same ministry, having access to the same Spirit. The empowering of the Spirit alone enables us to reveal Jesus to the world. It is this same empowering that brings unbelievers to a crisis of choice, producing either forgiveness or retaining of sins. Every believer can be filled with the Spirit toward these ends. It is a promise to the whole Church, with no exceptions.

"If you forgive the sins of any..." (v. 23)

The type of forgiveness referred to is freedom from the bondage of sins—the guilt, power, and presence of sins' corrupting our lives. The forgiveness of sins results in two things—a new vision of God and a new motive for life. When a persons' sins are forgiven, there is a new understanding of God. The separation is torn away and we see God in a fresh way. This clear vision of God becomes the impetus of a new motive for life—God's love flowing through the individual. The forgiveness of sins is a primary message believers declare to the world. No religion offers humanity freedom from the power of sin itself. Jesus told disciples He was sending them with the power to forgive sins. In John, the foundational message is through Christ it is possible for sins to be forgiven, their power destroyed, and a new life begun.

"If you retain the sins of any..." (v. 23)

The opposite of forgiveness of sins is retaining them. Forgiveness is freedom from sins while retaining means ongoing slavery. A person whose sins are retained is still bound by their power. They may try to get free in their own strength, but cannot. They have no vision of God and no motive for life surrounding God's love. Those receiving a living witness of Christ, culturally relevant with a demonstration of the Spirit and power (1 Corinthians 2:4), have two choices: sins forgiven or retained. Their response to the witness takes them down one or the other pathway.

Believers are commissioned by Jesus, empowered by the Spirit, bringing humanity to a choice—*the valley of decision.* As people hear and see the witness, believers using Jesus' authority either forgive or retain sins, according to the choice people make. It has been said the most important issue human beings must reconcile is what they do with Jesus. For those repenting of waywardness and trusting in Jesus, their sins are forgiven, no matter the nature of them. Others stand defiantly against Christ as the multitudes did, crying "crucify Him." To them, the commissioned believer says, "Your sins are retained." Our calling is witnessing of Christ, drawing people to gaze upon His glory and Kingship, making a choice. Upon their response, believers either forgive sins or retain them.

Together, these four commission passages reveal the mandate Jesus has laid before the global Church. In Matthew the global Church moves outward, discipling all the ethnic peoples, baptizing, and teaching them all Jesus commanded. In Mark, the global Church incarnates Jesus' love among the broken, needy, and outcast, identifying with suffering and pain, while impacting creation itself in the process. In Luke, the global Church become His witnesses, not only in words, but through transformation into His likeness. In John, the global Church reveals the Father and Son to the world through the forgiving or retaining of sins.

★★★

Having a clearer understanding of the commission itself Jesus has set before His Church, we can now consider what its fulfillment will be like. In the next chapter, we tackle this important subject, envisioning the future results of remaining faithful to the global Church's core identity.

7

Biblical Basis of Fulfilling the
Great Commission

We have already used the phrase, "the fulfillment of the Great Commission," many times without yet defining it. A vast majority of ministry leaders understand the phrase to refer generally to being involved in the Great Commission, yet this is incomplete. Few consider there is an end, finish, fulfillment of the commission Jesus gave His whole Church. Jesus' commission doesn't go on forever. There is a close, when all Jesus commissioned and promised will have been realized through His victorious global Church. Jesus meant His people to see the Great Commission as one day being fulfilled, pressing toward this purpose, hastening His return. The Bible often looks toward this end of redemptive history, prior to the second coming of Jesus.

As previously discussed, the core identity of the Church biblically is an ever-expanding, multiplying, reproducing body. Thus, grasping where God is leading history is essential to remaining faithful. In this chapter we consider what Scripture reveals "the fulfillment of the Great Commission" looks like, what its characteristics are, and how to measure where we are. Studying these truths breeds encouragement and faith, motivating the people of God to continue obediently in its pursuit. They help realign us over and over with the certainty of where the all-wise King is leading history.

BIBLICAL REFERENCES TO THE FULFILLMENT OF THE GREAT COMMISSION

The Bible as a whole consistently lifts our eyes from day-to-day existence to the big picture storyline of God's priorities—where redemptive history is going. This is purposeful. If believers and local ministries buy into the redemptive storyline of God, we find meaning in daily activities. Our families, jobs, and relationships matter in a new way. It shapes what we prioritize, think about, spend money on, how we use time and energy. Failing to see this grand narrative hinders our ability to walk in the destiny God has called us and is a denial of Scripture, distracted with tunnel vision. The Bible reveals that big-picture plan along with the end purpose itself, inviting every believer to see their life caught up in that big picture story, living in its light. God is orchestrating that big picture with a purposeful culmination in sight. History is not running off the tracks though challenges will continue to increase. Challenges are opportunities to grow in trust in God now, empowered for the greater, yet future challenges, all working toward a glorious, future culmination.

Great Commission Fulfillment References in Isaiah

The second portion of the book of Isaiah (chapters 40–66) has some of the most explicit references to a great harvest among all peoples at the end of the age.[1] This section of Isaiah highlights the "Servant Song" passages revealing the work, ministry, and mission of Messiah. There is much detailed information about God's plans and purposes related to the fulfillment of the Great Commission. Whereas the New Testament doesn't provide a lot of detail, the Old Testament prophets (particularly Isaiah) reveal much. Some passages refer to God's plan for the Jews while others to His work among Gentiles, across the nations. At the end of the age, both will come together in mind-blowing numbers, as the Lord undertakes to bring about the fulfillment of the Great Commission.

Isaiah 42:1–13—He Will Bring Justice to the Earth

Isaiah 42:1–13 reveals Jehovah as deliverer God in opposition to the worthless idols described in the last verses of chapter 41. The Lord's servant (Messiah) is described as vastly superior to idols. He is God's answer to a world void of divine revelation and light. Messiah will accomplish worldwide, permanent justice among all nations through Himself, partially through His first coming and completely through His second. Messiah has God's ultimate justice in mind, not only a fair and just society in the present. His justice restores people first to God, reconciling them with each other, while impacting societal structures and institutions with truth. This is the only way to attain true justice.

The type of justice referred to concerns the revelation of God provided to the world through the vehicle of His global Church. Subsequently proceeding to God's global justice experienced upon Messiah's second coming. Through Messiah (Jesus), God is revealing what the nations have lacked, namely a clear word of blessing and restoration from God. This is absolutely true among all unreached ethnic peoples, evidenced by the myriad of religious attempts to appease the divine. The passage goes on to reveal the result of Messiah's work. The peoples of the earth will praise, adore, obey Him according to His prescribed ways. Messiah has revealed truth to the nations (through the channel of His global Church) in Himself, planning global transformation among every people. As they find in Him the longing they have craved and sought elsewhere in vain.

Isaiah 43:1–13—I Will Say "Give Them Up"

In the previous verses of chapter 42, Isaiah described Israel as blind, disobedient, without spiritual understanding. Yet God's grace in chapter 43 will see to it that in time God has a people for Himself, mouthpieces to the ends of the earth. He has purchased, redeemed, and restored these uncountable people for Himself. Upon Messiah's first coming, and the outpouring of the Spirit at Pentecost, Israel (the Church) would be empowered as never before. The people of God would overcome fear as they proceed as Messiah's hands and feet among the nations. When they pass through life-threatening difficulties, as Jesus promised they would, His abiding presence would be with them, using these challenges to establish His glory among the peoples of the world. The lead up to the great harvest at the end of the age will be full of challenges, troubles, and difficulties. Yet Jesus is with us, turning difficulties into glory. The psalmist declared in Psalm 66:3, "How awesome are Your works! Through the greatness of Your power Your enemies shall submit themselves to You. All the earth shall worship You and sing praises to You." Such experiential knowledge changes everything. Multitudes from the east, west, north, and south will be gathered from every people group, a global gathering into His Kingdom that will astound the world, stirring opposition from the enemy and his wicked allies.

A Comprehensive Picture in Isaiah 49

Isaiah 49 reveals a prophecy looking directly to the completion of salvation history at the end of the age. In this extraordinary passage, God declares His plans to bring together Messiah's mission to Israel and the entire Gentile world, ultimately fulfilled during the present age, just prior to Jesus' second coming. In this passage God makes promises that have only been partially fulfilled. Today, we are asking Him to bring to pass the fulfillment of the prophecy among all the ethnic peoples of the world.

In the first section (vv. 1–6), the preincarnated Christ is reporting to the nations that His purpose will expand from the Jews (through His own physical ministry in the first century) to include all the non-Jewish ethnic groups of the world.[2] Messiah is the Servant, prophesying His own coming birth (first coming) as well as His reign (second coming). We see the profound power of biblical prophecy. Isaiah is privileged to see, hear, and record an exchange between God and His Servant (Jesus). Jesus will minister to the Gentile peoples in the same way He reached out to Israel. His salvation (deliverance) from the corroding effects of sinful nature is made available to all. The original relationship enjoyed between God and Adam can be completely restored among all who believe. This is the privilege and right of even the most distant peoples. None is exempt. This has been the eternal purpose and plan of God since the foundation of the world. Well before Jesus was born in Bethlehem, God determined His divine plan to reconcile the world to Himself through His Son.

God made Jesus as Messiah to the Jews and King to the Gentiles. Through Him, God will display power, glory, and splendor. This would happen through both Jesus' first and second coming. Each accomplishing a specific purpose in God's overall redemptive drama. Jesus' first coming was in hiddenness and humility, the necessary sacrificial lamb, through which all can find restoration before God. His second coming enforces victory over Satan and the powers of darkness, won through resurrection, defeating everything opposed to His rule and reign, setting up God's visible Kingdom on earth. The time period between these two "comings" of Jesus to the earth is when God is glorified among Jews and Gentiles. Jesus glorifies God through His Church being thrust out, scattered among every geographical area of the world. Every people and subcultural grouping having opportunity to voluntarily receive Jesus as true King. God is glorified when all peoples experience transformation through relationship with the Son.

Scripture, as a whole, advocates the following process of salvation history: In the final years leading up to Jesus' second coming, there will be an innumerable harvest of Gentiles (non-Jewish people) coming to saving faith in Jesus (Romans 11:25). This non-Jewish ingathering and the heightened moving of the Holy Spirit will provoke physical Jews to jealousy. They will see what has always been their inheritance through what the Gentiles are experiencing. This will produce Jews finding Jesus as their true Messiah by the millions in those culminating years (v. 26). Following Jesus' visible return, this uncountable group, joined by all true believers throughout history, will bless the world under Jesus' leadership as He restores the earth to His original Kingdom intention. Messiah's return will vindicate Jesus in the eyes of the world, His enemies, detractors, and rejecters.

Messiah promises Jesus as a light to the Gentiles that they might seek His salvation. This refers to every people having a viable "witness" living among them of the love and power of Jesus. At this point in history, we cannot say this prophecy has been fulfilled. It is God's heart each one receives an incarnated, culturally relevant witness that includes demonstrations of spiritual power. This is not yet the case as billions await such a witness. God's purpose stated here is directly connected to our being activated in the global Church's partnership with the Lord to serve the nations.

In verses 8–9, God is telling Jesus of the eternal victories Jesus will win through the cross and its impact on the peoples of the world.[3] Because of Jesus' victories God can give the Son as a promise to all peoples. The Father will make the Son a "covenant to the people," an unbreakable bond, uniting believers with God in fellowship. This "covenant" will have a direct role while they are alive, yet the full measure will come when Jesus returns. "In the day of salvation" refers to the specific, God-ordained time when God will send Jesus back to the earth a second time. Through the events surrounding Jesus' second coming, God will implement the full measure of His Kingdom and "salvation." Part of what will be accomplished at that time is the physical restoration of the earth. The verse relates to restoring ruins overrun by an enemy. God is promising Jesus will bring transformation to the physical earth upon His second coming. Part of His Kingdom purpose is reversing the effects of sin upon all things, including the earth itself.

Isaiah 52:13–53:12—God's Ultimate Plan of Salvation

This is a climax passage in the book of Isaiah, indeed, in all Scripture. God reveals His ultimate plan of salvation, sending His own Son to bear the sin of the whole world for those who receive it. The Servant (Jesus) is "exalted and extolled very high" (v. 13) while subjected to personal horrors and suffering (v. 14). That suffering leads to universal benefit and deliverance (v. 5) to all who willingly believe by faith. The number of those globally made righteous because of the Servant's suffering is described as "many" (v. 11). This is not a small number. It is uncountable, representing multitudes from every ethnic group. The servant's suffering bore the sins of those willing to receive it. In John 6:37 Jesus declares, "All that the Father gives me will come to Me." The *all* conveys large numbers, not merely a few remnant believers hanging on until the end. The last three verses of chapter 52 actually belong with chapter 53. They reveal what is happening in and through chapter 53, providing a commentary of the victory the Servant's obedient suffering achieved for all humanity. 1 John 2:2 provides a New Testament glimpse into this fact: "And He Himself is the propitiation for our sins, and not for ours only but for the whole world."

Daniel 12:3

The angel told Daniel, "Those who turn many to righteousness" shall shine like the stars forever (Daniel 12:3). The emphasis is not only on turning people to righteousness, but the sheer fact the angel used the word *many*.

This is the same word used in the Isaiah 53 passage above. "Many" will turn to righteousness from every people group globally during the time of the greatest difficulty (and greatest glory) known in human history. The years just prior to the second coming of Jesus. Daniel's prophecy is a direct correlation with the timeframe of the end of the age and the fulfillment of the Great Commission. Aligning with Jesus' own words in Matthew 26:28, "This is My blood of the new covenant, which is shed for many for the remission of sins." Jesus says His blood was shed for "many" as Daniel revealed.

Some argue this, citing Jesus also claimed at the end of the parable of the wedding feast in Matthew 22:14, "For many are called, but few are chosen." So, which is it? Are those who are saved few or many? Jesus is not affirming only a few end up being saved. He is not predestining some, while condemning others. He desires none to perish, but all to experience eternal life (2 Peter 3:9; 1 Timothy 2:4). Instead, a better translation of the original intent is, "For many are called, but few are *choice*." It is humanity's choice, not God's, whether or not they obey the invitation to the wedding feast, living according to the blessings, privileges, and responsibilities of that great Kingdom.[4] The call goes out to all humanity (many are called) and eventually all will have a witness among them (Matthew 24:14). But how many is a few who choose Jesus? If there are approximately 7.8 billion on earth presently,[5] a few are likely still at least one to two billion people, representing many from every single ethnic people group globally.

Joel 2:28–32 - The Outpouring of the Holy Spirit

Joel 2:28–32 introduces God's plan of releasing divine empowering toward His salvation being realized among all ethnic peoples. God has provided every spiritual resource necessary to accomplish this purpose. It was never intended for human beings to rely on abilities, strengths, and creativity alone to accomplish God's purpose. His purpose among the nations must be pursued in His ways. The New Covenant, inaugurated through Jesus' death and resurrection, provides more spiritual enabling than the Old Covenant (2 Corinthians 3:7–8). The Holy Spirit empowers disciples with the same Spirit Jesus walked in during His earthly ministry.

The prophet Joel looks forward to a partial fulfillment on the day of Pentecost in Acts 2. While looking beyond to a further future, end of the age, ultimate fulfillment during the timeframe of Matthew 24:9–14. Joel 2:28–32 refers to events that have never yet taken place to the degree mentioned. They are yet future, taking place in the final years just prior to Jesus' second coming. Joel speaks of an outpouring of the Holy Spirit (28–29) way beyond what was experienced at Pentecost, coinciding with a promised global harvest culminating at the end of the age (v. 32). These happenings will also coincide with the fulfillment of Psalm 110:3: "Your people shall be volunteers in the day of Your power," as more believers than ever before will directly engage in the fulfillment of the Great Commission.

The physical wonders of the Joel 2 passage (vv. 30–31) have never taken place historically. But at the end of the age they will happen, communicating the immediacy of the second coming of Jesus (Matthew 24:29). These crisis events will influence multitudes to seek God for deliverance and salvation (v. 32) while others harden their hearts in rebellion. Many will reject Jesus (Revelation 9:21), yet a great harvest of millions will be brought into the Kingdom from every ethnic group on the planet.

John 10:16

Jesus clarified in John 10:16, "And other sheep I have which are not of this fold; them also I must bring, and they will hear My voice; and there will be one flock and one shepherd." You can almost feel the palpable emotion in Jesus' voice as He thinks about the "other sheep." Who are they? Because Jesus' earthly ministry was focused almost exclusively on the Jews, the other sheep are easily understood as all non-Jewish people groups around the world (Gentiles). He created all to experience the highest levels of fellowship and communion with Himself. Multitudes of "other sheep" still wait (from Buddhist, Hindu, Muslim, and Spiritist backgrounds), yet belong in His fold, just like the rest of us.

Colossians 1:18

In Colossians 1:18, Paul adds a small line in the midst of one of his Christology passages, reflecting on the glories of Christ. He states, "That in all things He (Christ) may have the preeminence." It is easy to overlook as it is tucked away, surrounded by mountain peaks of glorious truth related to the majesty of Jesus as God. It is, in essence, a Great Commission phrase, proclaiming Jesus will have the preeminence "in all things." That means He will take His place of honor and glory, worshiped, and obeyed by many among all ethnic peoples, leading to His second coming. He will reign as rightful King amid every subculture of every unreached people group. Every person will either choose or reject Jesus, receiving His gracious work of restoration or condemning themselves.

Revelation 5:9–10

Revelation 5:9–10 is a glorious forward-looking picture, given to John. John sees the Lamb in verse 6 who took the scroll to open it in verse 7. When this happened, the four living creatures and twenty-four elders fell down in adoration in verse 8, breaking out in exuberant worship of the Lamb in verses 9–10: "You are worthy to take the scroll, and to open its seals; for You were slain, and have redeemed us to God by Your blood out of every tribe and tongue and people and nation, and have made us kings and priests to our God, and we shall reign on the earth." The scroll indicated the end was at hand, when the final events culminating with the second coming of Jesus would unfold step by step. Within that glorious, yet challenging, timeframe multitudes from every tribe, tongue, people, and nation will be redeemed, thrust into the Kingdom as part of the final harvest. These will reign with Jesus during His millennial Kingdom as Kings and priests before God. This is a powerful promise of what is yet to come with the creatures and elders specifying the detailed extent of widespread redemption. It is certain and will happen in the midst of the great conflict, challenges, and trouble of those final years before Jesus' second coming.

Matthew 24:14 and Revelation 7:9

Matthew 24 is a significant chapter related to the fulfillment of the Great Commission. It should be studied in depth by every believer to correctly grasp what Jesus reveals is coming. Jesus looks down through the course of salvation history revealing some of the dynamics, particularly near the end of the age and Jesus' second coming. In verse 14 Jesus prophesies, "And this gospel of the Kingdom will be preached in all the world as a witness to all the nations, and then the end will come." New Testament scholar George Ladd suggests, "Perhaps the most important verse in the Word of God for God's people today is Matthew 24:14…helping to ascertain the meaning and purpose of human history."[6] In this one verse we find Jesus linking the timing of His redemption being experienced with power among every people group on earth. Jesus reveals the extent of His plan for the gospel to touch everyone on earth with power.

Matthew 24:14 correlates with the vision Jesus gave John of the throne of God in Revelation 7:9: "After these things I looked, and behold a great multitude which no one could number, of all nations, tribes, peoples and tongues, standing before the throne and before the Lamb, clothed with white robes and palm branches in their hands." Who is this "great multitude"? Those brought into the Kingdom representing every subculture of every ethnic family (people group) on earth, the result of the mission movement through the global body of Christ. Particularly, the move of the Spirit during the final years prior to Jesus' return, ushering in the greatest global harvest ever known into the Kingdom of God. This will be the culmination of God's prophetic promise to Abraham that "in you all the families of the earth shall be blessed" (Genesis 12:3). This is no small group. John saw a great, uncountable multitude before God's throne.

THE CHURCH'S PRIMARY GOAL AND ITS CONTEXT

Matthew 24:14 signals "the fulfillment of the Great Commission," directly relating to Jesus' last command to His global Church before He ascended to the right hand of the Father—His Great Commission (Matthew 28:18–20; Mark 16:15–18; Luke 24:46–49; John 20:21–23). Referring to the Great Commission passages and Matthew 24:14, Ladd confirms, "Both passages speak about the same mission: worldwide evangelization until the end of the age. This fact ties together the Great Commission passages and Matthew 24:14."[7] Matthew 24:14 is the next great date on God's redemptive timeline. Verse 14 is our great goal as the body of Christ, the global Church's finish line, the primary purpose why she exists. The focal point of the unfolding of recorded history. It is the ultimate way the global Church partners with God to see the Son worshiped, exalted, obeyed, and adored among all peoples. Until Matthew 24:14 happens, we will not see the return of Jesus, making this culminating event, the most important focal point of the global Church in this age.

Yet the fulfillment of the Great Commission must be taken in context of the whole chapter (Matthew 24). Jesus is describing the lead up to the "end of the age" when the greatest transition ever known will take place—from the "present age" to the "age to come" under the physical leadership of Jesus on earth again. Jesus sets in context the challenges of that lead up, culminating with the fulfillment of the Great Commission. This background is necessary to rightly mobilize and equip the global Church. The primary mandate of the global Church in this age takes place in the context of pressure, persecution, challenge, and difficulty—a conflict of kingdoms. It is helpful to pause, take a moment, wrapping our heads around this truth. In Jesus' perfect leadership, He forewarns us. Jesus' global Church engages in the Great Commission with eyes wide open, hearts ablaze with love, walking in faithfulness, obedience, and perseverance.

We give ourselves no back doors of escape, pressing into the purpose of God among all ethnic peoples. It is the all-wise plan of a kind, good, and merciful God orchestrating global difficulties to create the optimal environment for the largest number of people to be thrust into His Kingdom of their own free will. This is the backdrop of the fulfillment of the Great Commission, helping us understand some of the wisdom of God in allowing great challenges, particularly in those final three and a half years. The global Church is privileged to partner with Jesus in the midst of this process as His hands and feet.[8]

As such, it is necessary that mission mobilization includes preparing the global Church to prevail in the midst of difficulties, not faltering at the first signs of trouble. Both Paul and Peter taught the New Testament churches in this precise way. The early Church saw the spread of the gospel within the hostile environment of the Roman Empire. Pressure and trouble were never far from these churches, yet they prevailed in spiritual strength. It is necessary to strengthen the body of Christ, preparing her to face the present, and coming challenges, with an overcoming spirit. The Lord's allowing of present difficulties of various sorts is a testing ground, helping His children be transformed into a steadfast people even as the heat is turned up. Proverbs 24:10 counsels, "If you faint in the day of adversity, your strength is small."

The Time of Greatest Spiritual Power Ever Known

Though a time of struggle, the simultaneous spiritual power released in that timeframe will far outweigh what we see currently or in history (Isaiah 60:1–3; Joel 2:28–32). Just as the challenges and difficulties mount, so does the powerful hand of God, exceeding the miracles and power of the books of Acts and Exodus (John 14:12–14). As the Holy Spirit reveals the glory, splendor, and attractiveness of Jesus throughout the earth, using His chosen vessel—the global Church—supernatural power and Holy Spirit activity will increase, becoming commonplace. The gospel of the Kingdom will cut to the heart, drawing whole clusters to Jesus through people movements to Christ, establishing reproducible, simple churches. While there will be increased hardship during this timeframe, the surpassing glory of God will be experienced in and through the Church in increasing measures.

Pressure & Shaking Produces the Great Harvest

The global generation facing the greatest pressure in human history will give way to the greatest spiritual harvest the Kingdom of God has ever seen. Crisis creates awareness of need in the human heart. The need was always there, yet when things are going well, we generally don't give much attention to it. Crisis in our families, or our lives being at risk, motivates receptivity to hear and respond to truth. As C. S. Lewis famously wrote, "We can ignore even pleasure. But pain insists upon being attended to. God whispers to us in our pleasures, speaks in our conscience, but shouts in our pains, it is His megaphone to rouse a deaf world."[9]

The growing crises will produce an atmosphere of responsiveness drawing millions into the Kingdom. Yes, multitudes of professing believers will be falling away (Matthew 24:9–13; 2 Thessalonians 2:3; 1 Timothy 4:1–2) and many true believers will be martyred for their faith (Matthew 24:9). Yet, simultaneously a great throng from every individual people group globally will be thrust into the Kingdom as the gospel is declared in word, deed, and spiritual power. Many will come to faith in the midst of crisis, even because of the crisis. The pressure of the years leading up to the end of the age is part of God's design to produce the great harvest prophesied in both the Old and New Testaments.

A parallel passage to Matthew 24 is Haggai 2:6–9. The prophet looks to a day when the earth will experience a great shaking by God's own hand. This shaking includes all we have seen in our Matthew 24 verses. The shaking creates a crisis environment where the glory of God is experienced at unprecedented levels. The crisis produces multitudes coming to the "Desire of All Nations," surrendering to His leadership. The shaking (challenges, difficulties, and trouble) actually produces the great harvest. God uses the least severe circumstances to produce the highest response of love without violating people's free will.[10] Shaking is increasing throughout history, culminating with the final years before Jesus' second coming, right alongside the increase of light and power and the great harvest.

Core Elements of the "Fulfillment of the Great Commission"

If Matthew 24:14 is truly a finish line for the global Church, what are core markers (measuring sticks) to be working toward? Rick Warren, pastor of Saddleback Church and director of Finishing the Task, suggests key items.[11] Each of the following characteristics are layers implied through Matthew 24:14 (supported throughout Old and New Testament prophecy).[12] Each will be considerably ramping up as we close in on the fulfillment of the Great Commission in the context of the final days before Jesus' second coming.[13]

1. Permeation of every subculture of every ethnic people group in every place (every person hearing and seeing) with the gospel of the Kingdom in a culturally relevant, age-appropriate way accompanied by the demonstration of the spirit and power (a result of God's people operating in the gifts of the Spirit like no time in human history) producing uncountable people movements to Christ[14] across every people group.

2. Rapid reproducing church planting movements (CPMs)[15] in every subculture of every ethnic people group producing culturally relevant, vibrant, spiritually alive churches (in a house,

building, office or otherwise) in every stratum of society, every neighborhood, and every apartment building within a 15-minute walk of every person. This implies an increase of millions of simple churches among unreached peoples.

3. A great multitude (several billion) of vibrant, wholehearted believers from every subculture of every ethnic people group around the earth living as true, New Testament disciples revealing authentic, apostolic faith—loving Jesus with all their hearts, standing firm in persecution with joy and victory. Jesus will have a zealous, surrendered, pure Bride in that day, not one that is casual and lukewarm.

4. A large proportion of wholehearted disciples (20 percent) voluntarily scattering themselves cross-culturally as message bearers (John the Baptist types preparing the way of the Lord) from every ethnic people group to other similar culture people groups nearby with the gospel of the Kingdom (15 percent) as well as some going further to distant culture subcultures of ethnic people groups (5 percent). They are not necessarily traditional, professional message bearers, but primarily lay leaders and lay people taking jobs and families, deliberately multiplying church planting movements and igniting people movements.

5. The completion of the translation of the Bible in the mother tongue of every person on the planet—in audio format among orality learners so that millions can go deep with the heart of God in their own heart language.

6. Breakthrough revival among Jews and the vast majority of living Jews coming to saving faith in Yeshua (right before the second coming of Jesus), living as wholehearted disciples (as a result of Jews seeing Arabs and other Gentile believers experiencing true faith, provoked to embrace their Messiah).

Spiritual Trends of the Timeframe

It is also helpful to be aware of overarching trends taking place during the years of "the fulfillment of the Great Commission." These are positive, spiritual trends the Lord will be emphasizing during the culmination of the great harvest in those coming years. These are in context to the intensifying of the negative sign trends happening simultaneously in Matthew 24:9–14.[16]

1. A spirit of revival and awakening (outpouring of the Holy Spirit, accompanied by experiencing the Spirit like no time before) experienced across the globe (simultaneous to the greatest darkness) propelling the people of God to live in astounding light and glory (Isaiah 60:1–2; Psalm 85:6).

2. Focused forming of every new believer in every ethnic people group as a true disciple—teaching them all things "I have commanded you" (Matthew 28:20). Teaching and imparting the apostolic faith at deep levels (2 Timothy 2:22), producing mature disciples partnering with Jesus in His global works. Also known as disciple-making movements.

3. Purposeful discipling of every corporate ethnic people group (not individuals) through Kingdom life and principles (Matthew 28:19). Penetrating seven spheres of society, pockets of societal transformation taking place as justice issues are tackled (Micah 6:8; Isaiah 56:1; Psalm 140:12).

4. The greatest measure of love across the body of Christ ever experienced (true spirit of unity of heart), rooted in loyalty to Jesus and His truth. Love for God, for His global Church and the lost. Revealing to the world the love of God according to what Jesus promised and prayed in John 17 (Ephesians 3:17; Philippians 1:9; Romans 15:5–7; 2 Thessalonians 3:5).

5. Miracles and spiritual power surpassing the book of Acts (John 14:12) and Moses (1 Corinthians 3:13) testifying to Jesus' supremacy over created order. The global Church marked like no other time in history by (a) anointed (cutting to the heart) preaching (b) healing ministry flourishing (c) deliverance of demonic bondage greater than during Jesus' own ministry. The body of Christ attaining to the fullness of Christ (Ephesians 4:13).

6. Widespread return to core messages, living out these messages faithfully across the body of Christ (the life of the cross; living in resurrection power; the Sermon on the Mount lifestyle; whole-hearted devotion; the Spirit-filled life; life in the Kingdom; Romans 3-8; victorious life in Christ).

7. The escalation of the global prayer movement in every corner of the earth (watchmen on the walls—Isaiah 62:6–7) aligning with Jesus' vision of the fulfillment of the Great Commission, crying out to God, "Come, Lord Jesus!" and "Let Your Kingdom come on earth as it is in heaven!" The global Church will sense the pivotal time they are in, responding accordingly in heightened, focused prayer and intercession like no other time in history.

8. Unprecedented number of men and women globally turning their hearts to the young generation and serving them through adoption, protection, coaching, mentoring, anti-trafficking, valuing them from God's perspective (Malachi 4:6).

9. Millions of disciples globally discerning the times (like the sons of Issachar—1 Chronicles 12:32), knowing what the Church should do as we face the challenges and the glory of the end times. They will understand the unfolding of the times, encouraging masses of believers in how to respond biblically (Daniel 11).

10. The use of technology and growing globalization to catalyze the gospel of the Kingdom among all peoples. As we progress in the accelerating interconnected world of economies, transportation, technologies, communications, trade, and more, the Holy Spirit will use globalization as a highway for the Word of God to run swiftly and be glorified (2 Thessalonians 3:5).

A "People Group" Worldview

Most of our Bibles include the word "nations" in Matthew 24:14. The word in the original language is better translated "ethnic peoples" from the Koine Greek: *panta ta ethne*.[17] Jesus is not referring to geopolitical countries, but individual ethnic people groups making up the geopolitical nation. For example, there are over 2,500 distinct ethnic groups in India.[18] God sees people as part of these groups sharing culture, language and customs. They make up our societies, giving meaning to life through vital relationships with others most like us. The gospel of the Kingdom has always spread primarily along these lines of community and trust. Groups within these communities often come to faith together through communal decisions. This is the norm of how people became followers of Jesus in the New Testament and is still true in most cultures of the world today.

An outsider brings the gospel to a people and subcultures among that people, yet it takes root by spreading along people group lines. We find direction toward fulfilling the mandate Jesus has given His global Church in Matthew 24:14. It is necessary to prioritize ethnic groups where the gospel has had little or no introduction or rootedness. We learn about the world's 13,000 ethnic groups,[19] researching their population of believers, targeting the 5,000 or so groups with followers of Jesus numbering 2 percent or less, called unreached people groups.[20] When all people groups have experienced the gospel of the Kingdom, with living witnesses in their midst, reproducing vital local churches, and potentially up to 50 percent of its people following Jesus, we will have seen Matthew 24:14 fulfilled.

***

Now that we've seen where we are going, having the end in mind, we can rightly grasp a foundational look at God's viewpoint, design, and core identity for the global Church. The global Church is at the center of God's macro plan for fulfilling the Great Commission. Unless we see this accurately, it is easy to get sidetracked in mission mobilization.

8

God's Macro Plan: The Core Identity of the Global Church

Rethinking global mobilization requires a clear biblical view of the nature, purpose, and identity of the global Church as God's missionary community. Only then can we break free of limited concepts of mobilization, instead helping the Church come in line with who she truly is. This chapter considers scriptural basis to understand who the Church is at a macro level—the one, true, universal Church of Christ. The next chapter proceeds to consider the micro plan of God—understanding a local church's core identity, what its biblical characteristics are and how it is meant to be an incubator of Great Commission understanding, passion and engagement in the purposes of God.

THE COMING OF THE SPIRIT AT PENTECOST

To biblically grasp our core identity as the universal global Church we return to the Church's birthplace. Acts 2 is the root of the great tree of the Church that has sprung up in every nation over the last twenty centuries. The global Church was birthed through the coming of the Holy Spirit as a completely new, unique entity (a mystery in New Testament language). Its purpose was to enable the people of God to walk in a profoundly new era of the historic people of God (unseen by the Old Testament prophets), aligning with God's will.

G. Campbell Morgan asserts Acts 2:1–4 provides a complete event within itself—the Holy Spirit's coming on the day of Pentecost. The 120 together in one place imparted with power dimensions.[1] Morgan reveals that on this event hinged a dramatically new era in salvation history. It is easy to overlook this. In the Old Testament the Holy Spirit did not "fill" people, living within them. He periodically "came upon" specific people, particularly prophets and priests, but did not abide within them. This is an entirely New Covenant phenomenon, as Ezekiel 36:26–27 confirmed, "I will give you a new heart and put a new spirit within you…I will put My Spirit within you and cause you to walk in My statutes." Ezekiel was looking forward hundreds of years to a time when Messiah would usher in a new era, officially inaugurated on the day of Pentecost.

Jesus clarified this same startling fact in John 14:17 stating, "The Spirit of truth, whom the world cannot receive…but you know Him, for He dwells with you and will be in you." On the day of Pentecost, the transition from the Holy Spirit merely being "with" to being "in" took effect along with all its vast implications. Immediately, the disciples had a new awareness of Jesus as Master, of themselves as part of His storyline and the massive shift happening through the event. Their lives, and how they related to God, were now completely different, possessing understanding of the previous three years with Jesus they did not grasp before. They were able to put the puzzle pieces together of what Jesus was doing, along with understanding how it fit into the redemptive plan of salvation, communicating to those around them. Hope came to the disciples through the resurrection. Yet not the meaning of the events. Meaning and clarity were provided through the coming of the Spirit at Pentecost.

Verses 1–4 provide the historic record of the origins of the Church. The lead up to this event surrounded Jesus fulfilling His Messianic mission during his three years of ministry. God was revealing Himself to the world through the incarnate Son. Though Jesus focused His ministry almost exclusively on the Jews, His Messianic purpose was unquestionably for all peoples. Israel forfeited its role by thinking God only cared for them, abandoning all other nations. This heresy cost them their place, for a time, in the grand narrative of God. In His ministry, Jesus gathered disciples around Him, training them to lead the Church into salvation history. Finally charging them to wait in Jerusalem to be filled with the Spirit for the widespread work set before them. It is not an overstatement to say a new age, very different from before, for the whole world, was launched on that one day.

Jesus was aware that only by His leaving would the Holy Spirit be given to His people. Subsequently making possible the work of global harvest as He commanded until the end of the age. The believing Jews' faith in Jehovah God was strong. Yet they needed to now adjust to the fact they were living in the last days, needing to embrace scriptural implications according to Peter's message in Acts 2:14 ff reflecting Joel's prophecy. This meant, in particular, they would now function daily in the power of the Spirit, something not available before. The believers had to learn a completely new paradigm.[2]

Acts 2:5 and following move into the results produced through the coming of the Spirit at Pentecost. The new body of Christ multiplied from one man (Jesus), to 12, to 500, to 3,000, 5,000 and exponentially across the centuries, transforming every culture, socioeconomic and status level. The key event on that day was the Holy Spirit filling the people of God, relating with them in a brand-new way never before experienced. This fact is the foundation on which the Church—and her progressing forward in her core mission—was birthed and empowered.[3]

If we break up the New Testament into two portions, we find the four Gospels make up volume one.[4] In the Gospels we are told of what Jesus began to do and teach. The Gospels detail His ministry and teachings up to His ascension to the right hand of the Father. Beginning with the book of Acts, we enter volume two, taking us into what some call the Church age. I like to call it the "global mission" age. Here, we are shown what Jesus continues to do and teach through the apostolic Church after His ascension. This implies there was much work left to be done that had not been completed through Jesus' own life and ministry. The rest of the New Testament takes place during the "global mission" age. Volume one concludes with the death and resurrection of Jesus.

Volume two opens with the ascension of Jesus and the curtain being raised on the life of the Church.[5] Accompanying this life was the coming of the Holy Spirit to continue the purpose of Jesus in the world. This age, according to the book of Revelation, continues until the second coming of Jesus. We are part of this age. The same Holy Spirit, who moved with power in the early Church, is seeking to do so today through a global, corporate Church available to function according to His prescribed ways.

The Purpose of the Filling of the Holy Spirit

The filling of the Spirit had specific purpose, as it does for every believer since. A simple interpretation of the Spirit's filling is for the purpose of revealing God. Wherever a believer goes, whatever they do, the primary purpose of the Holy Spirit's filling is enabling us to reveal and manifest God to others. Using this simple definition, we conclude the primary reason for the Holy Spirit's coming is empowering a corporate people who reveal God, as He is, in and through Jesus, to the world. The global Church, God's "missionary," Spirit-filled people, exists to reveal God to all the ethnic peoples of the world, bringing glory to Jesus as He draws multitudes to Himself, restoring them to what they were created for. Just as Jesus did not come to be served but to serve, giving His life a ransom for many (Mark 10:45), so do Spirit-filled believers serve the ethnic peoples in words and demonstrations of spiritual power. Laying down our lives willingly, even joyfully, as humble servants of the One who has done so much for us. Representing God to the world, attracting others to God, living that He may be worshiped, obeyed, and glorified in the earth, receiving the preeminence He is due.

The Correlation of Church and Mission

Therefore, the body of Christ globally, made up of millions of individual local churches and ministries all over the world, exists as a missionary people—our core identity—the corporate purpose God has put within us. Whereas every believer experientially knows Jesus, revealing Him to others, reproducing disciples, local churches too multiply themselves. Churches expand, influence, and reach out to yet unreached parts, not to merely get new believers into their one church, but multiplying and starting new simple churches. This expansion principle is in our DNA, the natural outworking of a healthy organism. To be a stagnant church or ministry, is an oxymoron, counter to divine order, a denial of who we are meant to be. Every local church is to spread through the day-to-day life of normal Spirit-filled people. Local ministries becoming ablaze with thriving vision, mobilizing, and equipping their own, influencing unreached people groups, are God's primary strategy in mission. Every local ministry, no matter its size, possesses a responsibility before God in the Great Commission. It has been said, "the Church exists by mission as fire exists by burning."[6]

Yet as Charles Van Engen insinuates, this correlation of Church and mission has in practice not fared so well.[7] It is uncommon to see Church and mission overlapping, but as separate entities—each with divergent purposes. This is a result of the historical development of the Church and mission and the particular context of each generation. Van Engen suggests a definition of the Church could be, "the one, holy, universal and apostolic community of the disciples of Jesus Christ, gathered from all families of the earth, around Word, sacrament and common witness."[8] Whereas Bishop Stephen Neill defines mission as, "the intentional crossing of barriers from church to non-church in word and deed for the sake of the proclamation of the gospel."[9] It is rare these two are interconnected as purposed in Scripture.

For the majority of Christians, "Church" and "mission" refer to two different, often conflicting, entities.[10] Lesslie Newbigin suggests Church is generally understood as devoted to worship and spiritual care, while mission is the propagation of the gospel through which new converts join existing "churches."[11] The situation is partly because mission organizations and "church" structures tend to function separate from one another. This general understanding reveals a disturbing problem as these two entities are meant to be closely related, even springing up together, as the DNA of the global Church is God's missionary people.

Over the centuries scholars and theologians have debated the relationship between "church" and "mission." Most today understand the biblical correlation as crucial, no longer able to be separated apart from doing great damage to Scripture. The Church's nature cannot be defined apart from its mission and mission cannot be defined as separated from the Church's life in the world. Johannes Blauw has said, "There is no other Church then the Church sent into the world and there is no other mission then that of the Church of Christ."[12] John Stott affirms the same, stating, "The Church cannot be understood rightly except in a perspective which is at once missionary and eschatological."[13] Newbigin agrees, citing, "just as we must insist that a church which has ceased to be a mission has lost the essential character of a church, so we must also say that a mission which is not at the same time truly a Church is not a true expression of a divine apostolate."[14]

As seen, before Jesus ascended to the right hand of the Father, He gave His disciples the Great Commission. Luke records a particular piece in Acts 1:8, not included in the commission passages of the four Gospels. He tells them, "But you shall receive power when the Holy Spirit has come upon you; and you shall be witnesses to Me in Jerusalem, and in all Judea and Samaria and to the ends of the earth." This verse has been interpreted in many ways over the years supporting all kinds of diverse mission positions. What if Jesus was simply clarifying the nature of the soon to be birthed "Church." Jesus is telling disciples they are to be a certain kind of people—ever-widening, multiplying outward in a ripple effect, as God's "missionary people."

Jesus appears to be laying out a blueprint in this verse. Revealing His true Church would be continuously spreading outward in ever wider concentric circles. The Church universal and every local ministry is an evolving organism, never static or stale, always growing into "the mature man, to the measure and stature of the fullness of Christ" (Ephesians 4:13). She is consistently changing, growing, developing into what God intends her to be. What the universal "Church" and an individual "church" are is not defined by what it always has been. She is dynamically adapting and responding to the Holy Spirit, aligning in a fresh way with the mission heartbeat she was always meant to possess.

THE TEACHING OF EPHESIANS ABOUT THE CHURCH

Charles Van Engen suggests an attentive study of Ephesians reveals an overview of God's eternal purpose for the Church—the core identity of His missionary heart.[15] Paul saw each local church as an organism continuously expanding through its mission expression. Reflecting the essential nature of God's mission through the overarching global Church of which it is part. Ephesians is considered by many to be the most holy place of Paul's writings,[16] taking us behind the curtain of what is seen, into the unseen realm of the nature and glories of the Church of Christ. What Paul reveals here is likely part of what he saw in 2 Corinthians 12:2 when he stated (referring to himself), "I know a man in Christ who fourteen years ago...such a one was caught up to the third heaven."[17]

The Greek word for Church is ecclesia, used at least 73 times in the New Testament, referring to an assembly who are "called out." Jesus, through His Church, is calling out an innumerable people for His name (Acts 15:14).[18] Paul reveals in Ephesians the core essence of the universal global Church, made up of multitudes of individual small, simple churches. The plural use of the term "church" biblically only refers to geographical locations of "gathered out ones" and not to the essential nature of the Church. There is only one church, according to Paul (Ephesians 4:4), continuously put together like a building. It is not yet fully built, having large portions of unreached peoples still outside His Kingdom [19]The explicit means of God's building process is global mission—the global corporate Church expressed through the exponential development of millions of small, simple churches. These are in geographical locations all over the world, continuously pushing the boundaries and multiplying outward, drawing in multitudes of presently unreached peoples into the "unity of the body of Christ."

Gathering Together All Things in Himself

The whole of Ephesians is one overarching message, revealing the mystery (hidden truth) of the global Church as the medium for achieving God's divine purpose.[20] The true Church is the body of Christ, every born-again believer functioning as a member of that body, with Jesus as supreme head. Through this body, every member in their assigned roles, Jesus is glorified throughout the earth, spreading experiential knowledge of God in Christ, the Church exponentially multiplied among all peoples.

In Ephesians Paul is laying down for all eternity the monumental calling of the corporate, universal Church. The global Church was hidden to Israel in the Old Covenant. The Old Testament prophets did not foresee the age of the Church, the timeframe between the first and second coming of Jesus. They had no idea of the entity God would bring into being to complete redemptive history, ushering in the fullness of the Kingdom of God through the second coming of Jesus. Paul states clearly in Ephesians 1:9–10, "Having made known to us the mystery of His will, according to His good pleasure which He purposed in Himself, that in the dispensation of the fullness of the times He might gather together in one all things in Christ, both which are in heaven and which are on earth—In Him." Howard A. Snyder refers to this one verse as revealing God's master plan.[21]

Henrietta Mears agrees, concluding that according to this verse God's eternal purpose is to gather, or reunite, all things together in Christ.[22] There are many areas of division and hostility this includes. The most important being that, apart from Christ, there is a vast chasm of hostility between God and humanity. Human beings were created to enjoy unbroken fellowship with God in paradise, yet have been separated through the inheritance of sin. But God has gone above and beyond, making a way at great cost to wipe out that division. Between human beings there is division as well. Paul uses the example of animosity between Jew and Gentile, yet how in Christ they have together been brought into one body, the Church. God desires every present division between races, ethnic peoples, economic status and education levels, castes, marriages, family members—healed and restored through His redemptive work. In and through Him all things find their unity. Division is also seen in creation itself, groaning until the revelation of the sons of God (Romans 8:19). This has both a present and a future outlook. We have hope, faith and confidence from Scripture that every one of these areas (and many more), presently divided, hostile toward one another, are being and will be "Gathered together in one" in Christ.

God's Channel for This Gathering—The Church

But how will all this oneness and gathering take place? What is the channel God has set up to accomplish this? The eternal, global Church. Howard A. Snyder states, "A remarkable phrase occurs in Ephesians 3:10. God's cosmic plan, Paul says, is that 'through the Church, the manifold wisdom of God should be made known to the rulers and authorities in the heavenly realms.'"[23] Within a divided and hostile world, God has set in place His unifying entity— the global Church. God's exalted view of the Church increases the seriousness of our response—living worthy of the gospel. "Gathering together in one" happens partially in this age as the ethnic peoples of the world receive

His transforming power, experiencing the Kingdom of God and then with completeness through His own second coming. Jesus is, and will be, the centerpiece overcoming every conflict. The Church of Christ globally stands as Jesus' vehicle to bring about one great goal—reconciling the world to God, breaking down the separation between God and humanity and healing the divisions and hostility brought about by self-centeredness.

Ephesians proceeds to reveal all this takes place in the context of great spiritual conflict (Ephesians 6:10–20) as the powers and principalities seek to hold captive the hearts and minds of human beings. We do not fight against human beings, but spiritual powers in heavenly places. Armed with God's armor, we wage spiritual war through intercessory prayer, worship, and obedience to God. As William Barclay puts it, "the Church stands for that purpose of world-wide reconciliation for which Christ appeared and in all their relationships with one another must seek to realize this formative idea of the Church."[24]

Every new believer enters a community of faith far superior than anything they have imagined. Paul doesn't write of joining denominations, church networks or associations, but a "body." By faith, we join a global family of unity, the universal global Church, while possessing individual gifts serving the nations toward the benefit of this corporate entity. Each member exercises their gifts as part of that body, equipping the saints for the work of ministry, toward the building up of the global Church.

Unity of the body does not refer to putting denominations together to get a larger whole. Instead Paul starts with the whole and works backward. The universal, corporate global Church defines the identity of its parts, millions of individual local churches around the world. The global Church is more than merely the sum of all these parts but can be understood like a tribe. Individual churches are important as a local expression (we will look at this in detail in the next chapter). Yet only as they see themselves as part of the global Church, local ministries obtain true meaning and identity as part of the whole. Paul clarified this in 1 Corinthians 12:14–27, using the image of an eye, ear or other body part by itself being insignificant. Yet when rightly connected with the oneness of the global whole, local ministries become more important as a part of the created whole.

Equipping the Saints

Mission mobilization empowers the global church to become actively engaged with God's purpose for the nations. Leadership is at the core of this plan of God. God's intent of spiritual leadership is equipping the churches and people of God for this great purpose. Paul's teaching in Ephesians relates to spiritual leadership within this global, universal body. What is the biblical foundation of true leadership? Who are leaders meant to be, what are their characteristics and what do they do? Ephesians 4 answers these questions, empowering individual churches and the global Church as a whole in its calling and purpose.

Apostles, prophets, evangelists, pastors, and teachers (as varieties of mission mobilizer functions previously mentioned in chapter 4) enable the body of Christ to proclaim the gospel of the Kingdom, doing the work of the ministry, both locally and globally. The early Church in the first century was activated in this way: discipling, baptizing, and teaching ethnic peoples. Paul's exhortation clearly implies local ministry leadership directly empowers believers to become involved in God's mission in the world in a multiplicity of ways.

Too often Christian leaders do all the work of ministry themselves—a one man show. Instead leadership exists to equip every believer within the local ministry to do the work of ministry. Leaders empower and enable the process of every disciple operating in God-given roles and gifts in the Kingdom of God. A reason little mission mobilization takes place is too many Christian leaders doing all the work themselves, falsely believing this is what is expected of them. A biblical theology of leadership always empowers and equips others to do the work of the ministry, never doing all the work ourselves. Paul laid significant leadership groundwork, revealing the primary means mission mobilization across the global Church transpires effectively.

The Focus of Ephesians 1-3

Ephesians can be broken up into two parts, chapters 1–3 and 4–6. The first three chapters reveal the heavenly calling, eternal character of the global Church, detailing the glorious riches undeservingly received as well as the Church's highest purposes.[25] These chapters detail the "spiritual blessings" the global Church has corporately received through the death and resurrection of Jesus. The Church is rooted and grounded in these "unsearchable riches of Christ." Every local church teaches these truths, empowering disciples growing in experiential knowledge.

Ephesians 1–3 gives us a stunning picture of Jesus' eternal intent for the global Church. Though presently far from this standard, God is moving us in this direction. The Ephesians, like many believers today, were rich in spiritual resources available to them, yet poor in what they were actually partaking. God wills His global Church to avail herself of all the "spiritual blessings" purchased for her." In doing so, she unveils to the nations, spiritual forces in heavenly places and ages to come, all God has purposed for His people. The "spiritual blessings" are rightly ours through Jesus' death and resurrection, yet have been minimized, misunderstood and abused in His global Church. Believers are grateful for them, in a general sense, yet often don't proactively lay hold of them within their lives in any specific way. Jesus' intent is His body operating in the "spiritual blessings" reflecting the indescribable, unsearchable riches of Christ.

Paul provides two core apostolic prayers in these three chapters. Ephesians 1:17–19 and Ephesians 3:16–21. Both are essential biblically recorded prayers used to stand in the gap in intercession for our families, communities of faith, organizations, and global Church. The prayers reinforce growing in spiritual wisdom and revelation related to the "spiritual blessings" just detailed by Paul. In Ephesians 1:17-19, spiritually grasping these truths does not come by natural intellect but revelation of the Holy Spirit.[26] This is why it is necessary to pray this way for the global Church.

In Ephesians 3:16-21, the Spirit empowers the Church with spiritual strength to overcome temptation, while taking us further in comprehending the depths, width, height, and length of His love. There is so much to be known about God, His work through Christ, His purpose in and through the Church. The way to mature in expressing God to the world is standing in the gap in intercession for the global Church. These prayers (as well as all the apostolic prayers in Scripture) are core mission mobilization prayers, seeking the Lord of the harvest to grow His body in the foundations of who we are becoming in Christ. Apart from this we cannot rightly reveal Him to the world. Every local ministry ought to pray these prayers regularly over every member of their community of faith. Through this growth, local churches experience God in deeper ways, in turn revealing Him to ethnic peoples.

The Focus of Ephesians 4–6

The second three chapters apply the "spiritual blessings" of Ephesians 1–3 to the practical life (conduct) of the global Church. The two sections are intertwined. Paul starts Ephesians with a sweeping vision of who the Church is (chapters 1–3) proceeding to show their practical outworking in how we live (chapters 4–6). Only by partaking of the banqueting table of all that is available to believers in Ephesians 1–3, can we hope to effectively live out our calling in practice in chapters 4–6.[27] Because of our great calling, the global Church embodying chapters 1–3, we live entirely differently, revealed in chapters 4–6. This releases spiritual authority necessary to be effective in the Great Commission. Mission mobilizers help local ministries internalize "spiritual blessings" and "unsearchable riches of Christ," an essential piece of "rebuilding ancient ruins" so the nations can flock to Christ in the great harvest.

Charles Van Engen reveals a core element of chapters 4–6 being the corporate nature of the global Church as a holy community of faith.[28] At first, this doesn't appear to have much to do with the Church's role in mission. Yet as we scratch the surface, we begin to see differently. God prioritizes holiness because holiness is who Jesus is as our head. Paul details a series of sinful practices in Ephesians. The Bible is a searchlight on every unique culture, exposing behaviors not according to His plan for humanity. They are laid down by believers, putting on the new man—practices in line with God's holy heart.

As Scripture enters a culture, transforming multitudes of individuals, over time the culture itself is changed. Members of local churches are "children of light" revealing the "fruits of righteousness, goodness and truth." Turning away from sensuality, lust, immorality, greed, stealing, bitterness, anger, lying, coveting, foul language. Paul is not merely speaking to individuals, but the collective behavior of a local community of believers. Community is affected by individual behavior, as members of one another. We don't merely live for ourselves but are in covenant relationship with the community of faith. Negative behavior impacts the whole community, even when kept secret. Paul specifies a local church's corporate holiness extends to its worship, organization and submission, marital relationships, parenting and an individual's work. Holiness is an all-encompassing core characteristic of both the universal, global Church and its local expressions around the world.

GOD'S REDEMPTIVE PLAN THROUGH HIS GLOBAL CHURCH

The restoration of the earth through the influence of the Kingdom of God (now by faith and upon His second coming by sight) is the eternal purpose of God, bringing Jesus the greatest glory. A major factor is His never-ending desire to experience unhindered fellowship with the gem of His creation—human beings. His divine patience holds back His return as He wants none to perish apart from voluntarily choosing His restorative love.

Those receiving His restorative death and resurrection, as a response, love Him with all our hearts, becoming like Him. Through this restored lifestyle, we become God's primary vessels in enabling others to experience this same restored life. Loving Jesus in an increasing measure, receiving His victorious life, and multiplying His restoration among others, is His purpose for every disciple between the time of Jesus' first and second comings. As Christopher J. H. Wright says, "this is who we are and why we are here" and what the fulfillment of the Great Commission is all about.[29]

The global Church are the descendants of Abraham and the inheritors of God's history-spanning covenant of "blessing all the peoples of the earth through you" (Genesis 12:3). God's redemptive process for all humanity started with one man, Abraham, extending to all his descendants. Who are these descendants? Christopher J.H. Wright affirms they are not merely physical Jews (literal Israel) but people of every nation believing in Jesus as Messiah, Lord and Savior, living in faithfulness and obedience to His ways, receiving His blessings.[30] The global Church is the direct descendant of Abraham, commissioned by God to spread the blessing of God we have received to the nations. When God commenced His plan of redeeming the planet, He didn't merely take people directly to heaven. He brought into being a global, cross-cultural Kingdom community with the twofold objective of loving God with wholehearted devotion and blessing all the peoples of the world.

Jesus' Prayer for the Church

This is why Jesus prayed in John 17:9, "I do not pray for the world but for those whom You have given Me, for they are Yours." At first this prayer seems strange. We may with surprise react, "I thought You love the world," and of course we would be right. We find the added piece in verse 21 when Jesus concludes, "That they also may be one in Us, that the world may believe that you sent Me."

Jesus' chosen Kingdom strategy, in full agreement with His absolute sovereignty, is the global Church becoming all He intended spiritually, which always overflows in blessing others. We are meant to climb to the heights of fellowship with God, growing in mature discipleship, walking in unity often neglected in local churches and ministries. Jesus at present is praying this same prayer over us. He is not praying this for the world, but for those who are His.

What is the purpose of Jesus' prayer? To see a mature, purified, refined Bride, walking in her Matthew 22:37 calling. Jesus told the inquiring lawyer, "You shall love the Lord Your God with all your heart, with all your soul, with all your strength. This is the first and great commandment." Jesus sets this focal point as the most important commandment. He goes on to declare, "And the second is like it: You shall love your neighbor as yourself." The second flows from the first. Unless the global Church is growing in maturity in loving God, progressing from elementary principles of the Kingdom to maturity in Christ (Hebrews 5:12; 6:1), she is unable to bring the nations to the feet of Jesus.

Unless the global body of Christ, saturated with practical unity toward one another, lays down accusations, betrayals, relationship clashes, forgiving those who insult, offend and hurt us and our people, the world will not believe. That is what Jesus is praying in this prayer. The world will see Jesus, believing in Him, as the global Church, full of new followers of Jesus from unreached ethnic peoples across the 10/40 Window (Middle East, Asia and North Africa), walk in practical love and unity. These are presently hostile to one another in the natural (think the animosity between Jew and Arab), yet will embrace meekness and humility, blessing one another, according to Jesus' empowering. An important application relates to our mission and ministry teams themselves. Relational conflict is common among message bearer teams, often hindering us from shining among an unreached people. Jesus invites us to face and overcome these relational challenges, resolving problems, reconciling with one another, and living in a spirit of oneness.

The New Testament's Prayer Emphasis

This is the same reason so many of the recorded biblical, apostolic prayers of Paul, Peter, and John are focused, not on the world itself, but on the global Church becoming all God intends spiritually. We see through a glass dimly, believing it most necessary to pray for the lost to come to Christ (this indeed is a crucial item of true intercession). The New Testament, however, provides a different emphasis, instructing prayer primarily for the global Church to arise in biblical discipleship. Rooted in wholehearted love for Jesus and agreement with New Testament standards and teaching. Through the global Church becoming transformed, ascending to a different plane than we see today, she is used to draw all peoples to Jesus in a very short time. This is where God is taking the global Church and we join Him through strategic intercession for the global Church.

Treasure in Earthen Vessels

Paul tells us we have the treasure of the Kingdom in earthen vessels (2 Corinthians 4:7). It is necessary to buy into the fact that abilities, personalities, and even gifts, are not how disciples influence others. Jesus' work through us makes all the difference. It is through embracing weakness (in light of the greatness of God) that we become worthy vessels of His Kingdom.

Paul reveals this key Kingdom principle in 2 Corinthians 12:9 as he recounts an encounter he had with the risen Christ, "And He said to me, My grace is sufficient for you, for my strength is made perfect in weakness." This one verse has so much insight packed into it and it seems like most of the global Church does not yet really believe this theological juggernaut. We still operate by the world's system of who and how things get done, believing that strength through power, finance, education, national background is what matters. In doing so we have brought the principles of the world into the Church's strategic thinking.

We wrongly perceive that lacking (having weakness) in certain areas means we cannot rightly participate with God in His global work. If we don't have resources, a well-known name, education, are from certain parts of the world, ethnic status, then we have nothing to offer God. In God's Kingdom this is backward thinking. Instead, God says, whoever you are, from wherever you come from, the very things you lack (that you think disqualify you) are actually the things qualifying you for My prevailing strength filling you. It is natural to rely on human "strength." Yet doing so is one of the greatest hindrances keeping believers from experiencing God's undertaking in circumstances. He wants to be all in all among us. Paul boasted in his weakness and lack (2 Corinthians 12:9) while engaging in God's mission purpose receiving His strength.

***

We have now considered core passages related to the macro, big-picture nature, essence, and purpose of the universal, global Church. Let's proceed to look at the grassroots of individual local ministries, grasping their characteristics and role in mission mobilization.

9

God's Micro Plan: A Local Church's Characteristics

While necessary to grasp the macro plan of God across the global Church as just seen, it is also important to come down to the grassroots, micro level. Understanding God's intent of an individual local church. Because God is calling local ministries to embrace their core identity, it is essential to grasp a local ministry's purpose in the heart of God.

Every local ministry (whether 10 or 5,000 members) is part of the grand storyline of redemptive, salvation history God is working in the earth. They are Jesus' hands and feet—an essential part of His body. No local ministry can say, "I am too small" or "I don't have resources" or "we have no education." Engaging in the Great Commission God's way overcomes every excuse. Every local ministry has responsibility before God to recognize and become activated in their core identity as a local ministry. We could rightly say God's greatest single strategy in fulfilling the Great Commission is a "local church" on fire for Him (rebuilding ancient ruins from chapter 5) and His purposes in the earth. Local churches, wholehearted communities of redeemed, are God's vessel in the world. Through them Jesus multiplies communities of faith, advancing His Kingdom among every family, neighborhood, village, town, city, district, province, and nation of the earth. God's Great Commission ministries align with core elements of who they are called to be.

ESSENTIAL CHARACTERISTICS

While a part of the global, universal whole, every local ministry, as subunits of the whole, have essential characteristics. Each individual church ought to take on a different cultural expression while possessing inner commonalities binding them together as part of the universal Church of Christ. The Bible is written to a communal culture—a community of faith operating in unity, not merely individual disciples acting according to their own will. Millions of individual local churches around the world embracing these characteristics is God's chosen vehicle to fulfill the Great Commission. The defining factor of New Testament churches is the abiding presence of Jesus, through the person of the Holy Spirit. Jesus' promise, "I will be with you always" (Matthew 28:20), describes the nature of the community—not His presence in a building, but within the people of God—the Church.

We start with a question, "What is a local church?" Seems pretty easy, right? An exercise I often do in our Global Mobilization Institute courses is invite students to list all the necessary pieces of a "local church." What are biblical, nonnegotiable elements of a church? I then ask them to list elements "Christian culture" or cultural traditions have added to a "local church." Unscriptural additions (not necessarily bad), based on culture, context, generation, tradition, and more. It quickly reveals how significant elements have been added over the centuries, often overshadowing the stripped down, biblical essentials of a local church.

For example, does a local church need a building? The early Church, according to George Ladd, "apparently consisted of several congregations which met in numerous larger homes forming 'house churches.'"[1] (Romans 16:5; Colossians 4:15; Philemon 2; 1 Corinthians 16:19; Acts 20:8). The concept of a church as a building is not found in the New Testament, appearing in the early AD 300s around the time of Roman Emperor Constantine.[2] What about worship equipment or sound systems? Are they essential to be a local church? How about "wearing our Sunday best" or setting up chairs in rows? Can a church sit on mats or cushions in a circle? It is helpful to assess cultural elements of a local church, comparing them to the nonnegotiable elements of the New Testament. These nonnegotiable elements are not lengthy as the Holy Spirit intends every local church to have the essentials, while culturally relevant to the particular culture they are in. The New Testament allows for significant diversity in expression of churches while not compromising core, essential elements.

Wendell Evans defines a local church as a grouping of followers of Jesus with sufficient structure to demonstrate corporate identity within its social and cultural context and carry out its corporate functions considered in this chapter.[3] This could be in a home, under a tree, an apartment high rise common room, a local government office, a business conference room, an elementary school's faculty meeting room or a host of other possibilities. "Sufficient structure" includes (1) a nucleus of at least twelve baptized believers (merely a helpful guide), (2) a particular place they consistently meet, (3) recognized, spiritually qualified appointed leader(s), (4) financially sustained from within their community, not reliant on outside funds.

Four Core Spiritual Elements

The book of Acts describes core characteristics of a local church, revealing church participation was a serious decision. According to scholars G. Campbell Morgan and George Ladd, Acts 2:42, refers to specific, core elements of local churches, not the sum total of their practices.[4] These four particular elements are mostly oriented to what the Church is among its own members, that which binds them together. We will consider more of the outward-oriented nature of local churches, part 4, of the book.[5] These four spiritual elements are necessary for a fellowship of believers to constitute a church. They are in addition to the four in the above paragraph related to a church having "sufficient structure." Those four speak to the structure, while these four to the spiritual elements within that structure.

You may notice that with these four core characteristics we do not find the core identity we have been discussing in this book. Because the concept of every local church as God's missionary people was so interwoven into the whole event of Pentecost, Luke did not feel the need to include it in any specific way. The Old Testament had laid out God being a God for all humanity, not merely Israel. Jesus' Great Commission messages had only weeks before been given, providing the overarching mandate of the body of

Christ—discipling all ethnic peoples, empowered by the coming Holy Spirit. There was no need for Luke to detail that again. Instead what is revealed are the core elements of this new community of faith known as the Church, of which the Great Commission emphasis would naturally show up in these four elements.

G. Campbell Morgan reveals, "Christian gatherings in the early Church were characterized by simplicity, possessing a profound sense of unity, oneness."[6] Directly after Pentecost, when most of the new believers were still from a Jewish background, they continued worshiping in the temple, while adding house church gatherings to the mix. The core elements of these house churches are defined in Acts 2:42. (1) Continuing steadfastly in the Apostles doctrine (2) Fellowship (3) the Breaking of Bread and (4) Prayers. This does not imply these were all the churches did. There are many other activities that were a part of normal early Church life, yet Luke records these four as above the rest. Without these four taking place, escalating us deeper in God, there is no local church, just a social group of people.[7] Let's break these down a bit.

1. The Apostles' Doctrine

To "Continue steadfastly in the apostles' doctrine" is to prioritize the anointed, impactful, effective teaching and application of the Word of God in every local church context. This may sound obvious, yet is anything but common. The global Church faces a crisis, a declining standard of teaching the Bible in a way that believers can relevantly grasp, applying it effectively to their lives. Fewer believers have a solid grasp of Scripture. They may know Bible stories yet cannot identify practical applications to their individual lives. The Bible is becoming sidelined among believers. Not because it is less relevant but because of not being presented in a transformative, applicable way requiring a constant response.

Of course, we teach something from the Bible at each meeting, yet that is far removed from the apostles' doctrine which set the early Church on fire in the first century. It is essential to regain, in a widespread way, the Spirit-filled, discerning, searching, teaching of the Word, increasing revelation knowledge and spiritual understanding to the hearer, producing direct application in their circumstances.[8] According to George Ladd, the apostles' doctrine is alive, pressed into the experiences of believers, applied within their life circumstances. The teaching ministry in local churches is under attack from the enemy. If Satan can get churches to exist on Bible leanness, he can easily defeat them. This first core element is a return to prioritizing a powerful, anointed teaching ministry in local churches.

Much of what we hear on Sunday mornings is what the writer of Hebrews called "The milk of the Word." In Hebrews 5:12–14 he distinguishes between milk from meat of the Word, milk being the elementary, introductory elements of the Kingdom of God (Hebrews 6:1–2). It appears much of the global Church has made these introductory principles the core of teaching and preaching, failing to progress to the "meat" of the Word—growing in maturity in God. God's intent is millions of mature local churches globally growing in alignment with His heart and ways, not merely rehearsing introductory elements over and over. Pastors and teachers are meant to go deep with God's Word themselves, able to teach, explain and counsel using it. True churches are continuing steadfastly in this process, putting themselves under the divine instruction of the Word of God. This likely means more than Sundays. Many cultures meet daily, while some meet two to three times a week.

The apostles' doctrine, documented in the twenty-one New Testament letters, reveal two interrelated focal points. First, growing in doctrinal understanding and second responding with action. These cannot be separated as is a tendency today.[9] Right understanding, experiencing God's truth and ways, must lead to right, obedient action. This is confirmed by Paul's continuous use of the word therefore in his writings, showing cause and effect. Paul lays out doctrinal truth then pivots to show how to apply that truth in a practical way. Take the book of Romans as an example. Paul reveals the glories of true salvation throughout the book, then in chapter 12 proclaimed, "I beseech you THEREFORE, brethren, by the compassions of God, to present your bodies a living sacrifice, holy, acceptable to God, which is your spiritual worship" (Romans 12:1). Because of the many forementioned doctrinal realities, present yourself as a living sacrifice unto God as a response.

"The apostles' doctrine" is the same as what Jesus called the "gospel of the Kingdom." Jesus talked more about the Kingdom than any other subject, as did Paul. The Kingdom was consistently the core of their teaching. The apostles' doctrine then has the Kingdom of God as its center. Many understand the "gospel of the Kingdom" being for bringing people to Christ alone, failing to recognize true discipleship means growing in the phases and teachings of the gospel of the Kingdom.[10] The apostle's doctrine guides local churches through each stage of the gospel of the Kingdom. In this way disciples are developed in all aspects of the Kingdom message, not merely a slice, becoming spiritually strong, courageous believers. An important part of the Kingdom message, or apostles' doctrine, is the concept of local churches taking responsibility in the Great Commission. This is integrated within the discipleship process, not an added, extra component. In this way mission mobilization becomes a part of normal church life.

2. Fellowship with God and One Another

The second core spiritual element of every local church, according to Acts 2:42, is "Fellowship." What is the biblical meaning of fellowship? The Greek word is Koinonia, meaning having all things spiritually in common together, sharing oneness in Christ with one another.[11] Jesus' love filling local churches, marking believers as they relate to one another. This includes talking together of the things of the Spirit, of their relationship and experiences with God, what He is teaching through His Word, how they are growing and personal accountability. George Ladd affirms, "the early church were persons who were irresistibly drawn together because of a consciousness of sharing a common blessing."[12] Local churches are "iron sharpening iron," humbling themselves in vulnerability with one another. In unity with the living Christ, and one another, they received the same Spirit and shared a new life, drawn together because of first being drawn to Christ Himself. Being members of Christ implied they were also members of one another. Undergirding everything in the life of a church is the core characteristic of love. This type of life with the members of a local church is God's design, His divine order, for growing into spiritual maturity.[13] It is not enough for churches to "Continue steadfastly in the apostles' doctrine." Without fellowshipping at a deep level of love with one another we will not become a church after God's own heart.

3. Worship and Adoration

What is the next core spiritual element of a local church highlighted in Acts 2:42? The new church continued steadfastly in "The breaking of bread." There is some confusion as to what this exactly meant. Was Luke referring to

Communion or to eating meals together among the believers? The context reveals the former as verse 46 goes on to cite, "So continuing daily with one accord in the temple, and breaking bread from house to house, they ate their food with gladness and simplicity of heart." Luke would not have been redundant. Verse 46 refers to eating meals together while verse 42 speaks of Communion, the Lord's Table or the Lord's Supper, a supreme act of worship remembering Jesus' death, body broken and blood spilled, until He comes again.

Communion, over time, has become an opportunity to confess sin or pray for God to do something in our lives. Biblically, Communion is not the place for either of these. Communion is exuberant praise, worship and adoration as we remember His sufferings and exaltation. A time for glorying in Him and His works for all humanity, thanksgiving for His substitutionary death and all it means.

It is thus necessary to broaden this spiritual element from only referring to Communion as a periodic activity to including the whole life of worship of the local church. Paul Pierson highlights that "communion has at its core the worship, adoration and exalting of Jesus as crucified King, it covers the essential calling of every local church to be deliberately growing in wholehearted love for Jesus."[14] When we are given consistent opportunities within a local church to grow in loving God through a wide variety of acts of worship and adoration, we are engaging in Communion.

4. A House of Prayer for All Nations

Fourthly, a local church engages in the core spiritual element of prayer. This is a priority in a local church. The whole company of people (no matter how big or small) continuing steadfastly, in individual and corporate prayer. Isaiah declared in Isaiah 56:7 what Jesus repeated in Matthew 21:13, "For my house shall be called a house of prayer for all nations!" At its essence the Church of God are a people of prayer and intercession. Not only for their own needs, but for all the nations to experience the gospel of the Kingdom in power. In the Lord's prayer, Jesus taught six distinct petitions (Matthew 6:9–13). The first three are focused on His name being glorified among the nations, the Kingdom of God to come and His perfect will to be accomplished on the earth. These are prayers centered in the fulfillment of the Great Commission, God's redemptive storyline being accomplished, ushering in the age to come through the full-fledged Kingdom of God on earth. The second three are prayers for ourselves and our needs. The sequencing is significant. First, intercede for His glory among the unreached and second, ask for personal needs.

A local church, as a corporate entity, is called by God to stand in the gap in prayer for the nations. To be a local church failing as a people of prayer is an oxymoron. This is a core piece of a local church's identity, expressing itself as a missionary people, interceding on behalf of ethnic peoples all over the world. Prayer could be defined as aligning with the will of God and calling that will into existence. Prayer is Jesus' primary way to release heaven's resources into the earthly realm.[15] God wants the spirit of prayer active in every local church, engaging in prayer and intercession. The power of God increased to push back darkness and release Jesus' light. The Holy Spirit is emphasizing prayer in a greater way in the global Church today, yet it is still rare to find local churches prioritizing prayer for all nations.

Practically, this may look like setting time aside during the Sunday service for focused prayer for the unreached, one evening a week for prayer for global harvest or installing an onsite prayer room. People can come throughout the week to intercede for the nations. This is done free from the inclination to make the meeting about something other than prayer and intercession.

Three Core Outward Elements

In addition to these four core spiritual elements of local churches there are three outward elements making a biblical local church. These three are adapted from Charles Van Engen's writings on this subject[16] and can be categorized as:

- Proclaiming and living out the confession, "Jesus Is Lord!"
- Sacrificial service to those in need
- Powerful witness locally and crossing cultures

1. Proclaiming and Living Out the Confession, "Jesus is Lord!"
After receiving the Holy Spirit in Acts 2, the disciples immediately progressed outward, proclaiming with clarity what was happening. Imparted boldness from the Spirit overcame timidity, communicating widely and powerfully.

Peter's message highlighted the Lordship of Jesus over all. This truth is at the center of a local community of faith. A local church bound together spiritually through the apostle's doctrine, fellowship, communion (worship) and the spirit of prayer embodies the rightful Lordship of Jesus over all. The early Church was known as a people unto whom, "Jesus is Lord!" The phrase became a confession and creed of the churches as a core element of faith and identity.

The Lordship of Jesus motivates a local church outward in proclamation of the gospel. Lordship means all belongs to Him. Jesus' sacrificial work of redemption, or purchasing back wayward sinners, is for all. Since the global Church's commission is bringing humanity, and the whole creation, under Jesus' rule as Lord, a local church proclaims truth to all in many diverse ways. This part of the essential nature of a community of faith is often overlooked, hindering it being the vehicle God intends to fulfill His Great Commission.

Members of New Testament churches naturally "gossiped" the gospel with relational connections at workplaces, markets and among relatives. The gospel runs fastest along established, relational lines of trust and observance. As believers confessed and testified Jesus as Lord over all, they spent time teaching friends these truths. In time many came to their own faith in Jesus. Then the small churches multiplied, starting new fellowships in another part of town. At times their multiplication of churches went further, starting new fellowships in other cities, provinces or areas with the same intent—crossing cultural barriers to reach those who had never heard. A local church scatters itself outward in concentric circles through simple, mobile, easily reproducible, fellowships—not merely gathering people into one large megachurch. The early Church understood the redeeming Kingdom of God as a universal Kingdom, meant for all peoples. Because Jesus is Lord, possessing all authority in heaven and on earth, local churches go forth, discipling all ethnic peoples.

2. Sacrificial Service to Those in Need

Because local churches are living fellowships of Jesus' disciples, they identify as the fellowship of the crucified. Jesus, the sacrificial servant of Isaiah 53, laid His life down to redeem humanity from the wrath of God. True discipleship then includes becoming sacrificial servants of others as He did. Ministries of service are part of a local church's worship of Jesus. Sacrificial servanthood is a crucial piece of being God's missionary people, demonstrating the gospel of the Kingdom.

This is not a side issue, done when convenient or when we have resources for it, but a core characteristic of what a local church is as well as a key piece of our Great Commission mandate in Mark. James reveals this same idea in James 1:27 teaching, "Pure and undefiled religion before God and the Father is this: to visit orphans and widows in their trouble..." The gospels cite a "disciple is not above His master" (John 13:16) and corporately local communities of faith reflect the servanthood of their Lord.

The Lordship of Jesus is on display through His Church identifying with broken humanity. Identification and culturally relevant communication of the gospel naturally proceeds to their restoration, redemption, and incorporation into local churches. Leading to potential multiplication of local simple, reproducible fellowships among unreached peoples. The Church's role is to demonstrate God's justice and righteousness in a broken world. God's definition of true justice is much different from the counterfeit justice movement often seen. His justice reconciles human beings with creator God, through whom they can be transformed, thus transforming institutions, structures, and circumstances around them. "Jesus is Lord," our pattern as the great Sacrificial Servant, not merely out of humanitarian, humanistic concerns.

3. Powerful Witness Locally and Crossing Cultures

Jesus provided the calling of local churches and individual disciples in Acts 1:8 instructing, "You shall receive power when the Holy Spirit has come upon you and you shall be witnesses to Me in Jerusalem and in all Judea and Samaria and to the end of the earth." A prominent interpretation drastically twists the meaning, asserting first prioritizing the local city, stating Jesus mandated the early Church to first reach Jerusalem. This is a misreading. Looking closely at the verse, it never says first be witnesses in Jerusalem or then in Judea. The words "either" and "or" are not there. The correct reading is to view every local's church's mandate as both to the local city and crossing cultural barriers to unreached peoples more distant.[17]

This line of thinking focuses on geographic expansion while overlooking a local church's witness both locally and beyond. A local church doing the four core spiritual elements (Acts 2:42) along with living out the confession,

"Jesus is Lord," and sacrificially serving those in need, provides a powerful witness of Jesus, revealing their core missionary nature. Every local church's existence in the world includes proclamation and demonstration. A local church makes the truth that Jesus is present in the world real and visible. Those outside His Kingdom come to Him through the presence, proclamation and demonstration of a local church, but not necessarily within its four walls. Every local church is witness in their own community and beyond. The nature of the Church is not to gather within but to multiply outward in concentric circles of influence.

An over emphasis on "witness" explicitly referring to what we say about Jesus has brought some confusion. We go out "witnessing" for Jesus. While a local church proclaiming the gospel of the Kingdom is accurate and indisputable, of accompanying importance is truth being realized within a believer, empowering words with spiritual weight. A "witness" bears witness to Jesus' Lordship and Kingdom. They've experienced truth deep in their life, finding Jesus to be Reconciler, Redeemer, Savior as well as Lord, Deliverer, and Healer. The gospel has transformed and continues to transform their lives, families, and circumstances. They are new creations in Christ experiencing the benefits, blessings, and privileges of the Kingdom of God. Witness falls on deaf ears if only speaking intellectual, religious information instead of experiential, proven truth.

***

We have come to the end of part 2, considering biblical foundations of the Great Commission. We looked at the four distinct commissions from the mouth of Jesus in the Gospels, each one giving a slice of the overall pie of our Great Commission calling as the global Church. We saw an overview of the redemptive storyline of Scripture, rooting us in that storyline, while also detailing what the fulfillment of the Great Commission looks like according to Scripture. We then considered the macro understanding of the nature of the global Church while also looking at the micro plan of God through every single individual local ministry operating in certain core characteristics. This has been an exciting part as our faith has been boosted to trust the promises of God in His Word of what is to come. Let's now proceed to look at what church and mission history reveal about mission mobilization.

Part 3

Historical Analysis of Mission, Mobilization, and Revival

10

Historical Eras 1 & 2: AD 30–1500

Reflecting on church history helps the global Church rethink global mobilization.[1] History is more than names, dates, and events. God has been gradually unfolding His master plan of redemption, in the midst of world history, since initiating His far-reaching covenant with Abraham 4,000 years ago (Genesis 12). The progressive nature of God's redemptive story within history is an important concept. God is working progressively in history, never doing everything at once. He is not in a hurry, having purpose in every era and century. Tracing God's global mission and mobilization heartbeat throughout redemptive history is the same. There are ebbs and flows, seasons where particular foundations were laid to prepare for the next progression. "Progressive" refers to the continual unfolding of God's redemptive storyline along a divine continuum, from its beginnings in Genesis to its fullness in Revelation at Jesus' return.

Dr. Wes Adams affirms God is not detached from history nor acting arbitrarily through events. He doesn't initiate events, movements, or seasons without planning and purpose. Neither is God reacting to forces (spiritual, political, economic, social, cultural) shaping world history. They do not take Him by surprise.[2] History is moving in purposeful progression from a God-initiated beginning to a God-appointed end. Adams puts it this way: "God transcends history as the Creator, descends into history as the Redeemer, and will return as the Bridegroom to unite with His prepared Bride."[3]

MISSION, MOBILIZATION, AND REVIVAL IN CHURCH HISTORY

The early Church in the first century began well, engaging in mission mobilization that produced a quickly spreading mission movement to the unreached (Gentiles). But how has the Church done through the centuries in mobilization? Where has the Spirit brought us and where is He taking us from here? What can we learn from history related to mobilization? This is what we consider in this part.

A 4,000-Year Grid for Interpreting History

To get the most out of church and mission history we need a grid, a lens or perspective, to interpret correctly. A grid enables analysis, helping us glean practical clarity. Through careful study, Wes Adams has concluded that in both biblical and redemptive history, from Abraham (Genesis 12) to the present, there is a recurring, overarching historical trend—a brand-new, noteworthy era has occurred every 500 years without exception.[4] With every 500-year portion of time, in biblical and redemptive history until the present (about 4,000 years), something shifted which introduced a new, important element into God's redemptive storyline. From a historical standpoint, this is quite remarkable as it never fails to show up. Let's quickly consider these 500-year eras in God's salvation history.

- Abraham as the beginning point of Israel: 2000 BC
- Moses, the Exodus, and the Law: 1500 BC
- King David and the tabernacle of David: 1000 BC
- Post-Exilic Jewish restoration: 500 BC
- Incarnation of Messiah, Jesus Christ: 0 BC
- Institutionalization of the Church: AD 500
- East and West division of Christianity: AD 1000
- Protestant Reformation: AD 1500
- Present day: AD 2000

141

   With each new era God restored (in a progressive way) core elements of faith, Christian life, and the expansion of the gospel, overlooked or laid aside. Each era was a major thrust forward in the overall purpose of God, though not necessarily discernible at the time. This historical trend indicates that around the year AD 2000, a shift to a new major era in God's redemptive storyline may be happening. I am confident this includes mission and mobilization progressively maturing across the global Church. Empowering the whole, global Church for the first time in history to deliberately engage in mission mobilization toward fulfilling the Great Commission.

The Bookends of Redemptive History

If we view the whole of redemptive history, from the day of Pentecost until the second coming of Jesus, as a timeline, the mission and mobilization emphasis started with a bang. The early Church, empowered by the newly poured out Holy Spirit, went out with zeal, spiritual power, and obedience to Jesus' last spoken command—the Great Commission. Herbert Kane states, "What began as a Jewish sect in AD 30 had grown into a world religion by AD 60."[5] Small house churches acted as training centers, preparing lay believers as witnesses and evangelists. They embodied the Church's identity as proclaiming and demonstrating the gospel of the Kingdom. That generation is a dramatic sign to the Church through the centuries. Their teaching, methods and life responses should be studied and reflected over and over, applying and interpreting them within our generation. They are the only generation in church history encapsulated in the Bible itself. This is purposeful, meant by the Spirit as an anointed, authoritative guide to every generation. To the degree we have either imitated or strayed from them, is the degree to which the global Church has been effective or not in cross-cultural mission.[6]

   Now to the end of the timeline, the generation fulfilling the Great Commission and the second coming of Christ, we see how things will end. The Spirit will have a global Church wholehearted for Jesus, surrendered to His purposes, victorious over compromise and complacency, walking with heart hunger for God, refined in faith, endurance, and perseverance, dynamically inspired by the timeframe they are living, emphasizing the Great Commission across every local ministry. That generation will be different from what we see today. Loving God for God, not what they can get from God. Through challenges and trouble, believers will choose. Multitudes will choose the latter, contributing to the falling away Jesus prophesied in the New Testament (Matthew 24:12; 1 Timothy 4:1-2; 2 Thessalonians 2:3). He is purifying His Church, separating wheat from the tares, real from counterfeit. This victorious global body of Christ, purified by trials, living the Sermon on the Mount lifestyle, empowered by the Spirit, emphasizing the Great Commission, scattered to all subcultures of all unreached people groups, is central to the great harvest at the end of the age.

These are the two bookends. But what about the middle? One would assume that following such a strong start, global mission and mission mobilization emphasis would grow, coming to a crescendo at the end. Unfortunately, that has not been the case. The great historian Kenneth Scott Latourette has divided church history into three large periods of time:

1. AD 100–500 (the first five centuries)
2. The 1,000-year period called the Middle or Dark Ages
3. The last five centuries (500 years)

We will use these three historical eras to break up our look at the history of mission, mobilization, and revival, seeking core principles and lessons.

HISTORICAL ERA 1: AD 100–500

Following the birth of the Church (AD 30) and mission expansion in the first century, the next 400 years (AD 100–500) found the Church slipping. Dependence on the ministry of the Spirit was less emphasized, while institutionalization increased—the Church reflecting the worldly and political systems of the cultures around them. Still around AD 290 it is thought about 10 percent of the Roman Empire were followers of Jesus.[7]

In the early 300s, Constantine the Great (AD 272–337), emperor of the Roman Empire, became a nominal Christian (AD 312), declaring Christianity the state religion of the Roman Empire, having lost much of its essential dynamic. It became institutionalized instead of maintaining its vibrant, vital core. During these years, buildings were first used as "churches" and paid clergy were introduced. Constantine wanted church leaders paid well, attracting unqualified people seeking money and prominence. Christianity became "popular" for all the wrong reasons, losing its cutting edge as the gospel ceased being the power of God among society, substituted by religious forms and rituals. "Christendom" was born in the mid-300s, referring to the financial support of the Church by the state and assumption that most, if not all, citizens were "Christians." This was the foundation of what would become the "Holy Roman Empire," the Byzantine Empire and the Roman Catholic Church. Being a Christian ceased to mean enthroning Jesus as Lord and obeying His teachings of discipleship, but being a member of the right institution.[8] The Great Commission mandate was greatly reduced as nominalism gripped the Church.

Mission in this era consisted of a few monks attracting followers to their ascetic lifestyle of withdrawal from corrupt society, fasting, prayer, meditation, and good works. Roman Catholic global mission was closely tied with politics and territorial expansion of the Empire. Outstanding missionaries of this era included Ulfilas and Patrick.

Ulfilas (AD 311–383) was one of the greatest cross-cultural missionaries of the 4th century. After studying in Constantinople under famous Bishop Eusebius, he served among a barbarian tribe, the Goths, outside the Roman Empire in modern-day Romania, translating the Bible into the previously unwritten Gothic language.[9] By AD 410, when the Goth army sacked Rome, it is believed that most Goths were followers of Jesus, a direct result of Ulfilas' earlier ministry. Patrick (AD 385–461) was born in Britain, but taken as a slave to Ireland at sixteen years old for six years. During which time he embraced the faith his parents instilled in him. Eventually he escaped capture, becoming a monk in Britain and had a dream of a man in Ireland calling him to return to reach the masses for Christ. He returned to the country of his captivity and had a successful, 30-year mission ministry among the unreached Irish.[10] This era generally consisted of one-off missionaries while the concept of mission mobilization inculcated within the life of the churches was basically nonexistent.

HISTORICAL ERA 2: AD 500–1500

This era of history, known as the "Dark Ages," from AD 500–1500, was so for a reason. Spanning the 1,000-year period from the fall of the Roman Empire (AD 476) to the rise of the Ottoman Empire (AD 1453), spiritual light was dim. Spiritual darkness and political compromise consumed the Church. Christianity (predominantly expressed through Roman Catholicism and Eastern Orthodox) and European politics were merged during this long period, becoming almost inseparable, creating a skewed understanding of the gospel and the Kingdom of God. The official church became more entrenched in institutionalization, religious forms, and rituals replacing a heart connection with Jesus. True faith was almost nonexistent, except for a few zealous monks in the monasteries.

The Celtic Mission Movement

In the early AD 500s mission zeal captured the Celtic church movement in Ireland, founded through the ministry of Patrick nearly a century before. Ruth Tucker, in her landmark book on mission history, notes, "There was a passion for foreign global mission in the impetuous eagerness of the Irish believers, a zeal not common in their day. Burning with love for Christ, fearing no peril, shunning no hardship, they went everywhere with the gospel."[11] Their first cross-cultural venture was to Britain, the country Patrick had come from. The missionary impulse was stirred up in the Celtic churches. Mission mobilization took place within each church entity, engaging believers in Bible study on God's love for all, prayer for peoples around them not knowing Christ and strategizing how to reach lost peoples. One of the greatest missionaries from this mobilization movement was Columba (AD 521–597)[12] who established a mission base in Iona, an island off the coast of Scotland. He ministered throughout Scotland, focusing on miracles, signs, and wonders to help the people see God as greater than their idols.

Gregory the Great

Probably the most important individual of the early part of this era was Gregory the Great (AD 540–604). Gregory was a significant mission mobilizer, one of the most able bishops of Rome (the leadership role that would eventually be called pope),[13] continually pressing the Roman Catholic church to send out mission teams. Before becoming bishop, he had a deep urgency to see the pagan tribes, beyond the borders of the Roman Empire, reached with the love of Christ. Though he himself was not able to do this personally, he was instrumental in helping mobilize the Church for cross-cultural mission, legitimizing it, engaging monks with this priority. This is often an experience of mission mobilizers—desiring to go out themselves yet for a variety of reasons are not able to personally do so. They resolve to send as many as possible in their place.

Gregory had significant missiological understanding, setting missionary policy followed in the Catholic church for centuries. He was well ahead of his time with clarity on missiological issues still faced today. To the question of what to do with pagan ceremonies and temples, he suggested missionaries not do away with them as of the devil, but instead destroy the pagan idols while adapting the temples (which the people were accustomed to) for worship meetings to the true God. As a replacement of sacrifice rituals to demon gods, he encouraged the appointing of festivals where oxen are slain in honor of God as His provision of their food.[14] Recognizing the wisdom of not taking away what a people knows, Gregory encouraged utilizing their forms and rituals, inviting the people to change their meaning and intent, making them tools of worship of the true creator God.

This is part of mission mobilization as seen in chapter 15—educating local ministries with the nuances, principles, trends, and strategies of cross-cultural mission contextualization. Which cultural forms should be used as bridges for the gospel, which ought to be abandoned? The latter question is not for the outsider to decide, but for the new believing community. Imposing from outside is where many mistakes have been made in mission history.

The Nestorian Movement

One of the greatest global mission and mobilization movements of the Middle Ages was the Nestorian movement of the AD 500 and 600s, becoming known as "the most missionary church the world has ever seen."[15] The movement took its name from Nestorius, an archbishop of Constantinople in the 400s. Nestorius himself was eventually called a heretic and deposed from his position in 431 over the struggles surrounding the definition of the two natures of Christ. Paul Pierson clarifies, "Later Nestorian leaders affirmed Chalcedonian Christology, that is, the doctrine of Christ espoused by the Church as a whole: Eastern Orthodox, Roman Catholic and Protestant."[16] After facing persecution in the Roman Empire they fled to Persia where the Nestorian Church grew rapidly. Believers in Nestorian communities were deeply committed to spiritual disciplines, possessing great faith, were mighty in Scripture (many of them memorizing entire books of the New Testament) and cross-cultural mission.

Their mission strategy, being restored today, was scattering out as bankers, merchants, doctors to the unreached of their day. They followed Paul's example of bivocational ministry through his tent-making business. Paul Pierson reveals this allowed their sending out large numbers of laborers without much money, as each person was a Kingdom worker while simultaneously working with their hands, earning a living.[17] These believers scattered themselves among the Huns in Central Asia, to India, Arabia, Tibet, Afghanistan, and China, planting church centers that functioned with discipleship schools, raising up a generation of zealous believers for the Lord. In the 700s and following this strong mission mobilization movement declined, particularly as the Islamic movement and the armies of Genghis Khan took over large segments of Asia.

Glimmers of global mission and mission mobilization shone through the remaining centuries of the Middle Ages through the monastic movements of St. Francis and St. Dominic, the two greatest missionary orders of the Roman Catholic Church of that era. While earlier monastic movements had gone to deserted places, these two leaders guided their monks into the cities and towns, as society moved in this direction. Though we cannot espouse all Catholic doctrine, many Catholic missionaries were motivated by true relationship with Christ and evangelical fervor. It wasn't until the Protestant mission movements in the mid-1700s that mission work was undertaken by non-Catholics.

Mission to Muslims

The series of Crusades against Muslims from AD 1096–1492 was a major setback for mission, contributing to animosity between Christians and Muslims still lasting today. The Crusades were a tragic misinterpretation of "mission" based in a wrong concept rooted in medieval Christianity. To them a true Christian was baptized into the Roman Catholic Church. If you regularly received the sacraments, you went to heaven. This resulted, among some, in doing whatever it took to help others get baptized, even at the edge of a sword.[18]

Economic factors also contributed to the Crusades. The years AD 970 to 1040 included 48 years of famine. The decade of AD 1085 to 1095 experienced an even greater famine across Western Europe, producing widespread poverty and social unrest, pushing the pope to find an economic solution. The Roman Catholic Church in financial need, sought to take by force the growing wealth of the Muslim world. Political reasons also motivated the Crusades as the Roman Catholic Church sought to win back the Holy Land from Muslims. Under the pretense of religious purpose—protecting Christians in the capital of the Eastern Roman Empire, Constantinople, from Muslim Turks—Pope Urban II launched the first Crusade in AD 1096.

Many true believers and movements of the later Middle Ages stood against this misunderstanding of Jesus toward Muslims. In the early AD 1200s, while the Crusades were raging, Francis of Assisi (AD 1181–1226) taught Muslims should be won by love, not violence and hate. He set out to reach Muslims, even meeting the Sultan of Egypt. His sensitivity to the Spirit's love for Muslim peoples paved the way for others to follow. One of the most influential of the Middle Ages was Raymond Lull (1232–1316). Lull was a visionary with great foresight, born to a wealthy, aristocratic Roman Catholic family in Spain. In his thirties Lull had a life transforming encounter with Christ that included open visions. Upon becoming born again, he surrendered his wealth to the poor, making it his life's focus to win all peoples to Christ.

In particular, Lull recognized the importance of churches having a vision to reach Muslim peoples, generally the most hated peoples at that time. Lull was a mission mobilizer. Because of his aristocratic birth, he found ways to have an audience with the pope, pleading with him to approve a school of mission for the Muslim world, preparing laborers by learning Arabic, even learning Arabic himself.[19] Finally, in AD 1311 the Roman Catholic Church formally adopted Lull's training school plan. Through his widespread travels he preached among multitudes of churches, mobilizing them with love for Muslim peoples, as part of the Great Commission, dedicating themselves to find ways to reach them. Lull's strategy for reaching Muslims was through Christian apologetics. He wrote over sixty books revealing the love he had for Muslims, wanting them to see the reality of Christ. Lull traveled to North Africa three times, preaching, and teaching among Muslims. On his third trip, he was stoned to death at 84 years old.

***

In this chapter we have observed a glimpse, an overview of the first 1,500 years of mission and mobilization in the Church. We now proceed to the most exciting of eras, the last 500 years, where we begin to glean significant insight into where God is leading the global Church. We are moving progressively in history and in God's redemptive purpose. As history progresses, we see the broad strokes of light moving us, step by step, toward the culmination of all history.

11

Historical Era 3: 1500s to Present Day—Sub-Eras 1 & 2

With this new era, we take a massive leap forward in God's redemptive plans in history. This is Latourette's final 500-year era, as well as the final 500-year period of the grid outlining major shifts every 500 years since Abraham. This overarching 500- year era marks the gradual recovery (restoration) of what was lost during the previous centuries of spiritual decline, particularly AD 100–1500. We will consider the restorations God has been recovering in this era. During these last 500 years, God has been accelerating the pace of His redemptive purpose, seemingly century by century. This 500-year era is alive with the activity of God, particularly with monumental revival, mission, and mobilization movements. Within the overarching 500-year era, there are several progressive revival, mission, and mobilization eras. Each one building on the previous, contributing to our understanding of where God is leading.

We find a unique dynamic during this 500-year era. The intertwining of revival, mission, and mobilization emphasis, together empowering the Church to progress in her calling. We will look in detail at four specific revival eras and four accompanying mission and mobilization eras. Each era is marked by a significant revival that dynamically impacted mission conviction, helping mobilize and equip the Church for Jesus' Great Commission. You cannot have one emphasis without the others. We have tended to isolate mission history, telling those stories. Yet without the backdrop of the revivals restoring key aspects of spiritual life and expression, we have an incomplete picture. This fact is one of the clearest principles of God's redemptive plan revealed in history: At pivotal times God revives and renews His Church, restoring core elements of her calling, and releasing them to spread the gospel to all peoples.

REVIVAL ERA #1: PROTESTANT REFORMATION (AD 1517–1648)

The Protestant Reformation, on the heels of the previous thousand-year Middle Ages era, proved as Paul Pierson describes to be a massive reordering of a "re-contextualization of the Christian faith in the new emerging Europe of the 16th century."[1] This revival season must be understood against the backdrop of the Middle Ages Catholic Church that lost its way, groping in spiritual darkness. The Church mirrored society as sin and corruption ruled the sociopolitical structures of the period. The common people suffered, without hope, care, or spiritual understanding. Experiential knowledge of God was replaced by institutionalized church life, irrelevant to the ordinary person. Christian life had become rules and regulations, void of true spiritual life. The Church and its leaders were manipulative, keeping the people in darkness, ignorant of the Bible. Salvation was diminished, reliant on works and merit instead of faith in the shed blood of Christ.

But God was intervening, restoring specific areas of faith that had been lost. Focal restorations God initiated during this tumultuous time of change and shaking included:

1. New understanding of core elements of the gospel long sidelined and overlooked
2. New ministry structures emerging more relevant to the masses
3. New church government
4. Greater emphasis on lay leadership—empowering every believer in their relationship with God and as vital witnesses of Jesus
5. New communication methods and worship styles introduced.

Each of these are areas of contextualization needed in every cross-cultural ministry endeavor as well.

Overall, there was a significant shift toward getting the gospel message to the common people, in a way they could culturally and intellectually understand. Something denied them during the Middle Ages. The Reformation, at its core, was a rediscovery of truth—the biblical gospel—that was personal, life transforming. The gift of a kind, good God through faith in Christ to restore people, families, societies to what He intended before the Fall. It also restored the crucial anchor of the authority of Scripture, not merely monks, popes, and other learned individuals. What mattered supremely was no longer what the pope said, but what the Bible said. This was an earth-shattering recovery, empowering every person to read and hear the Bible for themselves.

Classically understood, "revival" is a redemptive phenomenon that has appeared primarily since the Protestant Reformation began. There were pockets of revival and renewal in the early Church and throughout the Middle Ages. Yet revivals reinvigorating the Church in a widespread way, proceeding to impact society through that renewed church, are a fairly unique occurrence since the Reformation of the 1500s.[2] The Reformation unleashed the powers of heaven as the first fruits of the last 500 years of revival, renewal and awakening activity. From the Reformation revival fires began to burn among Anabaptists in Germany, Switzerland, and Holland, among Puritans in England and early Pietists in Germany and pockets across Europe, starting in the late 1500s and 1600s. These moves of God recovered what it meant for people to be saved.

The accusation that the Reformers (Martin Luther, John Calvin, John Knox, Ulrich Zwingli) were not concerned about cross-cultural mission is a valid one. They were on the front lines of pushing back an onslaught of wrong theology, structure, and belief systems. That generation needed the drastic transformation these key players and movements brought about. Yet it is helpful to consider further underlying reasons for the absence of mission vision and mobilization during the Reformation. These reasons help us understand why churches, even today, often become stuck in faulty outlooks on mission.

For example, Protestant theology defined the true Church as existing where "the word is rightly preached and the sacraments properly observed."[3]

This was a response against the Roman Catholic Church, in general good while evidently incomplete, lacking anything of the core missionary dimension of the Church. God's plan for the Church, made up of millions of individual, simple communities of believers in every city, town, village, and neighborhood, among every subgroup of ethnic people groups, consistently reproducing themselves. This reaction to Roman Catholic doctrine overlooked key areas of who and what the Church is.

Though used by God to restore needed focal points of the gospel, the Reformers had significant blind spots in their overall theological outlook. Martin Luther believed in the imminent return of Christ yet discounted the importance of cross-cultural mission. Somewhat bizarrely, he thought the Great Commission was only for the first century apostles, who accomplished it in their generation. According to him, every succeeding generation was excused from taking the Great Commission seriously. Calvin's often misunderstood doctrine of election made it appear global mission was pointless since God had already chosen whom He would save. This was evidently a misrepresentation of the heart of God in and through the gospel.

MISSION & MOBILIZATION ERA #1: THE MORAVIANS

We now proceed to what is commonly referred to as the modern mission movement. AD 1750–present witnessed the greatest thrust forward in Protestant mission to date, through the "great centuries" of mission. We find a significant increase in mission and mobilization overall during this era. It is necessary to reiterate the progressive development of history. Since the 1700s the widespread restoration of the Great Commission has been growing in camps across the body of Christ. Aided by the important restorations across the Protestant Churches through the Reformation. That restoration is not yet complete. It will continue to take place, culminating in a crescendo, into the next generation.

The famed Moravian movement, starting in 1722, paved the way for the modern mission movement launched by William Carey in 1792. The Moravian community at Herrnhut (the Lord's Watch), in Bavaria (modern day Germany) is a representation of core principles of effective Mission Mobilization Movements. For a local church or denomination desiring to practically engage in mission mobilization, the Moravian spiritual community is essential to study and emulate. Let's consider these core principles up close.

First, they had leadership infusing the vision of the Great Commission into every element of church life, in the person of Count Nicolaus Ludwig von Zinzendorf (1700–1760). Zinzendorf had spiritual foundations in the Pietistic revival in Germany and became bishop of the Herrnhut Moravian community. Zinzendorf felt Jesus' heartbeat for the world, believing every church community, because of all Jesus had done, should be ready to go anywhere, accepting any sacrifice to take the gospel of the Kingdom to the world. He was one of the greatest missionary statesmen of the last 300 years and a passionate mission mobilizer.[4] Cross-cultural mission and mission mobilization was no side issue for the Moravians at Herrnhut, but at the forefront of why the church community existed, constituting their core identity.

Second, the Moravian community experienced a significant spiritual awakening in August of 1727, binding them together, consuming them with love and obedience for their Master, wherever He may lead. They referred to this revival as their Pentecost.[5] The spiritual fire fueled their hearts for obeying Christ's commission. God uses seasons of corporate refreshing at pivotal times to spiritually empower His people to respond to His guidance. As Paul Pierson reminds us, spiritual revival and renewal are always precursors to growing mission vision gripping a community, aligning their hearts with the Lord's.[6] This principle reveals the importance the Moravians placed on spiritual maturity as a foundation for effective mission. They taught and lived wholehearted devotion to Christ, expressed through their mission sending movement.

Third, the Moravians recognized every member of their church community was called to global mission, whether or not they left the confines of the community itself. This is a core principle of mission mobilization—every believer expressing their role in the Great Commission with zeal and dedication. Lay leadership in mission is crucial. The task is just too big to rely on a few professional "missionaries."[7]

Fourth, devoted prayer sustained the community and its global mission work. Through careful planning, the Moravian community facilitated what has become known as the "100-year prayer meeting." An unbroken, around the clock, chain of prayer for wholehearted devotion in their community and global harvest among the nations. Devoted prayer literally went on day and night for a hundred years, breaking every twenty-four hours into one-hour prayer slots for two community members to engage in intercession.[8]

Fifth, cross-cultural ministry was not just for clergy in the community. The Moravians believed a large percentage of lay people in their community should go to near or distant cultures planting small, simple, culturally relevant churches. They were a scattering community, deliberately choosing the hardest, hostile, out of the way places of the day—the West Indies, Greenland, Labrador, American Colonies, South America, South Africa. One of every 13 people in the Herrnhut community (which never numbered more than a few hundred) went to a distant culture with the gospel,[9] a total of 216 by the time Zinzendorf died in 1760, while many others went out from the community to nearer cultures within Western Europe itself. The Moravians' spiritual battle cry was, "May the Lamb receive the reward of His suffering!"

Sixth, the Moravians sustained scattering a large number of laborers by not relying on the church funding their mission endeavors. Zinzendorf believed cross-cultural message bearers should take their trade with them to the unreached,[10] understanding voluntary contributions alone were not adequate to fulfill the Great Commission. The sheer numbers of message bearers necessary, made relying on home churches to finance them unfeasible. They followed the well-worn footsteps of Paul the apostle as a bivocational tentmaker. Moravian message bearers influenced the local communities they went with the gospel, while helping their local economies through their example and expertise in various trades.

Every generation has pioneers in mission the next generation learns from and reads about. This is how God has wired His people, influenced by the zeal and abandonment of those before us. The Moravians and Zinzendorf dynamically influenced the mission movement over the next 300 years. William Carey, in the 1780s, was familiar with the Moravian missionary example, using it to fire his own imagination. John Wesley visited Herrnhut and was profoundly influenced through a mentoring relationship with Zinzendorf.[11] He was marked by the spiritual depth and disciplines of the community itself. In particular, the Moravians' understanding of personal relationship with Jesus through faith, freedom in the Holy Spirit, radical commitment to prayer and their zeal for the lost.

155

REVIVAL ERA 2: THE FIRST AND SECOND GREAT AWAKENINGS (1730S–1840S)

It was the core principles of the Moravian movement that inspired so many. The Moravians and their deep spirituality were the precursors to the First (1730s–1770s) and Second (1790–1840) Great Awakenings in the US and England, which influenced the launching of the first Protestant mission societies. This era of revivals restored fundamental spiritual areas the Reformation overlooked. The era was characterized by powerful preaching, crisis conversions, understanding the new birth and experiential salvation. Along with the acute awareness of faith producing justice in society through compassion for the poor, righting wrongs and bringing salvation to the world.

The First and Second Great Awakenings brought about the great societal reforms of the mid-1700s and 1800s, including the abolition of slavery in England (1833) and the US (1865). It was on the back of the First Great Awakening, and the transformation it brought to American society, that a just democracy in the colonies of America was created and fought for during the American Revolution (1775–1783). These two significant revival movements were the first, since the early Church in the New Testament, to experience widespread salvation and spiritual awakenings.[12]

It is difficult to calculate the enormous influence of the First and Second Great Awakenings upon American and British society, and the mission and reform movements that came out of them. Both societies had been straying spiritually in the years prior to the revivals. Social evils were everywhere (drunkenness, poverty, slavery). When God is ready to do a new thing, He first renews and revives His people with a fresh outpouring of the Holy Spirit in their midst. These movements produced devoted Christian life rooted in a definite born-again experience. They also produced authentic faith within nominal society, applying Scripture to life and focusing on the power of the cross. The movements placed a great role on laity in churches, emphasized evangelism and mission, engaged in ministries of education and compassion for the poor, and sought to help their societies adopt the values of the Kingdom of God.[13] This is the legacy of the First and Second Great Awakenings, overflowing into their mission sending zeal to the nations.

MISSION & MOBILIZATION ERA 2: WILLIAM CAREY AND THE GREAT CENTURY OF MISSIONS (1792–1914)

In 1800, according to mission historian Stephen Neill, "It was still by no means certain that Christianity would be successful in turning itself into a universal religion."[14] At that time, Christianity was generally still a "Western faith" struggling in an age of rationalism and humanism in the Western world. But the evangelical faith was stirred by the Great Awakenings, and within the next 100-year period would spread with such focus that cross-cultural laborers would be found on every continent by 1900. The First and Second Great Awakenings are the backdrop of the impact, devotion, and message of what Kenneth Scott Latourette called the "Great Century of Missions."[15] Officially dated from 1792, when William Carey launched his Baptist Society, to 1914, when World War I broke out.

Ralph Winter has helped the Church immensely with a grid to analyze and interpret mission history since 1792.[16] Along with each revival era, Winter points out there was a progressive mission movement bringing new understanding and strategic focus to the mission endeavor. Three successive "mission eras" of modern Protestant mission history. Each coming through a particular mission leader of the day. The first era was from 1792–1865 to the coastlands, the second era from 1865–1935 to the inland peoples, and the third era from 1935 to the present to the unreached, hidden peoples.

The first key figure was William Carey (1761–1834), a Baptist lay preacher and part-time school teacher, supported through his trade as a shoe maker. It was through Carey that Winter's first era of Protestant global mission came to pass. Though of humble background, Carey was one of the most brilliant linguists in history, translating the Bible into many languages and dialects. Carey came to Christ during the First Great Awakening in England, a direct by-product of revival. He represents the dynamic relationship between revival and mission expansion throughout history. The one empowering the other. Carey was greatly influenced by Jonathon Edwards, the revival theologian in New England, and the journals of David Brainerd.[17]

As a relatively new believer, Carey learned about the wider world as the British Empire was growing as a global power and the English explorer,

Captain Cook, was exploring islands of the South Pacific. Carey began to dream of these far-off places, even praying for them, in time becoming convinced God was leading him to do something practically for the unreached peoples who lived so far away.[18] Small pockets of mission activity were going on, but nothing widespread yet at this point in history.

Through Carey, modern cross-cultural mission, and particularly mission mobilization would begin in earnest, primarily through the influence of a book he published in 1792. Carey wrote about the importance of "using means" to reach those in far off places. Many Christians in his day believed if God wanted to save those out of access of the gospel, He would somehow sovereignly do it of His own accord. Without the use of His people or Church and mission structures. Carey's own denominational leaders said this exact thing to him, influenced by an extreme hyper-Calvinistic theology. Others taught that the apostles of the first century had preached the gospel to the whole world already.

Carey's writing on "using means" referred to deliberately forming structures to send out teams of laborers to the unreached world. Carey illustrated such a "society" wasn't only about those who went, but needed the prayers and financial contributions of those in the home church as well. His little book mobilized his generation of Christians to envision God using them in far off places in the Great Commission, challenging believers to "expect great things from God; attempt great things for God."[19] Carey is known as the "Father of the Modern Mission Movement" because he was the first to envision a mission society, set apart for sending workers to other parts of the world. Many of his ideas can be traced to the Acts 13 model of the Antioch church sending the first organized mission team in the New Testament— Paul, Barnabas, and John Mark.

Among other roles and functions, Carey was a mission mobilizer. Through his influence a widespread Mission Mobilization Movement was developed, on the heels of the Great Awakenings, which swept the churches in England and America.[20] His activities add to core principles of effective Mission Mobilization Movements—they use media and literature to communicate their message, distributing widely across the Church. Stimulating new understanding, clarity, and even spiritual vibrancy, surrounding Jesus' Great Commission and practical responses to it. The distribution of effective mission literature, media, teaching, and education is at the center of effective Mission Mobilization Movements.

Through his book and the influence of the First and Second Great Awakenings, an explosion of mission societies in England came into being in the late 1700s and early 1800s. Including the London Missionary Society (LMS) in 1795, sending famous missionaries Robert Morrison to China and David Livingstone (the great missionary-explorer) to Africa. The Church Missionary Society (CMS), connected to the Anglican Church, was started in 1799. The Wesleyan Methodists in England launched a mission society in 1813.[21] It became apparent to all that Carey was right to envision organized efforts (mission structures), essential to the burgeoning missionary movement. The idea the Church should organize, sending out laborers to the unreached would eventually become an accepted and standard pattern.

Carey's mobilization efforts reached America in 1806 as five college students at Williams College in Massachusetts had been reading his book, hearing his vision and the beginnings of his mission society. They regularly met for prayer, seeking God for the salvation of the unreached around the world. Effective mobilization becomes contagious as it spreads from group to group. On one summer day a thunderstorm drove these five students to shelter under a large haystack, yet they continued praying, offering themselves to reach the nations when they graduated. Their inspiring story has become known as the "Haystack Prayer Meeting," commemorated by the only monument to a prayer meeting in history, still standing on the campus of Williams College in Massachusetts, USA. They started the first ever student Mission Mobilization Movement on a college campus in America, quickly spreading across New England.

The result of their mission mobilization was the founding of the first ever American mission sending society (patterned after Carey's) in 1810, called "The American Board of Commissioners for Foreign Mission." This society was launched through a Mission Mobilization Movement of dedicated college students, the forerunner to the eventual Student Volunteer Movement, probably the greatest Mission Mobilization Movement in history. Influenced by the rediscovery that world evangelization was the direct responsibility of the Church and every generation of Christians around the world. There was a spiritual kindling taking place, along with a theological shift of lay people being trained for mission. The floodgates had opened from only clergy being allowed to minister the gospel. This shift has continued, yet there is still room to grow to achieve the practical expression of Martin Luther's "priesthood of all believers" doctrine across the global Church. It is coming and will influence mission and mobilization in the same way these historical movements did.

***

Carey and others he inspired (Adoniram Judson in Burma; Robert Morrison in China; Henry Martyn in India and Iran; Alexander Duff in India; Robert Moffatt in South Africa; David Livingstone in Africa; Karl Gutzlaff in Thailand) during the first era of Protestant global mission from 1792–1865 landed, lived, and ministered primarily along the coasts of Asia and Africa. There were so few of them, and the needs were so great, that trying any ministry beyond the coasts was next to impossible. It would take another revival era, and a progression into the second era of Protestant global mission and mobilization to see the push to the inland areas of frontier countries take place.

12

Historical Era 3: 1500s to Present Day—Sub-Eras 3–4

The hand of God continued to progressively restore areas lost and forgotten over the centuries. Imparting mission strategy necessary to go to the next phase of seeing all unreached frontier peoples reached with the gospel. The century of the 1800s included significant revival movements through William and Catherine Booth and the Salvation Army and the famed Keswick movement in England, Andrew Murray and the revivals in South Africa, the revivals of Charles Finney, the Methodists, the Frontier Camp Meetings, the Holiness revivals in America. The predominant restoration of these revivals was deeper spiritual life in Christ. Whereas the Great Awakenings of the 1700s restored the experiential nature of conversion, the revivals of the 1800s emphasized growth of the inner life of the believer. These revival movements stressed the sanctification of the believer, both experiencing God's power to sanctify and a progressive growth in one's inner life character—biblical concepts not dealt with much during the Great Awakenings of the 1700s.[1] The revivals of the 1800s too saw significant societal reform and changes, particularly in England and America, in addition to fueling the new mission thrusts.

MISSION & MOBILIZATION ERA 3: HUDSON TAYLOR & THE INLAND PEOPLES (1865–1934)

Ralph Winter's second era of Protestant mission history starts in 1865 through a young British man named Hudson Taylor (1832–1905).[2] The revivals of the century were deepening the spiritual lives of the believers, empowering them to live wholly for God, responding to His "compelling" desire to reach the world for Christ. Through careful study and prayer, Taylor began to discern God wanted His people to reach the inland peoples of China. Doing so had not been considered prior as Carey and his generation focused on the coastlands alone. Taylor saw how the vast, teeming multitudes had been overlooked by staying along the coasts. God opened a window of clarity to His Church through Taylor related to mission strategy that would progress the mission movement deeper into geographic countries than ever before.

As with Carey 75 years prior, Taylor faced great opposition. People told him it was impossible for foreigners to live in inland cities of China. Discouraged, Taylor continued seeking God. One day His voice broke through to Taylor, "you are not sending them to the inland, I am."[3] Undeterred, Taylor remained fixated on the need to reach the large numbers of peoples in the inland parts of China, founding the interdenominational China Inland Mission (CIM) in 1865. It was not until twenty more years that other mission structures and denominations caught on to what Taylor had discovered—the importance of pressing to the interior of countries where the vast majority of unreached frontier peoples lived.

About forty new mission structures were organized through Taylor's direct influence including Sudan Inland Mission (SIM), Africa Inland Mission (AIM), Heart of Africa Mission, Unevangelized Fields Mission, Regions Beyond Missionary Union (RBMU). This was a mobilization movement, helping the body of Christ understand the previously unseen peoples of the interior across the frontier nations. Well-known missionaries God raised up during this second era of Protestant global mission included Jonathan Goforth to China, John Paton to the New Hebrides, Lottie Moon to China, Amy Carmichael to India, Mary Slessor to Nigeria, Gladys Aylward to China, C. T. Studd and the Cambridge Seven to China, Samuel Zwemer to Arabia, and many more.

As in the first era, a student mobilization movement arose around the same time, fueling the colleges with mission vision and fervor. In the first era we noted the Haystack Prayer Meeting, which gave rise to a focused student mobilization emphasis at Williams College in Massachusetts spreading to other New England Colleges from 1806–1810 and beyond. The same happened in the second era of Protestant global mission through the Student Volunteer Movement from 1886–1930. These zealous young people were stirred up by God through the deeper spiritual life revival movements of the late 1800s, growing in understanding of the Great Commission, and surrendering their lives.[4] Campus ministries integrated biblical understanding of the Great Commission, with prayer for the nations, discussing inland peoples and strategies to reach them. The student volunteers who joined mission structures in the late 1800s and early 1900s contributed greatly to the remarkable "Century of Missions."[5] By 1930, 20,000 recent college graduates from England, USA, and Canada had joined missionary ranks, progressing the mission movement forward substantially.

REVIVAL ERA 4: THE 20TH CENTURY

Let's now consider the revival era of the 20th century (1900–1999) that helped ignite the two eras of mission progression straddling the same time period. The 20th century was marked by tremendous spiritual revivals that, unlike all their predecessors, became truly global. This was largely due to global systems coming into their own (particularly during the first ten years of the 20th century), enabling the message of the revivals to spread widely to many nations overnight through the electric telegraph and newly invented telephone. Communications and transportation technology were growing, inventions making life more convenient. This revival era restored core elements to the spiritual arsenal of the body of Christ. Going beyond the restorations of previously neglected focal points from the revivals of the 18th and 19th centuries (1700s and 1800s).

The restoration during the 20th century focused on the Holy Spirit's ministry to and through believers and the gifts of the Spirit. This emphasis was intended by God to bring the global Church back to her book of Acts origin.[6] The Church rediscovered the third person of the Trinity, along with His presence and power. This global rediscovery included His healing, deliv-

163

erance, gifts, miracles, and power evangelism, in ways unseen since the first century church. God has been restoring New Testament Christianity right in our midst. As a result, many have called the 1900s the "Century of the Holy Spirit" and rightly so.[7]

This revival era started with a bang. In fact, the decade between 1904–1912 saw an almost unbroken chain of revivals taking place around the world. Revival historians regard this decade as the most concentrated time of global revival ever in Church or biblical history. Yet God was preparing the way for revival well before it broke out in 1904. He was sovereignly stirring many believers around the world to pray for worldwide revival, mobilizing His praying Church as the instrument for what He wanted to bring about. God was highlighting an important principle of revival—relationship with His Bride. The Keswick movement of those days played a major role in drawing believers into greater reliance on breakthrough prayer.

Revival commenced in 1904 with the great Welsh revival (1904–1906) spreading quickly to other nations, notably the Far East of India, Korea, and China as well as Indonesia, Japan, South America, and Africa, where revival fires burned.[8] "Wales was ablaze for God" with 20,000 converts recorded in the first five weeks of the revival and 100,000 in the first six months. Churches were filled night after night with meetings commonly extending all night. The powerful, manifest presence of God swept through villages and towns, to the point that theaters, taverns, and dance halls closed for lack of business, while jails and courts were deserted for lack of crime. Literally everywhere in the country people were talking about God as the fear of God (awe, reverence) was felt deeply.[9]

The decade of revival, sparked through the Welsh revival, touched all nations, crossing all major denominations—Anglican, Baptist, Brethren, Congregational, Lutheran, Methodist, Presbyterian—and was marked by hunger and thirst for God, extended worship in God's presence, conviction of sin and the need for God's mercy. This move of the Spirit brought "God consciousness" among the people.[10] Jesus was visiting His people with His powerful presence. Emphasis was placed on removing everything doubtful from a person's life and a prompt obedience to the Holy Spirit in all things. Church membership soared around the world during this decade as unbelievers, even the most hardened, sought salvation through Jesus. Many sensed, at the time, God's purpose for these revivals was to empower His people to fulfill the Great Commission before Christ's return. The unprecedented growth of the Pentecostal and Charismatic movements that spread around the world during the 1900s is dynamic evidence of this possibility.

The Welsh revival was quickly followed by the Azusa Street revival in Los Angeles (1906–1908), called the catalyst of the Pentecostal outpourings of the Holy Spirit, impacting every continent. Azusa Street included the same elements of the Welsh revival, yet added other characteristics including dramatic healings and speaking in tongues. The same powerful presence of God manifested in the meetings—sometimes so thick it was like a cloud in the room, charging the atmosphere with awe and fear of God.[11] But the greatest characteristic was fervent love for God kindled in the hearts of all involved, seeking Jesus above all else. Many missionaries were scattered from Azusa Street to many nations and within a few years the revival had spread to fifty nations. Joining the Welsh revival as the first truly global revival movements ever.

Following this initial revival decade, the century progressed with a growing restoration of the ministry of the Holy Spirit and His gifts to the global Church. This was the core rediscovery of this era of revival. In the 1700s it was the recovery of the new birth experience, in the 1800s growing in the deeper life of sanctification and in the 1900s the ministry of the third Person of the Trinity as the Bible reveals Him, propelling the global Church forward in the Great Commission. The 1900s gradually saw the Spirit's activity brought into the mainstream churches, becoming normalized and generally accepted over time. An estimated 520 million people were impacted through the Pentecostal and Charismatic movements worldwide, particularly across Africa and Latin America, changing the expression and understanding of Christianity globally in one century.[12] Some of the revival movements of the second half of the 1900s included the Healing Revival (1947–1958), the Charismatic Renewal (1958–1985)—also known as the "Third Wave of the Holy Spirit," the Jesus Movement (1967–1975), and the "Toronto Blessing" (1994–2000).

Each successive revival in the second half of the 1900s helped integrate the ministry, gifts, and manifestations of the Holy Spirit into the overall body of Christ in a way never experienced before. For example, a seminary course was offered from 1982–1985 at the interdenominational Fuller Theological Seminary called "Signs, Wonders and Church Growth" under the leadership of Peter Wagner and John Wimber (founder of the Vineyard Church Movement). It was an "experiential" course—the first half of each class session given to lecture and the second praying for one another for healing. It was by far the largest course registration at the seminary in those years, generating great interest and controversy.[13] Healings and miracles took place within the course itself as practitioners learned to operate in the Holy Spirit's power. Such a course, at a major, globally renowned Seminary, had never happened before.

The "century of the Spirit" has been a huge part of God preparing the global Church today to be scattered to the unreached, obeying His commission. Though the baptism of the Spirit had been available since Pentecost, this experience throughout history was largely neglected. There was a corporate rebaptism that transpired during the 20th century and a recommissioning of His global Church to embrace her core identity and take the gospel of the Kingdom to all ethnic peoples. As a result, we see a corresponding massive progression in the mission and mobilization movement during the 1900s that is continuing now, growing in its intensity in the AD 2000s.

MISSION & MOBILIZATION ERA 4: CAMERON TOWNSEND AND THE UNREACHED PEOPLES (1934–PRESENT)

The third era of Protestant mission expansion started in 1934 through Cameron Townsend and Wycliffe Bible Translators. Several other key missiologists were also involved in this crucial era. If the second era opened up the previously unconsidered concept of the interior, inland peoples—the third era went even farther. The first two eras focused on geographical areas—reaching coastal peoples and then inland peoples—while the third era shifted to identifying "people groups." Particularly looking for "hidden peoples," mostly tribal peoples often not having a Bible or portions thereof in their own mother tongue. Townsend founded Wycliffe Bible Translators [14]to focus on these peoples, providing them with the translated Bible in their own language.[15]

The concept of identifying "people groups" was not limited to tribal peoples alone. But was expanded to consider the cultural and sociological categories of particular groups sharing culture, language, leadership structure, customs and worldview. No longer looking at geo-political countries alone but recognizing that countries are made up of a vast tapestry of individual "people groups" who are different from one another. If Jesus gave the Great Commission to reach all individual "ethnic people groups" then mission strategy had to change from its previous geographical focal points. Donald McGavran, the first Dean of the School of World Mission (1966) at Fuller Theological Seminary in Pasadena, California, identified differences of caste and economic status as major barriers to the spread of the gospel. His influence helped missionaries and structures begin to identify and prioritize people groups for mission focus.[16]

Ralph Winter, founder of the US Center for World Mission (now Frontier Ventures), also in Pasadena, California, who worked alongside McGavran, helped to clarify and publicize the "people group" concept at the 1974 Congress of World Evangelization in Lausanne, Switzerland. The title of his paper was carefully chosen: "The Highest Priority: Cross-Cultural Evangelism." Donald McGavran called Winter's presentation a watershed moment in global mission history.[17] It was through this presentation that Winter shifted global mission strategy from a focus on political boundaries to a focus on distinct people groups. Winter argued that instead of targeting countries, message bearer teams needed to target the thousands of individual people groups worldwide, over half of which have not been reached with the gospel message.[18]

A recognition was made that it was necessary to do church planting and evangelism along the line of a similar ethnic people group. Doing so produced greater fruit and potential people movements to Christ, when these people-defining factors were brought to the forefront.[19] Through this process of identifying ethnic peoples, the term "unreached peoples" was introduced. Over time this term has come to be defined in the following way: "An unreached or least-reached people is a people group among which there is no indigenous community of believing Christians with adequate numbers and resources to evangelize this people group without outside assistance. They generally have an evangelical population of less than two percent. They need outside help to grow their indigenous Christian community."[20] Such "unreached peoples" could even be in largely Christianized countries, but due to particular cultural identities have remained isolated from the gospel.

The student mobilization movement corresponding with this third era of mission expansion was started in 1936 through the influence of Robert C. McQuilkin, then president of Columbia Bible College in South Carolina. A group of 53 students from a variety of Christian colleges possessing mission vision met with McQuilkin, forming a committee to consider starting a new mission thrust among college students that would "dedicate itself to the awakening of missionary interest among students." This led to the founding of the Student Foreign Missions Fellowship (SFMF) which would dynamically influence thousands of college students in America.

In the early 1940s the InterVarsity Christian Fellowship (IVCF) movement was gaining momentum on campuses in the US and Canada. At this time IVCF did not have a global mission emphasis. In 1946 leaders from SFMF and IVCF met to discuss a merger of their organizations, with the SFMF piece being the fuel for global mission.[21] It was the SFMF influence that led to the formation of a student missionary conference in 1946 that was the first of what would become the influential triennial Urbana Student Mission Conventions still taking place today. Urbana has helped keep global, cross-cultural mission on the front burner, focused on within the campus ministries of the US and Canada.

Mission mobilization, as a focused entity of the overall mission movement, took a great leap forward during this era as mobilization tools were developed and distributed more widely than ever before. The "Perspectives on the World Christian Movement" course, developed by Ralph Winter was started in 1974. This is a mission education tool helping believers understand the foundations of global mission and mission strategy. Over 130,000 people and counting worldwide have taken the course.[22]

The AD2000 and Beyond Movement with Luis Bush in the 1980s and '90s fueled the imagination of the global Church with the possibility of "a church for every people and the gospel to every person." It was a powerful worldwide influencer of global mission vision, particularly among majority world, non-Western churches. This movement helped spark many non-Western churches and ministries to first consider how God was calling them to engage directly in global, cross-cultural mission to unreached peoples. The Kairos course was launched in 1994 providing education and understanding in cross-cultural mission and is serving a growing number of people annually.[23] These and other tools and initiatives paved the way for the mission mobilization movement God is trumpeting around the world today.

★★★

As we have seen in these historic chapters, God is certainly a progressive God, unfolding His plans and purposes in the earth in stages, phases, and seasons, not all at once. We see from this analysis that we are on the verge of extraordinary breakthroughs in cross-cultural mission and mission mobilization. The Lord has been restoring core aspects of faith, beckoning us onward into the fullness of His redemptive purposes. We have progressed into potentially a final era—characterized by truly global mission and mobilization movements, empowered by transformational revival spreading around the world.

13

Global Systems as Great Commission Platforms

It is important to note how growing secular trends of the day, world systems of influence, contribute to shaping the mission, mobilization, and revival thrusts of history. This understanding helps us today to effectively "launch out into the deep and let down your nets for a catch" (Luke 5:4). It also helps us effectively call the global Church to her core identity. Both Colonialism and Industrialization had far-reaching effects on the expansion of the gospel during the "Great Century of Missions" (the 19th century), opening doors among unreached peoples otherwise closed. The Industrial Revolution brought new dominance to Europe which was accompanied by a desire to exert that dominance globally. Colonialism and imperialism would soon become the common governmental policies of nations, exploiting other nations through dominance for their own financial and territorial gain.[1]

THE GLOBAL SYSTEM OF COLONIALISM

Though in no way endorsing the morality of these systems, the mission societies of the day sent laborers to the ends of the world, in the well-paved footsteps of the commercial and colonization platforms. As Patrick Johnstone concedes,

> Today we abhor the competing nationalisms, arrogance and greed that drove the colonialism of the supposed civilized "Christian" nations of Europe. We see the negatives—the subjugation, enslavement and even genocide of peoples, the trading monopolies that transferred the world's wealth to the West, the consumerism, cultural imperialism, etc. However, there were distinct positives, too. The greatest benefits were religious freedom and the chance to proclaim the gospel. Colonialism allowed Western missionaries to sow many seeds in many nations.[2]

The infamous East India Company, for example, made it possible for William Carey and his band of laborers, to take up residence in India (though the East India Company despised the work of the missionaries). This historic tie between Colonialism and mission history has left a bad taste among many non-Western peoples, lingering to this day.

Most missionaries had no desire to exploit people as their colonizing governments or industrialized companies did. Instead, they sought to enhance social progress through the power of the gospel, the democratic approach to government, schools, hospitals, universities, and political foundations.[3] They used the open door into these countries as avenues to preach the gospel, reaching people for Christ. Though all too often, they did so with the introduction of Western culture, leading at times to the destruction of indigenous traditions.

Throughout mission history, the spread of the gospel has often expanded through particular eras of world systems. In no way does this excuse the horrible exploits done by governments through the policies of Colonialism or entrepreneurs of the Industrial Revolution, nor mistakes made by former generations of missionaries. Yet, it reveals the fallen global system factors contributing to the spread of the gospel in global mission. The point is that global systems of various generations have often been tracks across the nations upon which the gospel can and has progressed.

The Pax Romana

Paul utilized one of these global systems of the Roman Empire as a track in the first century. The gospel went forth in power in the first century across the Empire, spreading far and wide in a relatively short period of time. The Roman Empire and its policies, made it much easier for the early Church to multiply as it did. There were world system forces of the day which God used to contribute to the spread of the gospel across the Roman Empire.

The most prominent was the *Pax Romana,* or "Roman Peace," put in place in 27 BC by Roman Caesar Augustus, lasting until roughly AD 180.[4] The Pax Romana produced unprecedented peace and economic prosperity across the Empire, the government providing Roman citizens with security, law, order, engineering, and unhindered travel across the Empire. To maintain their widespread Empire, the Romans built an extensive system of high-quality roads, many still existing today. These elements contributed to the New Testament church expanding all over the Roman Empire, "running swiftly and being glorified" (2 Thessalonians 3:1). Entrusted with the Great Commission, it is necessary that local ministries discern the wide variety of world systems at play and how God may choose to utilize these for the spread of the gospel.

In the Middle Ages, there was also a system in place, providing tracks for the small thrust of global mission in that period. It was monasticism. Though a religious system, as we've seen, the Church of the Middle Ages was inextricably linked with the state. This provided protections, to some degree, to the few missionaries who scattered out in that day. Without the monastery system in place, under the protections of the Roman Catholic Church, it is almost impossible to imagine anyone having the ability to move about in that era with the gospel.

The Printing Press

The monumental invention of the printing press by Johannes Gutenberg in 1440 was an incalculable secular development through which the Reformation of the 1500s blazed forward. The explosion of the Reformation can be directly linked to the ease of widespread printing and distribution of writings across Europe. For the first time in history people could produce spiritually revolutionary writings and get them into the hands of thousands of common people. Before the printing press this was impossible. The printing press was a track the Reformation ran on. The circulation of information and ideas transcended borders, capturing the masses during the Reformation, threatening the power of political and religious authorities. That invention is seen by many as a key turning point in the history of the world, no less Church history.

Over the last 300 years tracks which revival, mission and mobilization have run on included continuously progressing technology. From the printing press and books, to the advent of newspapers, radios, televisions and today the internet and streaming video, from anywhere to anywhere. All these enabled mission and mobilization to be done differently, spreading the message farther, faster, quicker and in a more connected way. Another track is transportation progressing from horseback and carriages until 1830 when the railroad was introduced. That gave way to the advent of the automobile in the late 1800s and a progression from ships to the airplane in the early 1900s. Though not global systems necessarily, each of these technological advancements made the world a little smaller, empowering the revival, mission, and mobilization movements to more effectively spread, having greater impact.

THE GLOBAL SYSTEM OF GLOBALIZATION

That leads us to the present. Is there a secular world system in place now that could contribute to the spread of the gospel among all ethnic peoples much quicker than before? The answer is a resounding YES! That world system is globalization.

Globalization sprung onto the global scene following the breakdown of the Cold War global system and communism falling apart in 1989. According to global analyst Thomas Friedman, "technology accelerations and globalization accelerations mean we are now living through one of the greatest inflection points in history," perhaps unequaled since Johannes Gutenberg launched the printing revolution in Europe in the 1400s.[5] "Globalization is not a trend or a fad but the international world system that replaced the Cold War system. Having its own rules, logic, pressures, and incentives, it affects everyone's country, company and community, either directly or indirectly."[6]

A simple definition of globalization is the interweaving of markets, technology, information systems and telecommunications systems in a way that is shrinking the world, "enabling each of us to reach around the world farther, faster, deeper, and cheaper than ever before, and enabling the world to reach into each of us farther, faster, deeper, cheaper than ever before."[7] Globalization connects the whole world like never before, from businesses to banking to supply chains. No one is an island unto themselves anymore, reliant on others across the world. Smartphones have dramatically changed our lives within a 15-year period, the first iPhone being introduced in 2007.[8] Zoom and Skype, free global video calls, have transformed our capacity to be connected in ways only dreamt of just 10 years ago. Instant messaging, streaming video, the cloud—all are a byproduct of mind-boggling accelerations in technology that have utterly transformed how human beings do life and have been centered around warp speed development of the internet. Now you don't have to go to physical meetings, able to meet online at no significant cost. Everyone is able to do this because of the tremendous internet technology advancements of the last few decades.

Friedman continues, "Globalization means we increasingly know how each other lives—able to read about, watch a YouTube video, FaceTime across oceans, peering into one another's worlds. When we all increasingly know how each other lives, we start to want what others have. Whether that's a certain lifestyle, effective business, political freedoms, better education, clean water, safety and protection or much more. When we can't get the things we see others have, we stand up for ourselves."[9] The Arab Spring (2010) would not have happened apart from globalization, nor would the international pressure on the Myanmar generals to release Aung San Suu Kyi in 2010 have had impact. Through globalization and accelerated technology every country and culture are able to view the lifestyles of people around the world while also becoming aware of every news story affecting governments around the world. Globalization has and is changing everything. It is more difficult than ever for a government or religion to keep its people from seeing and experiencing what those outside live like. Globalization is putting shackles on everyone in leadership around the world today. You cannot run and you cannot hide.

From the end of WWII to 1989, the dominating world system revolved around the Cold War, which was based on one overarching feature—division. All threats and opportunities as a country or company tended to flow from who you were divided from. That system was symbolized by the Berlin Wall. Like the Cold War global system, globalization as a global system is also characterized by one overarching feature—integration. Instead of being divided from the world as most people were pre-1989 (end of Cold War), the world was moving toward exactly the opposite—significant integration with one another in finance, economy, business, education, media, entertainment, and even ministry. In globalization, threats and opportunities flow from who you are connected to, symbolized by the Internet. Since the fall of the Berlin Wall and Communism in 1989, the end of the Cold War, we've gone from a world of division and walls to a world of internet without walls. During the Cold War, two nations were in charge: the United States and the Soviet Union. In globalization, we reach for the Internet, a symbol to which we are all increasingly connected. The central logic of globalization mirrors the logic of the internet. We are all increasingly connected, but nobody's in charge.[10]

Eighty percent of globalization is driven by technology. "The technology exists to overcome walls, tying people together, getting access to the best technology and cheapest wages of Taiwan, Mexico, or Mississippi."[11] Globalization is driven by technology, what technology empowers you to do. Because technology is advancing at an exponentially fast pace, the globalized world is only to become more so, not less. When you wire the world into networks and remove the walls, we can all increasingly work on the world stage directly, unmediated by a state or any other hindering entity. What globalization does by wiring the world into networks and removing the walls is super empower individual people, both for good and for evil.[12]

What does all this have to do with mobilization? Globalization has paved the way for mobilization in unprecedented ways, making it possible for multitudes of small mobilization efforts and initiatives to spring up. One major impact of globalization is that it has decentralized everything. No longer is one person, leader, organization, or movement in charge. No longer are there only large, mega organizations and denominations in the world. In the last thirty years, mission has become tremendously decentralized. We have seen a shift, potentially influenced by the accelerations of technology and globalization, from large centralized mission organizations to a much flatter decentralized model of organization, church, and networking. Any church, independent ministry, mission structure, or mobilization effort can more easily spring into existence and multiply as a result of the globalization system. This seems to be a major factor in the explosion of independent ministries globally. Anybody can start a ministry, just like anybody can start a business, publish a book, make a movie, etc. This can pose a challenge as some independent ministries should likely not be in existence due to lack of accountability, questionable doctrine, practice, and more. Yet, it can also serve in seeing multitudes of empowered, decentralized groups contribute to the fulfillment of the Great Commission like never before. Everyone now is truly enabled in ministry, if they want to be.

Globalization and the speed at which digital technology is developing have empowered multitudes of digital platforms and social media. These are being used now for mission and mobilization, yet will go to a whole new level through yet future insights and ideas of how to effectively reach ethnic peoples through these platforms. Globalization is empowering any mobilizer anywhere in the world to have the tools needed in an instant to mobilize churches and ministries in their area. Globalization has empowered training as now some training can be done effectively online. As a reminder, we are not excusing immoral uses of this global system (or seeking a debate as to the goodness or ills of globalization) only highlighting its existence, that it will only increase and the importance of utilizing it for the glory of Jesus and the extension of His Kingdom. Deep thought and careful action need to be extended, while seeing all the benefits as well. As all the global systems before it provided tracks for the gospel to run on, so does globalization.

***

The world system enabling the gospel to run swiftly and be glorified globally is in place, similar to the Pax Romana for the early Church. The whole body of Christ engaging with the whole world is possible under the globalization system, where it was not during the Cold War system, with all its divisions. It is the argument of some that globalization has empowered the global Church in a way never known before in history. I believe the increasing technology and globalization system are a part of the Lord's plan to orchestrate circumstances in the earth that are conducive to reaching all subgroups of every unreached people group with the power and love of Christ.

14

Where Are We Now: A New Era

We've covered a lot of ground in these historical chapters. We've seen the sweep of the 4,000-year history from Abraham to AD 2000 and the unmistakable trend of the 500-year eras where a new catalytic event took place defining each era, progressing it into the next. At the same time, we saw the broad strokes of progressive global mission vision over the last 2,000 years. The year AD 2000 brought us to the end of a 500-year era since the Protestant Reformation of AD 1500. We spent extra time considering this last 500-year era because of its significant emphasis on revival and restoration movements resulting in growing global mission and mobilization concern and strategic concepts. We considered four revival eras and four mission and mobilization eras within the last 500 years. We are now entering another catalytic mission and mobilization era that will define the way forward and that you and I are a part of.

ADDING TO WINTER'S THIRD ERA

Now that the previous 500-year era, which included an almost unbroken century-by-century progression of revivals and subsequent mission and mobilization expansion, is complete, what is the Spirit saying today? Where do we go from here? It has been debated whether a "fourth mission era" can be identified and added to Ralph Winter's three eras of Protestant mission history. To consider this, it is important to differentiate what Winter's eras focused on and what they didn't. Winter's eras highlighted target strategy used in each progressive era to reach peoples—coastal peoples, interior peoples, and finally a cultural, linguistic breakdown of ethnic peoples. There is no better strategic understanding than the concept of "ethnic people groups," distinguishing those who are reached (though unsaved) as opposed to unreached, helping the global Church target those who have not rejected the gospel, but have little access or opportunity to hear it. I dare not advocate moving on from this core missiological and biblical understanding of how to reach peoples for Christ.

However, in addition to the core "unreached peoples" designation of Winter's third era, it can be helpful to target megacities. The world's unreached megacities have often been overlooked in mission as they are so big and a melting pot of ethnic peoples and cultures. Some of the largest include Tokyo, Japan (38 million), Delhi, India (31 million), Shanghai, China (28 million), Mumbai, India (23 million), Beijing, China (21 million), Dhaka, Bangladesh (21 million), and Karachi, Pakistan (17 million).[1] Fulfilling the Great Commission means faithfully reaching every subgroup of every ethnic people group within a particular area of these cities.

This emphasis has been growing in global mission circles over the last 40 years and will continue to do so. As urbanization increases and the cities of the world swell with people looking for jobs, it is necessary for local ministries to have a focused strategy scattering multitudes of message bearer teams into targeted city blocks, neighborhoods, apartment blocks, and streets with the gospel. This scattering must be systematic, empowering every church, denomination, or organization to take their piece of the city, thus multiplying church planting movements toward igniting people movements to Christ.

A New Era of "Who" Is Scattering

This leads to another characteristic of the present "mission mobilization" era—the "who" of the mission sending movement. Winter's three eras focus on the target people, overlooking "who" it was that was doing the sending.

178

The "who" is important to distinguish because this has been shifting over the last 50 years. In the first mission era, William Carey sailed for India from Great Britain in 1792. The United States of America came into being in 1776, sending its first missionaries in 1812 (Adoniram Judson). Great Britain, the USA, and Canada were the primary mission senders for the next 150 years, including Winter's second era with Hudson Taylor. With the third era (1934) targeting the hidden, unreached peoples, particularly later in the era (last fifty years), a massive new trend of "who" is doing the sending has emerged.

We could also say that these three eras emphasized the "going" or "sending" aspects. Whereas the premise of this book is that God is presently "changing the face of missions," empowering the global Church to emphasize the Great Commission message, internalizing it through the multiplication of Mission Mobilization Movements across national churches. This is the needed precursor to the sending and going aspects. This seems to imply the shifting toward a new era.

Over the last 50 to 60 years, emerging sending movements have come about from many non-Western African, Asian, and Latin American national churches. As Jesus told Peter in Luke 5:4 and that we have seen as a core theme in this book, "launch out into the deep and let down your net for a catch." The net of national churches raising up laborers is widening, and for the first time in recorded history, we have a truly global body of Christ able to fulfill their assigned roles in the Great Commission. Previously, it was never realistic to speak of actually fulfilling the Great Commission, though each generation did. The early days of the modern mission movement (1792–1865) reached the coastlands, Taylor and the student volunteers in the second era pushed inland, yet all that was done through the Western Church, primarily from Great Britain, Canada, and the USA.

Now, in the latter part of the era of reaching every subgroup of unreached peoples, the work is in the hands of a truly global Church and mobilization thrust for the first time. If the global Church can be awakened to her core identity, through multiplying Mission Mobilization Movements, the fulfillment of the Great Commission is realistic in our generation, culminating in Jesus' redemptive purpose in this age. This scattering Church will not be content sending a few, it becoming normal for every local body scattering 20 percent of members in message bearer teams to near and distant culture peoples. The whole church engaged in her corporate responsibility in scattering the gospel of the Kingdom among all subgroups of all ethnic peoples with power. This has never happened before in church and mission history. Jesus will have a truly global Church engaged in His Great Commission.

A New Era—A Truly Global Mobilization Movement

For this reason, some mission mobilization leaders suggest we have moved into another mission era[2]—not in geographical or cultural people focus (as Winters' eras brilliantly highlight), but in the Great Commission emphasized across the whole global Church. I completely agree with them. Steve Shadrach puts it this way stating, "If the third Era is about taking the gospel to all ethne, then the fourth era is about all the reached ethne remaining faithful to press on to finish the job. It could be that God is handing us a new template He wants us to operate from…in order to mobilize national believers to reach the unreached."[3] Shadrach then defines the goal of this potential fourth era: "A global mission mobilization movement in which the whole church rises up to powerfully advance Jesus' Great Commission to the ends of the earth. Each of us has a strategic part to play."[4]

This takes place through a broader, comprehensive implementation of mission mobilization. We are in a transition period in how global mission is understood and acted upon through Jesus' global Church. For the first time in history, we have a truly global Church, empowered by the doctrinal and experiential restorations of the last 500 years. God has positioned His global people today for massive spiritual breakthrough among all nations. It is this truth the enemy fears most and has sought to keep from happening. We are truly moving toward redemptive fullness at the end of the age.

Some may argue that the numbers of new traditional missionaries and the mission emphasis in national churches of traditional mission-sending nations are going down. Yet the surge of growing mission awareness and understanding across traditionally mission-receiving nations is increasing. This is only going to continue through effective mobilization among them in the coming decades. This will also be affected as traditional models of mission-sending are tempered, transformed into biblical, Spirit-led means of scattering indigenous workers. Whereas most don't feel they can sustain sending the traditional way, they get excited when shown how to do so in ways even the poorest churches in the world can engage with.

I believe this eye-opening understanding will progress to cultivating Mission Mobilization Movements across the spectrum of church denominations and networks within every nation. Empowering churches to experience firsthand the restoration of the core identity of the global Church as "God's missionary people," prioritizing the Great Commission within their local fellowships, engaging every believer in their assigned roles. These results can take place through a reenergized, redefined understanding of mission mobilization.

TOWARD TRANSFORMATION REVIVAL—THE RE-VIVAL ERA OF THE 21ST CENTURY

What about the revival eras? Does God have a subsequent plan to the "century of the Holy Spirit" during the 1900s? Is there a simultaneous revival to empower the burgeoning global mission and mobilization movements? As the Church was armed during the 1900s with the rediscovery of the ministry and gifts of the Spirit, global mission progressed with new vigor. As the whole, global Church is rediscovering her core DNA as existing for Jesus' Great Commission, she will go forth in the power of the Holy Spirit restored during the 1900s revival era—with spiritual authority, anointed proclamation of the Word, and demonstration of the power of God, along with increased signs, wonders, healing, and deliverance.

As the world gets spiritually darker, the light of Christ among His people gets incrementally brighter (Isaiah 60:1–2). This clash of light and darkness creates the perfect storm of spiritual conflict. Disciples and local ministries experience victory through tribulation, not escaping it, used by God to burn away the chaff from the global Church (those following Jesus for themselves, not for Jesus' glory). Some struggle with God allowing believers to go through troubles. Yet this is the way of the Kingdom, the Spirit's mechanism for strengthening the spiritual muscles of His people, how Jesus produces a global Bride, near the end of the age, ushering in the greatest global harvest the earth has ever known. Abandoned, wholehearted devotion to Jesus will be the norm in the final decades before the Lord returns, producing increased Great Commission vision and activation. This "revival" among His people is beginning to happen.

Transformation through message bearer teams impacting the spiritual, societal, ecological, relational, and physical realms with the power of God will be widely seen. God moves into communities, taking up residence, resulting in massive transformation within that place, among those people. Revival that impacts all areas, producing transformation, not only of individuals, but the whole integrated realm. Transforming revival is a corporate encounter with a supernatural God that is tangible, measurable, and observable by all in the visitation location. God's presence brings accompanying fruit that characterizes His nature and His Kingdom, with transformational changes at every level—individuals, families, church, society and land.[5] It refers to the entire process of change a community undergoes as a result of God's manifest presence and subsequent spiritual awakenings. Transforming revival always impacts both the Church and society.

All this requires openness to change the Holy Spirit is orchestrating in the global Church right now. Moving from the traditional model of a few professional "missionaries" to the biblical, Spirit-led model of multitudes of spiritually qualified, lay leaders and lay people scattered in teams to near and far culture subgroups of ethnic peoples. Living among them, taking jobs with them, engaging in church planting movements, resulting in transformation and harvest ignited through people movements to Christ. These obedient millions, empowered by the Lord Himself to do the "greater works" (John 14:12), used by God as vessels of "transformation revival" among unreached peoples.

***

We are living in a time of unprecedented activity of God across the earth in the midst of growing difficulties, chaos, betrayal, and persecutions. Let's continue to the final part of our book, considering the four strategic focal points of the Holy Spirit toward the fulfillment of the Great Commission. Answering the crucial question, what do we mobilize the Church to do?

Part 4

Mobilized to Do What?
The Holy Spirit's Four-Point
Strategy

15

Multiplying Mission Mobilization Movements

We now proceed to part 4. So far, we've looked in detail at what mission mobilization is along with understanding more about the role of mission mobilizers in part 1. In part 2 we rooted ourselves in the biblical background of the Great Commission, its fulfillment, and the primary vehicle in that fulfillment—the global Church and individual local ministries. We've seen that mission mobilization is calling the global Church into agreement with God's redemptive strategy to accomplish His plans and purposes. In part 3 we considered the history of mission, revival and mobilization and what lessons we can glean and apply today.

Yet what exactly do we mobilize the global Church to do? In a global mission landscape full of often random activities and divergent focal points, it is necessary to bring biblical and missiological emphasis. Moving beyond good ideas and hit and miss activities, embracing His direction in what the global Church is mobilized to do in mission.

We start with some questions. Are there specific biblical, Spirit-led means of advancing the Kingdom? Are there particular strategies God is seeking to employ to produce the great harvest? Does the Spirit have a progressive plan or is God somehow piecing together all the random efforts?

The answer is yes, God has particular strategies, set forth in the New Testament and confirmed by the Spirit throughout history. The next four chapters represent big-picture, Spirit-led strategies the global Church mobilizes and equips disciples and local ministries to engage within the Great Commission. Each of the four builds on one another, unfolding progressively. We cannot proceed to points two, three, and four without seeing the foundation of point one firmly in place, which is why mission mobilization needs emphasis across the global Church right now. Point two progresses to point three and so on. We best understand God's big picture intent when considering the widespread multiplication of these strategies across every people group globally, not in pockets here or there.

Many years ago, mission practitioner Roland Allen affirmed, "Far from being an indifferent or secondary matter, the ministry strategy used in cross-cultural work is of the utmost importance."[1] Not from the perspective of implementing a "formula," guaranteeing fruitful results, but embracing biblical principles the Holy Spirit emphasizes and the Word of God advocates. Strategy of itself does not produce fruit, yet strategic models aligning with principles of the Kingdom produce great fruit. Many don't like the concept of methods as it is thought these somehow limit the Spirit. In fact, quite the opposite. The Spirit used means and strategies (not rigid formulas) throughout the New Testament and mission history, progressing the Church in global mission. We need a return to biblical models of how and why the New Testament Church proved so successful in mission in the first century.

Let's see a quick overview of the four-point progressive strategy of the Holy Spirit and then jump right into strategic point one. These concepts are steeped in scriptural foundation as we will see as we consider each one.

First, it is the will of God to multiply millions of individual local ministries across denominations, church networks and organizations emphasizing the Great Commission, putting it at the center of their local fellowships, mobilizing and equipping every disciple in their roles.

Second, the Holy Spirit wants to scatter at least 20 percent of these disciples from every local ministry (mostly lay leaders and lay people) to near and distant culture unreached peoples, geographically near and far to that local ministry.

Third, what is it this exponentially large number of Jesus' laborers are doing among unreached peoples? Multiplying thousands of reproducing church planting movements (CPMs) within neighborhoods, villages, towns, apartment buildings, in areas the Spirit guides them. They take the Church to the people, not expecting the people to come to them.

Fourth, through the witness of these exponentially increased simple, reproducing churches planted, "people movements to Christ" are ignited across the many webs of relationships—family, neighborhood, work colleagues, universities—culminating in every subculture of every unreached people group globally hearing the word of Jesus, millions coming to saving faith and discipled.

STAGES OF MISSION MOBILIZATION MOVEMENTS

It is important to analyze the global Church's progression in mobilization emphasis in history. We looked in detail at the overall historical development of mission and mobilization in part 3 of this book.

Mobilization from the Outside

Mission mobilization over the last fifty to sixty years has consisted primarily in effective mission education courses and mission conferences being offered to those already having some kind of interest in global mission. We call this "mobilization from the outside." This is a first stage in developing a widespread or localized Mission Mobilization Movement. These tools are a significant part of any mobilization effort. A small percentage of participants becoming engaged in a meaningful way in global mission as a result. Research reveals, however, a large majority involved in mission education courses, conferences or experiencing a traveling group promoting mission, never get involved in their assigned roles in the Great Commission.[2]

An observable problem arises in these situations. A believer has participated and been inspired in some way about global mission. They want to continue to grow. But how and where? Sometimes there are further steps through "mobilization from the outside." At some point, however, that person returns to their own local ministry where the leadership isn't necessarily engaged with these same interests. No one from their local ministry experienced what they did. The enthusiasm they had is often squelched within the local ministry because others don't yet share the mission vision. Their vision for the nations is dulled because there was no ongoing mission fuel at the local ministry level. They had to go outside the local ministry to be envisioned for mission.

How much better for these and other mission mobilization tools to be experienced within the life of local fellowships instead of needing to go outside the local ministry. Of course, there is nothing inherently wrong with an outside mission education course or conference. These have a tremendous place in the overall mission mobilization process. The point is making sure the primary context for mission mobilization is within the local ministry itself, where the group is together growing in being educated, inspired, and activated. This foundation is then supplemented, developed further, through mission conferences and education/ envisioning courses.

Mobilization from the Inside

I suggest there are two further stages of Mission Mobilization Movements. The second is, "mobilization from the inside." This is when a growing mission emphasis takes root within an existing local ministry. Where that ministry is developing wholehearted disciples understanding their redemption as including partnering with Jesus toward the fulfillment of the Great Commission. The ministry is geared toward every disciple grasping the Great Commission, internalizing it. They may offer mission education courses and other tools, but in the context of the local ministry, not going outside to gain mission clarity. These ministries are aligning with the core identity of the Church considered in chapters eight and nine. I am confident the Spirit is seeking local ministries and overarching ministry structures to progress from reliance on "mobilization from the outside" to prioritizing "mobilization from the inside," while utilizing outside tools as supplements.

Campus ministries during the Student Volunteer Movement (SVM) of the late 1800s and early 1900s were of this sort. They had large student mission conferences happening every three years. Yet the individual campus fellowships did not wait for that next exciting conference to engage their fellow students with Jesus' heart for the nations. Regular activities within the life of their fellowships included Bible studies looking at the theme of global redemption in the Bible. Prayer groups seeking God for the raising up of laborers and for the unreached themselves were also a mainstay. Information distribution and awareness of what was happening in global mission, including mission strategy, were the norm. This is a reason that movement saw such large numbers of message bearers scattered out. They engaged in "mobilization from the inside," not relying only on "mobilization from the outside."

Mobilization Fruitfulness

This leads to the third stage of Mission Mobilization Movements, the "mobilization fruitfulness" stage. As individual local ministries and church network/ denominational structures multiply Mission Mobilization Movements, the numbers of believers identifying and engaging in their assigned roles in global mission exponentially grows. That means growing waves of intercession for the nations, giving to the unreached, mobilizing others to become involved, advocating for specific niche Great Commission focal points, and reaching out to unreached peoples in the home community. And finally, yes, increased responding to the Spirit's call to become message bearers, both among near and distant culture peoples geographically. We want to progress, as the global Church, from individual local ministries giving lip service to global mission, to those ministries set on fire with wholehearted devotion to Jesus which inevitably overflows into passion for His global heartbeat. This process requires "mobilization from the inside."

WHAT ARE MISSION MOBILIZATION MOVEMENTS?

Having established "mobilization from the inside" appears most strategic, we now consider what this practically looks like. Particularly, as we considered in chapter one that God seems to be preparing the environment for His global Church to "launch out into the deep and let down your nets" (Luke 5:4).

There is generally a low standard of responsibility in local ministries to mobilize and equip believers. When looking around the world, grappling with the large number of unreached people groups remaining in the world (over 5,000) and relatively small number of professional "missionaries" serving around the world (430,000 full-time workers),[3] we must conclude our concept of mission mobilization has been too thin, needing change, giving way to a comprehensive viewpoint. It is time for a shift, a new paradigm in our local ministry settings.

Over the last decade, I have been asking the Lord a question, searching Scripture and church/ mission history for answers. Just as we may be familiar in mission strategy with "saturation church planting,"[4] is there a corresponding concept of "saturation mission mobilization"? I have come to believe there is. I am convinced part of the answer is working toward the multiplication of Mission Mobilization Movements (MMMs) (see glossary) across every level of the body of Christ in every nation. Every disciple, every local ministry, denomination/ church network, national evangelical alliance and mission association has a role and responsibility in fulfilling the Great Commission. Jesus' heart longs for a mobilization movement prioritizing the Great Commission within the life of every local ministry as intended. This concept is not mere theory but a recognition of evident facts.

My friend Tshepang Basupi, a Botswanan mobilizer now living in South Africa, tells his story.

In 2016, whilst busy doing mobilization in Botswana we were not getting the needed results. A few people who were mobilized were eventually unable to go because their churches were unwilling and unable to send them. The main issue we later discovered was the lack of vision and understanding of the Church's role in God's global mission. The Church in Africa is growing and has such a huge potential to be a major player in global missions. But why is it that only a handful of Africans are taking the gospel to the unreached. According to Operation World, there are over 182 million evangelicals in Africa today.[5] However, less than 50,000 message bearers have been sent from Africa, which is even less than 0.01 percent of the evangelicals in Africa. In August 2016 I joined 1400+ other young leaders from over 140 countries for the Lausanne Younger Leaders Gathering in Jakarta, Indonesia. During the Gathering, I listened to Dr. David Lim share a bit of his journey of mobilizing tent makers. He shared about the Filipino believers being sent into China and all across the Middle East and the vision of the Filipino church to mobilize 200,000 message bearers. As he was speaking, the Lord spoke to me. "Can you trust me for one million missionaries (message bearers) from Africa?" I was stunned? One million? This was a huge challenge to my faith and all that I have ever known and imagined.[6]

How does God intend to mobilize one million African message bearers (and many more from other parts of the world)? Tshepang highlighted a significant hindrance. Local ministries lack vision and understanding of God's global mission and His intent for them to be actively involved, even if they never leave their hometown. How can this be realized? Through multiplying Mission Mobilization Movements across the body of Christ.

Mission Mobilization Movements can be defined as any entity (whether a local ministry, denominational, organizational, or church network structure or national evangelical or mission association) where the Spirit of God is emphasizing the message, vision, and strategies of the Great Commission, as a natural overflow of wholehearted, abandonment to Jesus, activating every member in assigned Great Commission roles, spreading mission mobilization in a contagious way to other local ministries.

Characteristics of "Movements"

A professor and mentor of mine at Fuller Seminary, Dr. Bobby Clinton, has studied movements for many years. Not only Christian movements, but secular movements, religious movements, historical movements, social movements—looking for common principles. His conclusion is that movements have similar characteristics, no matter their type. Clinton defines a movement as a "groundswell of people committed to a person or ideals and characterized by the following important commitments" with five common commitments made on the part of those involved: 1) commitment to personal involvement; 2) commitment to persuade others to join; 3) commitment to the beliefs and ideals of the movement; 4) commitment to participate in a non-bureaucratic, cell-group organization; 5) commitment to endure opposition and misunderstanding.[7] We can apply these five commitments as we seek to multiply Mission Mobilization Movements as well.

The World Christian movement, started in the book of Acts, had each of these five. Those exalting Jesus are part of a movement with committed roots.

It is difficult to claim to be committed believers yet withhold ourselves from the global Christian movement as a whole. The most effective Mission Mobilization Movements have been, and will be, among those who buy into these five characteristics with zeal and sacrifice. Mission mobilization movements are based on the fundamental principle that God is interested in not only mobilizing individuals but mobilizing and equipping entire local ministries. As many of the world's cultures are communal in worldview, it is necessary to mobilize them as "communities."[8]

Individual Local Ministries as Mission Mobilization Movements

I first met Mirna Santa Cruz in Asuncion, Paraguay. After sharing during a workshop for a COMIBAM conference for the Southern Cone region of South America, she excitedly told me about her student ministry called Red de Universitarios y Profesionales Cristianos and her passion to infuse Great Commission emphasis within the life of its fellowship. We began a friendship that day and many years later Mirna has seen that student ministry implement the core principles of a Mission Mobilization Movement, producing great fruit among those students and professionals. Influencing them, their core identity now reflects God's multiplying, reproducing, missionary people.

Local ministries of this sort provide teaching, discipleship and fellowship which builds up every member toward spiritual maturity, preparing them to embody their role(s) in the Great Commission. They make deliberate plans to integrate mission vision into the life of that fellowship. The ministry becomes an incubator for growth in mission awareness, understanding, education and local implementation. The ministry becomes fueled by the conviction they all are responsible before God for becoming involved, with local and global mission to the unreached in some way. Admittedly, this can sound unrealistic because we have generally given such a low priority to the Great Commission in our local ministries.

Although the Great Commission tends to be an afterthought in our local ministries, it is meant to be on the forefront of our hearts, ministry plans, and strategies. Ministries that prioritize cross-cultural mission are God's primary strategy in mobilizing and equipping His people for the Great Commission.[9]

Local ministries as Mission Mobilization Movements align with Jesus' Great Commission through committing to the following three purposes:

1. Educating every disciple with a passionate understanding of God's heart in the Great Commission
2. Inspiring every disciple with a vision of ordering their lives around the fulfillment of the Great Commission, even if they never leave their hometown.
3. Activating every disciple in their God-given role(s) in the Great Commission. [10]

In addition, they hold the following action points:[11]

1. Cultivating **abandoned devotion for Jesus** (see glossary) among disciples under their influence
2. Implementing four core components for mobilizing and equipping their members
3. Developing and executing a sending strategy from their members to near culture and distant culture unreached/ unengaged people groups.

Instead of taking a one-by-one mobilizing approach, it is important for local ministries to prioritize mobilizing the whole of their ministry to grasp the Kingdom's outworking among every ethnic people group. This includes not merely periodically mentioning cross-cultural mission, but making it an integral part of their ministry's focal points on an ongoing basis. Instead of Jesus' global commission being sidelined as a department or committee, it is meant to grab the imaginations of every believer in that ministry. This does not mean every member will become a cross-cultural message bearer, yet it does mean they will understand and value global, cross-cultural mission, identifying and becoming activated in their role(s) in the Great Commission.

Four Core Mobilization Tools

A primary way a local ministry influences its members is through the implementation of four core mobilizing tools used by God throughout history in awakening His people for the nations. They are not new or trendy but help the global Church return with faithfulness to the basics of faith and discipleship. These four can be implemented and reproduced in any local church, campus ministry fellowship and Bible School in any part of the world. They are simple, user-friendly tools. Local ministries using these tools with perseverance, over time, will see fruitfulness in mobilization as a result of their implementation. Most believers possessing Jesus' heart for mission have been influenced by one or more of these four tools throughout history.

1. Small group Bible studies within a local ministry encountering God's mission heart and passion from Genesis to Revelation.

2. A committed prayer ministry that engages the whole local ministry body in intercession for abandoned devotion in His global Church and harvest among the unreached and unengaged.

3. Monthly or quarterly meetings within the life of the local ministry providing crucial information about aspects and nuances of the Great Commission most believers never hear about.

4. Making faith-filled, Spirit-led commitments to be scattered with one's family and job for long-term ministry among near and distant culture unreached and unengaged people groups.

Denominations/ Church Networks as Mission Mobilization Movements

Let's progress beyond one local ministry as a Mission Mobilization Movement. What might it look like for a whole denomination, church network or campus ministry organization within a particular nation to multiply individual local churches and fellowships within their ministry structures to prioritize local and global mission? Such efforts become Mission Mobilization Movements across a wider spectrum than one individual local ministry. They are self-sustained, self-reproducing mobilization initiatives utilizing a step-by-step strategy enabling a saturation style mobilization emphasis within denominational, church network and organizational structures.[12] For example, a particular denomination/ church network may have 100 local churches in a certain nation. Is it possible to see core principles of mobilization implemented within the life of every one of these 100 local churches?

This is what we are referring to.

Randy Mitchell, international director of One World Mission, affirms the concept of mobilization movements: "We believe it is possible to see mobilization occurring within churches, denominations, associations, networks and even nations as movements."[13] He goes on to reveal, "This means we can speak of them being fully mobilized or not at all or somewhere along a continuum of mobilization. A church, church network, denomination, people or even nation can be mobilized by degree. If a people can be mobilized or not mobilized we should be able to speak of them being partially mobilized and that percentage could through the right combination of efforts be increased."[14]

Take the body of Christ in Myanmar, for example. Operation World cites 8.98 percent of the total population are Christians.[15] This is one of the highest percentage of followers of Jesus in any South East Asian nation. What happens if that population of believers is mobilized to internalize Jesus' Great Commission emphasis within the life of their fellowships. Some of them voluntarily crossing ethnic barriers in their own nation, relocating with family and jobs. How can this be realized? Through multiplying Mission Mobilization Movements within their churches and ministry network structures.

Or consider South Sudan (gaining independence as recently as 2011). Operation World records that 62.3 percent of the total population are Christians.[16] What is strategically exciting is while their official national language is English, the entire population also speaks fluent Arabic, having been part of Sudan for generations. This means South Sudan has a large number of Arabic speaking believers and local churches strategically placed to influence the Horn of Africa and all of North Africa, overcoming the significant hurdle of learning one of the world's most difficult languages.[17] Yet right now South Sudan churches have little worldview of Jesus' Great Commission plan. What is needed? Multiplying Mission Mobilization Movements within their local ministries and ministry structures.

Utilizing a strategic plan, senior leaders appoint others within their particular ministry structures to be trained to multiply mission mobilization emphasis within the grassroots local ministries in a particular district, area or region. These appointed leaders are released across an area of oversight within the ministry structure to in turn train and overall advise local ministry leaders to implement core principles of Mission Mobilization Movements.[18]

Many, if not most, denominational/ organizational structures have leadership positions such as "Mission Director," "Evangelism Director" or the like. I have observed many leaders having these titles yet with little clarity as to how to mobilize local ministries in their denominational/ network structures for the Great Commission. Empowering such leaders is a significant way forward.

My friend Jimmy Fundar was in this category when I first met him. He was appointed by the Federation of Southern Baptist Conventions in the Philippines as their "National Missions Mobilizer." Yet he was unclear on what exactly this meant or how to go about his role. As were the denominational leaders overseeing him. Around that time, he learned of a GMMI Mobilizer Equipping School and thought this might be an opportunity to learn to do his role. He is now implementing core principles of Mission Mobilization Movements systematically across the 1,200 local churches of the Federation of Southern Baptist Conventions in the Philippines.

COMMON CHARACTERISTICS OF MISSION MOBILIZATION MOVEMENTS

Local ministries and denominational/ church network structures implementing effective mission mobilization emphasis have common characteristics, observed in historic and contemporary ministry structures. We will look at seven such characteristics. These are meant to be expressed by leadership in culturally relevant ways within ministry structures themselves. We pray these characteristics will be exponentially increasing across thousands of local ministries and denominational structures in the coming years and decades.

1. Prayer Movement

A local ministry becoming ablaze with local and global vision for the unreached is a praying ministry. Intercessory prayer is Jesus' primary way of moving His eternal plans and purposes forward. Intercessory prayer can be defined as prayer on behalf of people, families, cities, nations, and situations, as we stand in their place contending for the will of God, transformation, conviction of sin and the influence of the Kingdom of God among them.[19] Prayer and intercession give expression to the Spirit's inner longing in us to see God's glory and Kingdom known and experienced in families, cities, nations, and the world. As disciples are moved to ongoing, faithful, consistent prayer, God's purposes in the earth are accelerated. Through prayer, we partner with God to change the future of nations, people groups, cities, and villages. Intercessory prayer is the most important of ministries, yet generally the least utilized.

A local ministry praying corporately in a consistent, ongoing way finds the Spirit touching the hearts of more disciples within that ministry. I have observed that getting people to pray for the fulfillment of the Great Commission on a regular basis is one of the greatest means of mobilizing them. The local ministry is growing as a "house of prayer for all nations" (Isaiah 56:7), extending spiritual victories among the nations and pushing back the powers of darkness.

God promises to answer prayer in line with His will. How can we be confident we are praying in line with His will? By praying according to the promises of His Word and that He reveals by His Spirit. Praying the recorded prayers of the Bible over circumstances, nations and unreached peoples is a powerful way to pray. The New Testament is full of apostolic prayers that Paul, Peter, John, and others prayed for believers and the body of Christ.[20] A careful look at these prayers reveals an emphasis on praying for believers to be growing spiritually. Scripture puts more focus on praying for disciples than on the lost themselves. The implication is prayer for the spiritual development of believers creates impact on others for the sake of Christ. The global Church growing in spiritual maturity, becoming the Church after God's own heart, naturally overflows in blessing the nations.

2. Cultivating Abandoned Devotion for Jesus

Local ministries growing as Mission Mobilization Movements prioritize true biblical discipleship. There is a cry arising in the hearts of multitudes of believers for a more relevant walk with Jesus. The human heart was created to experience the highest levels of love relationship with God. This is what we mean by "abandoned devotion" to Jesus. A posturing of the whole heart and life before the Lord, His working in us an ever-increasing blaze of love for God over a lifetime. Abandoned devotion is to forsake all in pursuit of

Jesus alone. Abandoning things considered dear yet interfering with obeying Jesus. "Abandoned" describes the extent of devotion. Devotion is no longer casual, comfortable, or convenient but costs time, money, security, friends and family. We don't obey when it is merely convenient, but surrender everything to Jesus.

First John 4:19 reveals, "We love Him because He first loved us"! This is different from merely believing the doctrine of God's love for us at an intellectual level. The biblical exhortation is believers saturated with truth that God is not mad at us but filled with enjoyment (Psalm 16:11). Yes, when we willfully rebel, His heart is hurt. Yet He still enjoys the relationship, drawing us back. He is not like human beings who keep records of wrongs. Experiencing His kindness and mercy motivates a response, affirming, *No matter what it takes, I will love this God who loves me so greatly!* This is the foundation of abandoned devotion.

An appropriate corporate prayer of believers in these types of ministries is, "Lord, reveal Yourself to me!" This happens in small steps, not in one moment. We may not feel we want to know Him more, yet pursue it anyway. Over time we are transformed, feeling something missing when we don't spend adequate time in His presence. This is a core process of growing in abandoned devotion.

A believer prioritizing abandoned devotion for Jesus intentionally cultivates their spiritual life. They are not casual in discipleship, but purposeful about spiritual disciplines. They care how they spend time, money, and energy, knowing they will be held accountable before the Lord. They get around people who inspire a deep passion for Christ. They are careful about every word they speak, aware of the high standard Jesus places on words. They have eternity in their hearts, seeking first the Kingdom of God. They respond to the convicting checks from the Holy Spirit, repenting quickly over shortcomings and mistakes. Dwelling with the Lord, they become sensitized to His voice and guidance.

Each of these elements and many more are characteristic of a local ministry prioritizing mission mobilization. Mobilization is not about championing a cause, but about calling the global Church to freshly fall in love with Jesus so that what is precious to Him becomes precious to us and what is a priority for Him becomes a priority for us.

3. Leadership Embodying Vision for Local and Global Mission

Local ministry pastors, pastoral leadership teams, campus ministry leaders, and Bible school faculty possess an essential responsibility before God— inspiring, educating, and activating disciples in the Great Commission. We have already seen the fulfillment of the Great Commission is the primary purpose of the body of Christ. The chief end of local ministry leadership, therefore, according to Ephesians 4:12, is "the equipping of the saints for the work of the ministry, for the edifying of the whole body of Christ." We have already considered this crucial principle in chapter 4 in our discussion about types of mobilizers. Spiritual leadership provides a spiritual environment to guide, envision, and empower the people of God under their care toward the formation of Christ within and activation in their primary role(s) in the Great Commission. Local ministries not properly equipping disciples will not find themselves useful in the great harvest.

The secret of enabling local churches and campus ministries to effectively engage with unreached and unengaged people groups globally is one of leadership. Due to their positions, pastors and spiritual leaders are a force for the Great Commission. History reveals the global body of Christ has made its strongest Great Commission headway when local churches and campus ministries, led by leaders ablaze with vision and anointing from the Spirit, are becoming mobilized and equipped.

4. Every Disciple Involved

Despite the unprecedented technology and advancement in modern life, billions remain unreached, and millions unengaged. There is indeed cause to believe the situation would be different if every believer was operating consciously in their God-given roles at home or on the field in the Great Commission. Yet too few people are currently involved. The task is left to a small number of "professionals" whose job it is thought to evangelize the world.

But every believer has a role. The call to disciple all nations is not just for a few Christians but every believer irrespective of status, background, education, etc. What are these roles? How can we identify and fulfill those roles effectively? Why are we not all operating in our different roles? These are important questions to answer. Imagine what would happen if every member of a local ministry was actively playing their roles.

Traditionally, we talk of four distinct Great Commission roles: *praying*, *going*, *giving* or *sending*, and *mobilizing*. However, two more roles are available now, typically referred to as *welcoming* and *advocating*. These six roles are not mutually exclusive. One cannot say, "I'm a mobilizer, so I don't need to give." Believers should be involved to some extent in all or as many of the roles as possible, as opportunities are available, but should prayerfully determine the one consistent role they commit themselves to long-term.

5. Insight from Scripture of the Centrality of Mission (through group Bible studies, individual study, preaching, books, and more)

Mission Mobilization Movements prioritize the authority of Scripture resulting in believers grasping and feeling the heart of God for all humanity. Jesus became man, laid down His life, paying the penalty required for the restoration of humanity. God's creation of human beings and Jesus' work to redeem them, reveals the global universality of the purpose of God. His redemption is for all! From Genesis to Revelation, the Bible is the story of God's rescue effort to redeem His wayward world. Many believers, however, have not connected with it in this way. Failing to engage God's heart for the world because they've not seen it in the Bible themselves. It has never been presented like this in their experience. Once we start to see for ourselves the theme of Scripture as His great rescue effort, our whole worldview as a follower of Christ can shift. We have already seen some of this in previous chapters.[21]

6. Distribution of Great Commission Information

One of the proven ways God envisions His people with a heart for the nations is information. Mission Mobilization Movements are proactively distributing, teaching, sharing Great Commission information, statistics, and stories. Without information, it is difficult to develop burden. Without burden, it is next to impossible to receive God-given vision. Information gives us a picture of how things work and what is happening in the mission movement. Without relevant information on a host of topics of the cross-cultural mission movement, it is challenging for believers to practically understand the big picture and get involved in specific ways.

In Nehemiah 1, we find a biblical example. Nehemiah is serving in the king's palace. A group returned from Jerusalem informing him of the state of things in his beloved city. The walls are broken down, the people vulnerable to attack. Nehemiah is moved with concern, receiving a burden from the Lord. Without the information about the status of Jerusalem, Nehemiah would not have understood the need nor developed the burden. As Nehemiah sought God's face with this burden, the Lord released a vision of what he was to do about the situation. Nehemiah then makes plans to return to Jerusalem to rebuild the walls. It all started because Nehemiah was given information about the situation and was motivated to action.

It is the same today. Local ministries need information about the world, its needs, where the unreached are, strategies God is using, how unreached peoples come to Jesus, the means to enter unreached areas, and more if we are to partner with God in the Great Commission. Information resources like Operation World[22] and Joshua Project[23] have helped the global Church significantly. Information leads to an impartation of vision among ministry members. We want to be taught key items to adequately understand the Great Commission among unreached people groups, effectively participating with Jesus.

7. Executing a Sending Strategy

In the next chapter, we provide an overview of the concept of "scattering church members to near and distant culture unreached peoples," embodying this seventh characteristic of executing a sending strategy. Thus, we will not spend much time on this subject here. It will suffice to state a local ministry becoming a Mission Mobilization Movement develops a plan for scattering message bearer teams to near culture unreached peoples as well as distant culture unreached peoples. These teams are made up of lay leaders from the local ministry whom God has marked to move outward with the gospel from their local ministry situation. This is how the early Church spread so quickly—lay people on fire for God scattering out to surrounding areas with the gospel.

Local ministries are committed to seeking God as to where He would have them multiply within near culture and distant culture groups. God's strategy of planting simple churches all over is much bigger than we have understood—within a given city, every neighborhood, every high-rise apartment building, every office building with a simple church. This requires some level of coordination between churches in a given area, carefully dividing up a community. This will result in many more simple churches being reproduced. This is part of developing a local ministry's sending strategy.

✱✱✱

Now that we've seen the significant foundational strategy of the Spirit of multiplying Mission Mobilization Movements among local ministries and across denominational, network, and organization ministry structures, we can progress to the Spirit's second strategic point—scattering message bearer teams from these local ministries to unreached peoples.

16

Scattering Message Bearer Teams to the Unreached

ocal ministries prioritizing the Great Commission through multiplying
Mission Mobilization Movements inevitably progress to the next level of
the Holy Spirit's strategy. This is a natural step forward as a ministry aligns
with Jesus' core identity for His global Church as God's multiplying, reproducing people. It is also a natural step in what the Church is mobilized to do.

WHAT IS SCATTERING?

In the modern global Church, it is common to gather in a building called a
church. Yet this is counter to the natural process among a true community
of faith. The way of the Spirit compels His corporate and individual people
outward—"scattering," multiplying, reproducing itself.[1] Let's consider this
Holy Spirit inspired phenomena in detail.

Every Believer Compelled—The Natural Response

Renowned mission practitioner and author, Roland Allen, suggested God
has put within every believer a natural instinct to communicate the gospel of
the Kingdom and influence others of their own initiative.[2] This isn't forced on

them or even something that necessarily needs to be encouraged. It is innate to a follower of Jesus because the Holy Spirit has taken up residence within that person. The fulfillment of the Great Commission is dependent upon believers embracing this natural inclination, not squelching or resisting it. This inner drive is powerful, even moving the people of God to risk their lives to impart life-giving faith to others. The hope of the gospel, and the experience of its power, cannot be held for long without grieving the Holy Spirit. The Spirit longs for the gospel to be rooted in unreached families, villages, and towns, conveying His love to believers, producing inner desire for others to experience the transforming of Christ and His Kingdom.

"Scattering" begins when an individual believer helps those around them when natural circumstances arise. Believers live in relationship with many unbelievers. Life realities allow natural circumstances where a believer can demonstrate the message in relevant ways the unbeliever understands. They help the hearer be sympathetic to the message, producing confidence in the message's truth. Spiritual power is conveyed because the believer speaks from experience. They are not communicating an unknown subject, but one dear and personal. The message is their own truth, experienced in the crucible of life. The hearer (unbeliever) has then entered into another's experience of truth before they themselves have encountered it. This is the power of true witness.[3]

The profound power conveyed to a believer declaring their experience to others is often overlooked. Their ability to express it grows and develops. Through the telling, it is clarified, understood further and with new perspectives and insights. Verbalizing the message deepens it, shedding new light. It becomes increasingly real, its power and meaning becoming clearer. Discussing with others truth they have experienced, produces accountability to live in light of that truth in word and deed.

The believer becomes increasingly bound by the implications of being a disciple. Each time they share, the message's hold upon the believer is strengthened and deepened. Additionally, in expressing their faith a believer learns areas of truth they may be ignorant about. This increases desire to grow in particular aspects of faith and truth. They search Scripture for answers to difficult questions, humbling themselves, forced to think about the implications of the message and how to help others understand its nuances. They do not rely on canned answers failing to touch the heart. This entire process strengthens individual believers themselves while simultaneously communicating truth to those around them through natural relationships.

The Common Unnatural Response

Contrary to above, what is common today is for believers to remain to themselves, hidden in their cluster of Christians, acting as if the Church is to be isolated from society at large. Believers in Indonesia, for example, may rarely interact with their Muslim neighbors, co-workers, or peers in university. This is largely due to the societal divide among Christians and Muslims and the fear sown related to the other, reinforced over generations. This could be repeated over and over among minority Christian communities in places like Nepal, Pakistan, India, Egypt, and more. This is never the intent of Scripture. God wants to be right in the midst of society, relating with the broken, the worldly, the religious, revealing Himself through His hands and feet—wholehearted disciples. This means embracing the Spirit-imparted drive within to deliberately relate with those whom the Lord has put in our spheres, finding ways to naturally share the message and power of the Kingdom of God.

THREE LEVELS OF SCATTERING

"Scattering," has multiple layers.[4] It is safe to say biblically speaking every disciple of Christ is meant to "scatter" in one way or another. What happens when a local church made up of such believers acts on inner impulse, engaging natural relationships around them in work environments, school situations, neighborhoods, or family relatives. The result is a chain reaction where believers relate with unbelievers in their natural environments and unbelievers, over time, begin to respond to Jesus.

Level One Scattering

The believer naturally asks those receptive to the message if they would like to learn more by studying the Bible together. This is all done in a thoroughly natural way, as part of the relationships they already possess. This is always the place to start and every believer should be encouraged to consider their natural connections and who the Lord is asking them to begin sharing naturally with. This can be understood as **Level One Scattering** (see glossary). To be "scattered" refers to going out from the local ministry and entering the world they are already part of as Jesus' "message bearer." It is important to overcome the natural pull to use a traditional understanding of "missionary" when considering "scattering." We are merely referring to every believer in a local ministry considering their natural relationships and deliberately engaging receptive people with natural God-talk in their day-to-day conversations. This appears to align with the intent of the New Testament for every follower of Jesus.

A natural example is workplace evangelism, where conversations about God become a part of normal daily interactions within an office, work or campus setting. Every believer can and should be equipped for Level One Scattering within local ministries. To lead conversations, in a natural way, to things about God, culminating with inviting new relationships to study the Bible together in a nonthreatening, encouraging environment. Through Level One Scattering the gospel naturally infiltrates all sectors of society[5] instead of expecting unbelievers to come to our churches (which most will not).

The Lord evidently desires His people to have a plan for responding to the inner drive to express their faith. We need a strategy, a means, to guide others through core elements of the gospel of the Kingdom.[6] Every local ministry emphasizing the Great Commission ought to train their members with such a vital tool, adequately enabling them to express the gospel in a clear-cut way. Not only those with a leaning toward evangelism, but every member. My friend Vihaan, a Muslim background believer (MBB) in India, spends much time training churches across India to naturally engage those around them with the gospel. He is promoting and training churches toward Level One Scattering.

Following is an overview of *Level One Scattering*. Those "scattered" are members of local ministries committed to reaching the communities God has divinely placed them in—their university, workplace, social networks, neighborhood, extended families. They use natural relationships as bridges to connect with unbelievers who are receptive, open to spiritual things. As they begin to meet with a small group of unbelievers to discuss the Bible, considering the phases and points of the gospel of the Kingdom, they do so with the prayers and blessing of the local ministry. The leaders encourage them, acting as a resource. But they (the leaders) do not take over the small groups or seek in any way to control what is happening.

Scattered believers then, in their natural environments, are used by God to influence others in a natural way, spreading the influence of the Kingdom. In time some of these unbelievers become believers. It is at that time that an important consideration takes place. Do those believers become incorporated into the existing local ministry? Or is the background and traditions of the new believers so different from the local ministry that it proves impossible for them to naturally incorporate into that local body of believers? Most often, this is the case. Most traditional churches today are far removed from the cultural understanding of most unreached unbelievers, making it next to impossible to appropriately incorporate them into existing churches.

Instead, they need their own simple, cell-group style gatherings of people like them. The small group that has been meeting, studying the Bible, and praying together, can become its own brand-new simple local ministry in the same geographical area. This new entity can and should be connected with the existing local ministry but released to develop separately, on its own. Particularly related to cultural issues and making the group relevant to new believers. This is the power of scattering, reproducing, multiplying—the core identity of the body of Christ and the advancing Kingdom of God among all people groups.

Level Two Scattering

In addition to *Level One Scattering,* further levels of scattering include specific groups scattering from the local ministry, reproducing, and multiplying ministry among unreached peoples. We call these **Level Two and Level Three Scattering** (see glossary). The numbers scattered in these two levels are meant to be much larger than most local ministries have imagined. Local ministries with a vision for global mission may have a goal to send one or two "missionaries." Instead, the Spirit apparently has a different approach, intending local ministries to "scatter" even 20 percent of their members in message bearer teams in *Level Two and Level Three Scattering.* If a ministry has 200 members, this means 40 are scattered. If 40 members, 8 are scattered. Admittedly, most of us have never considered such a scale of sending before.

Let's consider what these two levels of scattering look like.

Level Two Scattering is when a team of believers (lay leaders and lay people) from a local ministry, previously faithful to *Level One Scattering*, respond to the Spirit leading them to a near culture unreached people within a 50 to 200-mile vicinity of the local ministry. They identify a section of a city, neighborhood, apartment complex, or company that comprises a subculture of an unreached people. This group is similar in culture, language, and worldview to the team, yet different ethnically. These are called "near culture peoples," as they are culturally near to the message bearer team, speaking the same language, having the same general worldview. For example, a message bearer team of Pakistani believers in a particular section of the city of Lahore sense God leading them to a particular subculture from a different ethnic background in another district of Lahore, 50 kilometers away. They are still Pakistani, sharing similar cultural qualities, speaking the same language, yet are different in ethnic background and are unreached.

Not all subcultures are divided by ethnic differences but can also be categorized by interests, age, generation, and life experiences. Examples of such subcultures in Lahore, Pakistan, for example might include factory workers, mothers of young children, taxi drivers, day laborers, football players, street kids, and many more. Hence the team's ministry is still crossing cultural barriers (though small), while reaching out to those having little access to the gospel (the unreached).

The message bearer team's purpose is to multiply simple, reproducible churches among the "near culture" community. They start by reaching out to their targeted subculture, building natural relationships, looking for receptive people to spiritual things, similar to *Level One Scattering*. These are their "persons of peace." They work through "persons of peace" within the community building trust, credibility, and reputation as godly, trustworthy people. They invite natural connections of their "persons of peace" to study the Bible together, learning about the Creator God whose Kingdom is available to all. These Bible study groups, over time, as some come to saving faith in Christ, become small embryos of a local church. We will look in detail at this concept in the next chapter.

I am convinced many more in local ministries are meant to be involved in *Level Two Scattering* to "near culture" peoples within 50 to 200 miles around them than currently are. I suggest a goal of at least 15 percent of members of local ministries being scattered in this near culture way. Most believers understand "global mission" as going across the world. Yet, today, many followers of Jesus are now in unreached nations where God wants to use their similar culture as a bridge to engage the unreached. The traditional ideas must give way to the Spirit-led realities of today. That is why their number is high. Relocating one's family and job 50 to 200 miles away to a similar culture of unreached people as one's own is possible for large numbers of believers. They serve in this way for a few years giving a new embryonic, simple church the greatest opportunity to grow, develop, and reproduce itself.

Level Three Scattering

Level Three Scattering takes us into the more traditional approach of mission sending. *Level Three Scattering* is when a team of believers (lay leaders and lay people) from the local ministry embraces God's leading to a distant culture unreached people. These may be within the same geopolitical nation where they are, in a neighboring country or even farther away, crossing continents. Similar to above, they identify a subculture of an unreached people group the Spirit is leading them to. That group is quite different from their own cultural background. They do not share the same language, basic customs, or world-view. There is a much larger learning curve to enculturate the gospel within that particular cultural understanding.

Level Three Scattering message bearer teams engage the same process as *Level Two Scattering*, prayerfully seeking "persons of peace" open to spiritual things and acting as an entry point into spheres of influence in the new community. They then engage some of these with Bible studies working through the stages of the gospel of the Kingdom, laying necessary groundwork for those from very different worldviews to culturally grasp the gospel. Over time some of these then become believers, the nucleus of a new simple church. I am convinced it is the will of God the number of *Level Three* message bearer teams also is higher than typically understood. If around 15 percent of church members are called to *Level Two Scattering*, it is consistent to suggest 5 percent of members from the sending local ministry are called to *Level Three Scattering*.

At *Level Two and Level Three Scattering* it is necessary to work together with other churches, denominations, and sending agencies in both near and distant culture situations. God has given every local ministry (no matter how small) specific "scattering" assignments. A local ministry should discern where God is leading? What specific neighborhood, building, part of a slum? It is necessary to discern these targets, then coordinate with other ministries toward a systematic coverage of "scattering" of neighborhoods, villages, and apartment blocks. Several years ago, I was riding in a taxi to a meeting in Bangkok. As I passed apartment block after apartment block, my minds' eye drifted to imagine a local church established within each apartment block, systematically reaching out to all the tenants in each building.

To reach all subcultures of every unreached people group globally local ministries must be specific in targeting as well as comprehensive, seeking to blanket an area (not only our own message bearer teams but in cooperation with other churches and sending agencies). The Spirit seems to be highlighting a significant paradigm shift toward the goal of simple churches multiplied within every square block and apartment building in a particular city or town.

Why 20 Percent?

If the premise of this book is accurate from a theological (study of God), ecclesiological (study of the Church), and missiological (study of God's mission and that of His people) perspective, couldn't we infer God intends to "scatter" many more than are currently doing so? If the church's core identity really is a reproducing, multiplying, missionary people in this age, shouldn't that be reflected to a greater degree in the number of those responding to the inner compelling of Christ from each local ministry?

Though in no way an exact number nor reached in a scientific manner, the concept of a local ministry scattering 20 percent or so of its members in *Level Two and Level Three Scattering* raises the global Church's sights from what has traditionally been done. It is meant to provoke faith-filled consideration about how much more local ministries can engage in "scattering" and multiplying.

Biblical principles anchor this concept in Scripture. God reveals at least 10 percent of personal income is to be set aside for Him, with additional offerings going beyond this. The 10 percent is an introduction, starting point, foundation of what is given to God. Never in Scripture are we taught to remain at giving ten percent. It is common to find believers increasing their tithes and offerings periodically by percentage points. Some adopt the "double tithe" principle, tithing 20 percent of their income. Conversely, if God has called His people to obey Him in giving at least 10 percent of income, even increasing to 20 percent, can we not apply the same principle to local ministries scattering members to near and distant culture peoples in *Level Two and Three Scattering*? Is it only money God is getting at with such a principle?

Tithing did not originate in Scripture with the Mosaic law. In Genesis 14:20, Abraham tithed a tenth of all his goods to Melchizedek, 400 years before the Law was given to Moses. Jacob did so as well in Genesis 28:22, also living hundreds of years before Moses. Abraham and Jacob represent that all belongs to God in the first place. Giving back to Him is a voluntary response of gratitude for all we have been given.

Through the law of Moses in Deuteronomy 14–18, the principle of giving a tenth of income to God became normalized—not as duty but a loving, trusting response that God is provider. In addition, Leviticus 27:30 reveals, "A tithe of everything from the land, whether grain from the soil or fruit from the trees, belongs to the Lord: it is holy to the Lord." And Proverbs 3:9 agrees: "Honor the Lord with your possessions, with the first fruits of all your increase." As Dave Ramsey highlights, "the Bible explains that tithing is an important part of faith for those who follow God and that your tithe should be money you set aside first. You're giving your first fruits instead of your leftovers."[7] With this understanding it seems an acceptable application to consider our churches scattering 20 percent of our members in *Level Two and Three Scattering*. Just as God invites us to trust Him with money, He also does so with those He intends to scatter to near and distant people groups.

THE STUMBLING BLOCK OF FINANCES

A significant factor in *Level Two* and *Level Three Scattering* is the global Church's viewpoint of finance. In almost every circumstance I teach these concepts, the first thing I hear is some variant of, "We want to engage with the unreached. But we are a poor church. How can we send twenty percent of our members to engage with unreached peoples, both near and distant? We cannot even support one."

I suggest a major piece of how God is "changing the face of global mission" (as cited in the introduction) surrounds shifting financial models. Responding to the above question, I often reply, "Did Jesus only give His Great Commission to affluent churches in affluent nations? Did God's promise to Abraham of blessing all the ethnic families of the earth only refer to those who had sufficient financial support to send?" Obviously, the answer is no. As established, God intends every local ministry to engage in fulfilling the Great Commission through implementing a "scattering" strategy to the unreached. The question is how a poor local ministry can send 20 percent of members in *Level Two* and *Level Three Scattering?*

The answer is simple, yet changing the engrained mission/ finance paradigm in our ministry structures, is more difficult. It is helpful to examine the New Testament and early Church, seeing how they were financed, taking cues from them. The norm of the book of Acts apparently was those "scattered" to the unreached (Gentiles) were financially sustained, not by support from a local ministry and other friends (the expected practice today), but through their profession or skills. Paul famously was a tentmaker, using this skill to earn a living as he went place to place planting new churches (Acts 18:1–3; 20:33–25). Priscilla and Aquilla did the same throughout their own ministry.

We can easily apply this to *Level Two and Level Three* message bearers taking their profession, trained skill, or career, deriving an income through this. This strategy overcomes the financial pressure the sending ministries experience. A quick study of Act 13, and the initial sending of the first organized mission team of Paul, Barnabas, and John Mark, reveals no money was promised or even sent with them. It was understood they would relate with the culture of the places they went by working with their hands. This would also provide for their livelihood.

The idea of a home church financially supporting message bearer teams is largely a modern concept birthed during the missionary movement of the last 300 years from affluent nations. This model has proven impossible for emerging sending nations to imitate (though many have and still are trying). I suggest it is time to relieve them of this financial support model, instead counseling a return to the biblical model of message bearer teams scattered to unreached people groups (both near and distant cultures), using skills and professions to derive an income.

This means of funding is not the case across the board in global mission work, but definitely for message bearer teams scattered to near and distant culture unreached peoples doing church planting. It does not refer to the financial needs related to projects and administrative/executive oversight. Every local ministry should determine their financial situation and if they are able to sustain large numbers of message bearer teams. If not, the tentmaking model should be adopted. More than only providing necessary financial income, this model immediately gets the message bearer into the community they have come to serve. Instead of being disconnected by receiving income from outside the community. Being seen in the community as working with your hands in some way puts message bearers into a credible box understood by the local community you have come to reach.

The Moravian Finance Model

The historic Moravian mission movement in the 1740s is a stellar example. Though an affluent noble, the Moravian leader, Ludwig Von Zinzendorf, chose to "scatter" his Moravian missionaries with no financial support. Prior to being "scattered," he instilled within them a vision of using the skills already present within the team for their long-term sustenance among the unreached. Each person or couple on the team considered what skills, abilities, or giftedness they possessed which could be used to derive an income. John R. Weinlick, official biographer of Zinzendorf reveals, "Even had the brethren been able to support their early missionaries by sending them money from the home churches, Zinzendorf would not have permitted it. He believed it highly important that the missionary earn his own living."[8] They were observed by the locals in a way the locals could relate. The idea of being financed from churches hundreds or thousands of miles away does not make sense to unreached local people. If they don't understand us, they won't trust us. If they don't trust us, they won't listen to our message.

The Moravian teams took this plan to every country they went, implementing it as soon upon arrival as possible. The message bearers understood finances sustained the team, not only individual persons and families, pooling their funds. Some had agricultural skills, farming land, while others started small entrepreneurial businesses, still others used their education and training to bring in an income.[9] All was then brought together to serve the group. They did so while remaining attentive to their time, prioritizing the proclamation of the gospel, a common argument to this approach. History cites the Moravian denomination as some of the most effective cross-cultural workers in mission history.[10] Their financial model ought to be considered by many today, particularly in emerging mission sending nations.

Objections Based on Church History

Some object, stating Jesus and the twelve disciples were financially supported during His three and a half years of ministry by the women who also followed Jesus. This is true as Luke 8:3 reveals. Peter and other apostles in the early Christian Church in Acts also devoted themselves entirely to their ministry, living off the money donated by Jerusalem church members (Acts 4:34–37). Both these examples were in a Jewish context. Once the books of Acts shifted from a Jewish focus to a Gentile one in chapter 13, there is also a marked shift in how finances were derived in ministry.

Still others refer to Jesus' own words, "The laborer is worthy of his wages" in Luke 10:7 and Matthew 10:11. Jesus was giving specific instructions to the 12 and 72 He sent out on 2 to 3-month preaching tours. These are not meant to be taken as universal principles of mission as is clearly evidenced. Jesus told them to only go to Israelites (the house of Israel) which obviously was a particular instruction for those specific outreaches. Later to be shifted to going to the Gentiles. That instruction was important, however, as Jesus knew Jewish culture. Being Jews themselves, the 12 and 72 would be received, shown hospitality as a bedrock of the Mosaic law. In fact, the more accurate rendering of Luke 10:7 is, "The laborer is worthy of their hire." We have typically interpreted the verse as someone being paid for gospel ministry. Yet this idea was likely nowhere on Luke's mind as he tells the story. When a Jew entered the house of another Jew showing hospitality, the visitor stayed two days free of charge. Staying additional days meant the visitor helped the head of the household in their profession or livelihood. They were "hired" to work with them to continue staying in their home. This was an understood hospitality principle among Jews of the day.[11]

Jesus was not teaching that message bearers throughout history should have their financial needs taken care of by others in every circumstance. If that were the case most leaders of churches in the New Testament did not obey the Lord in this matter. Jesus was not providing a comprehensive model of financial sustenance through His own situation. There is ample biblical evidence, following Jesus' ministry and into the book of Acts, that the church did not financially support the early apostles.

The early Church economic situation was similar to much of the global Church today—lower class and poor. Mission mobilization, then, includes helping local ministries incorporate a suitable financial model of "scattering." Using their skills or profession to derive a sufficient income to live at a similar level as the local people they came to serve, while opening doors of relationships among the people. This model allows local churches to scatter more members than the traditional finance model while aligning overall with God's plan.

Overcoming False Assumptions

Embracing this paradigm shift requires overcoming some unfortunate false assumptions in the global Church. It is common in some settings to measure whether a believer is a true person of faith by if they have cut themselves off from natural forms of income. This is true across the African continent as well as in several Asian contexts. It is believed having a natural income equals lacking faith and cutting off such possibilities, "fully entrusting oneself to God," is the way of true faith. This is a mishandling of Scripture as all sustenance comes from God to begin with, whether through a supernatural form or a natural paycheck. He is the source of it all, providing for the needs of His people (James 1:17–19; Romans 11:36).

God loves to supernaturally provide for His people. He did so with Elijah, providing the raven who brought him food and the brook which provided water (1 Kings 17:2–16). He did so with the 4,000 (Matthew 15:29–39) and then 5,000 (Matthew 14:13–21) by multiplying the bread and fish. Yet supernatural provisions in Scripture were never sustained indefinitely. They are tokens of remembrance producing faith that Jesus is supreme, overruling in created order. God does not intend believers to live perpetually from supernatural sustenance. The brook dried up for Elijah, the raven ceased bringing him food. God's normal plan is using means to supply natural provision while periodically breaking in supernaturally during unusual situations. I have many personal testimonies of this. Those supernatural injections of provision did not supply in an indefinite way, however. Jesus teaches directly about this crucial subject in Matthew 6:25–34. It appears the global Church needs this exhortation to progress correctly related to finances in the global purpose of God.

Matthew 6:25–34—A Financial Case Study

In Matthew 6:25–34 of the Sermon on the Mount,[12] Jesus focuses on worry of not having enough today and anxiety about the future. Worry and anxiety about finances are a snare Jesus wants to keep us from. This passage never teaches believers are not responsible to provide for our families, but to do so free from anxiety and worry. The whole counsel of Scripture teaches parents provide for their families and a lazy person does not eat (2 Thessalonians 3:12).God calls human beings to duties and vocations and to diligence in them. We consider the future financially and how we can meet those demands as they come. Jesus' exhortation is that because we have a faithful Father, we can be free from undue worry and anxiety regarding the supply of daily living.

"Look at the birds of the air."

To reveal His capacity to care for every need, Jesus guides us to observe birds free from anxiety in relation to their food. We are to contemplate the birds' actions and find something to emulate. "They neither sow, nor reap, nor gather into barns (as human beings do) yet your heavenly Father feeds them." Yet they do build nests from the natural means about them, seeking worms to sustain themselves and their young. Many birds faithfully migrate to warmer climates during the winter to have the substance needed throughout the year.

Jesus is not forbidding planning for the future nor taking sensible steps for financial security. He is rebuking our propensity to be anxious and worried in such concerns. Wise consideration of the future is right while consuming, tormenting, distracting worry is not. The point Jesus is making is birds are provided with food apart from incessant striving and anxiety in the process.

They are out working hard and beyond their own abilities, God supplies their needs. We are not encouraged in this passage to fail to work hard. Quite the opposite, throughout Scripture we are called to hard work.

God sustains us through means

Birds cannot "sow, reap, and gather" like human beings can, yet they have what they need. Humans have much greater advantages and skills than birds do. The birds use no means of their own, yet are fed, how much more should we (given much more capacity) trust God when He has provided so much to us through a myriad of means in our sphere. Hudson Taylor, famous missionary to China in the 1800s, once said, "The use of means ought not lessen our faith in God and our faith in God ought not to hinder our using whatever means God has given us for the accomplishment of His own purposes."[13]

It is crucial then we prayerfully consider what the "means" God has set around us to sustain us. For many it is a job, degree, business, farm, government, or special skill. For others it is relationships, networks of churches, contacts, companies, foundation, and more. We diligently engage the means God has ordained to meet our needs, asking Him, *How do you want to meet these needs?* Waiting instead for a sustained "miracle" reveals a fundamental misunderstanding of how God has set up His Kingdom to supply needs. It has too often been this faulty interpretation of "living by faith" that is a reason for worry & anxiety found in some of the body of Christ in the first place. Instead of diligently utilizing means, we have wrongly assumed God wanted to "supernaturally" provide, in an ongoing way.

EXAMPLES OF SCATTERING FROM THE NEW TESTAMENT

It is necessary to root this larger "scattering" concept in Scripture. In the church at Ephesus in Acts 19 we find a similar phenomenon. We will consider this account in further detail in the next chapter about church planting movements. For now, it will suffice to highlight that Paul set up a training school (school of Tyrannus) to equip the house churches connected to the overall church in Ephesus. Paul's teaching trained lay leaders and lay people in the church of Ephesus to be scattered outward with particular ministry strategies (we will consider what they did in the next chapter).

We are told in verse 10 the result of Paul's training: "And this continued for two years so that all who dwelt in Asia Minor heard the word of the Lord Jesus." By putting Scripture together, we conclude the church in Ephesus "scattered" multitudes (likely two by two) of lay leaders and lay people all over Asia Minor (some to near and some to distant cultures). They left their homes in Ephesus, taking their families and jobs for an indefinite period of time. Paul ministered in Ephesus, "equipping the saints," and the believers (saints) in Ephesus "scattered" out, "doing the work of the ministry" (Ephesians 4:12). The church at Ephesus is a powerful, fruitful example of a local ministry "scattering" a considerable number of disciples to the unreached. Apparently, "all of Asia Minor hearing the word of the Lord," can be traced back to the faithfulness of the church in Ephesus "scattering."

Let's also consider Jesus as He "scattered" the 72 disciples in Luke 10. These were in a different category than the twelve apostles, whom the Lord was training and who would then "turn the world upside down" in the book of Acts. The 72, on the other hand, were what we understand as lay leaders and lay people. Jesus sent them in groups of two, going to every city and village He was planning to travel. Jesus "scattered" them to preach the Kingdom of God and heal the sick, giving them power over demons. When they returned, having been successful, Jesus rejoiced with them. The 72 (lay leaders and lay people) being "scattered" was a first-fruits of what Jesus intended to do through His global Church on a much wider scale in the coming centuries. The central idea is that Jesus didn't just "scatter" one or two, as we are used to considering, but a large multitude of disciples as He still intends to do.

The Great Commission: Matthew 28:18–20

Let's quickly consider "scattering" as a survey of the New Testament. In Matthew 28:18–20, Jesus provides marching orders for His global Church until His second coming. The implication of this passage encompasses the central calling of the global Church to scatter. We move outward, sharing the gospel of the Kingdom through natural relationships God has put in our midst.

Acts 1:8: "You Shall Be My Witnesses..."

Acts 1:8 provides a blueprint to understand the book of Acts. Paul Pierson affirms, "The book is laid out with focus on three geographical areas, focusing on ever-widening concentric circles."[14] The first portion (Acts 1–7) details what took place surrounding the newly birthed church in Jerusalem following Pentecost. The second section (Acts 8–9) highlights God's works in and through His church in Judea and Samaria and the third portion (Acts 10–28), even further to the uttermost parts of the known world of that day.

Jesus clarified in Acts 1:8 they were to be moving outward from Jerusalem. But a problem happened. Between Acts 2 and 7, the Jerusalem portion, most scholars believe several years transpired. The Jerusalem church was almost exclusively Jewish believers, learning what it meant to live in relationship with the risen, invisible Christ through the newly poured out Holy Spirit. Yet most had forgotten Jesus' words in His commission. They were not looking outward from Jerusalem, having become comfortable. Believers had homes, families, and jobs. They still saw the gospel and Jesus' Kingdom as Jewish. They weren't quite clear on how "good" Jews could rightly relate with Gentiles as part of the body of Christ. Their Jewishness was so engrained, it was almost impossible to see beyond it. Many believers today are in the same situation. We struggle with understanding how the gospel could really be for all others, particularly those so culturally different, believing in idols, who may oppress and persecute us.

Acts 8:1–4: A Great Scattering

As a result, in Acts 8:1–4 the Lord stirred up a persecution within Jerusalem against the believers, propelling them outward, being "scattered." In this case, persecution was God's tool to help the early Church faithfully move out in mission. It was the Lord orchestrating the situation with the intent of moving the believers outward in mission.

In verse 1 "all" believers were "scattered" out of Jerusalem into other areas that had not experienced the power of the gospel. The verse specifically says the apostles, or head leaders, did not go with them, but stayed back in Jerusalem.

What does this reveal? That regular disciples (lay leaders and lay people) were tasked by the Lord with "gossiping" the gospel, gathering new believers in simple house churches everywhere they went outward from Jerusalem. Verse 4 tells us, "Therefore, those who were scattered went everywhere preaching the word." They had been equipped in Jerusalem over the previous several years and were now ready to reach others, planting churches among them, "as they were going." This is a key model of scattering the Holy Spirit wants us to emulate today. It was through normal, everyday believers, that local churches in the Judean region were planted and became fruitful.

Matthew 13:1–9; 18–23—Parable of the Sower (Scatterer)[15]

In Matthew 13 Jesus teaches eight parables related to the Kingdom of God. The first, the parable of the Sower (Scatterer), reveals Jesus' outlook on our subject of "scattering" among the nations. Let's look at Matthew 13:1–9; 18–23 in detail. If viewed correctly, this parable has significant missiological implications. We suggest generally across Church history this parable has been misinterpreted, skewing its original meaning and intent.[16]

The parable describes a man (Jesus) "scattering" seed on ground. We find four seeds of varying quality being "scattered." Jesus reveals the "scattering" of seed is not only the Word sown into people, but the "scattering" of believers into a certain generation with the gospel. It is not truth alone being "scattered," but as G. Campbell Morgan suggests, "believers."[17] Seeds are sons and daughters of the Kingdom whom God "scatters" throughout the earth with the Word of God living and active in them. The "Word" referred to by Mark and Luke is not the written Word itself, but the incarnate Word within a believer, growing in spiritual quality day by day.[18] In the next parable (wheat and tares), Jesus identifies "seed" as "the sons of the Kingdom" (v. 38). Symbols in Scripture rarely change. Jesus is concerned in this parable with the seeds, not the soil. We find in this parable the method of Jesus' work globally in this age—"scattering" sons and daughters of the Kingdom into the world to produce fruit. Every believer globally is in view here. The parable describes them as "scattered" into the world by Jesus, put in their families, surroundings, towns, and cities by Him.

To the seed (believer) that understands and obeys the Word, aligning their lives with Jesus' terms of discipleship, the age responds and a fruitful harvest comes forth. These influence the generation they live in, bringing it under the leadership of the King. According to Jesus, around one-fourth of believers fall into the category of producing fruitfulness (v. 23). The believer which does not understand the Word finds the well-trodden ground of the age hard (v. 19), unable to produce any harvest. The believer with no root in themselves finds the persecuting age destroying them (v. 21). The believer concerned about the things of the age are themselves absorbed and choked by the age (v. 22). Three fourths of believers do not produce fruit when "scattered" into the world. They are in contact with the truth and ideals of the Kingdom, yet do not produce the fruit of the Kingdom.[19]

The American Standard Version (ASV)[20] has the most accurate translation from the Greek, stating in verse 19, "This is he that was sown by the wayside." Most versions read, "This is he who received seed by the wayside," changing the entire meaning. The "he" is a believer "scattered" on the soil.[21] The key to understanding the parable is this phrase: "He that was sown." The parable and Jesus' explanation have everything to do with the method He has prescribed to see the Kingdom introduced and advanced in every generation until He returns. Jesus' method is "scattering" seeds (believers) into every generation, who have internalized the standards of the Kingdom. Through these seeds Jesus will bring a global harvest into His Kingdom.

Jesus describes four types of believers (seeds) to reveal different conditions among professing believers. The first seed condition Jesus gives is, "He that was sown by the way side" (v. 19). These believers hear the words of the Kingdom yet do not gain spiritual understanding and wisdom. They are superficial Christians. "Then comes the evil one and snatches away what had been sown in his heart" (v. 19). They heard it and believed for salvation, yet did not make it their own through experiencing its power in their circumstances. They did not understand God's purpose of discipleship, serving His purpose in the world. They are saved, but far from what God intended for believers. As a result, there is no Kingdom influence through their lives.

The next type of seed (believers) is "He that was sown upon the rocky places" (v. 5). They "hear the word, and straightway with joy receives it; yet he has no root in himself, but endures for a while; and when tribulation or persecution arises because of the word, straightway he stumbles" (vv. 20–21). This believer goes further than the first. They are familiar with the word of the Kingdom, taking joy in it. The Kingdom truths, however, have not been surrendered to in the life. The hardships and persecutions of the age come along and derail these believers because they have no real roots. Multitudes of sincere believers fall into this group. They sit in church weekly, attending Bible Studies and prayer meetings, going through the motions, yet producing no real fruit.

Who is the believer sown among thorns? "He that hears the word; and the care of the world, and the deceitfulness of riches, choke the word, and he becomes unfruitful" (v. 22). These have gone further than the first and second. They are born again with the life-giving power of Jesus inside, but are distracted by other desires fascinating them. The cares of money, power, pleasure, materialism, social status, political correctness, religious spirit, and more hinder them from becoming what God intended. This is another common grouping in Jesus' body. Hearing the Word, receiving it, yet not going on in growth in God because of deceitfulness of the world, its cares, worries and anxieties. This common type of seeds is also unfruitful before the Lord.

Finally, who is "he that was sown upon the good ground" (v. 8)? They obey the Word of the Kingdom, yielding to the rule and reign of the King. The word has been applied to their lives through the Spirit and become life. They produce fruit in the generation they are scattered by the Lord. The distinguishing factor of seed "scattered" on good ground is that they are fruitful. The fruit of the Holy Spirit is developing in their life. Their life and witness prepare their generation for the return of the King. Jesus never says the good ground is completely void of stones or thorns, only that they are not sufficient to hinder the fruitfulness of the seed. The seed is not overcome by them as the others are. These believers will obviously still have to fight the same temptations of the other seeds yet they are fruitful because they overcome each one.

Even among these fruitful believers there are varying levels of production: hundredfold, sixtyfold, and thirtyfold (v. 23). Jesus speaks of fruitfulness primarily as internal fruitfulness and external faithfulness and obedience. The Bible values inward growth of the fruit of the Spirit, developing in the ways of God, hungering after Him, cultivating spiritual wisdom and revelation and living in obedience to the Word and the guidance of the Spirit. If we are not developing inner life fruitfulness in growing dimensions, external fruitfulness, in bringing about a harvest among others, will not be evident either.

The Lord is incredibly gracious. We are never locked into one of the three negative seeds. Through admitting our wrong and changing those choices, actions, and priorities we are able to move into the category of the fruitful seeds sown in good ground. Jesus asks only that we confess our misguided ways, forsaking them and align ourselves with the ideals, values, and requirements of His Kingdom ways.

We find significant implications for the Great Commission in this parable. Fruitful believers possess the essential life of Jesus on the inside, conforming to His standards of discipleship. They are not perfect yet live free from the distractions of the other three seeds. We long to see local ministries scattering "good seed" (fruitful believers) among unreached people groups. When scattered, fruit springs forth over time, as the Spirit takes their witness, pressing it upon those surrounding them. When a son or daughter of the Kingdom is scattered among a people hostile to the Kingdom of God, in time (and through suffering and perseverance), they influence them with the realities of the Kingdom. This is why we trust the Lord for the highest spiritual quality of believers becoming activated in all three levels of scattering.

To pull this parable out of the abstract and give it some practical feet, consider the following. Current statistics tell us there are just over 2.5 billion Christians on earth.[22] If we took Jesus' teaching literally in this parable that three-fourth of Christians "scattered" by Jesus for His glory, produce no fruit, this would total 1.87 billion unfruitful Christians. This leaves potentially 620 million believers in the category of fruitful believers "scattered" globally, producing fruitfulness through their lives and ministries. Pause for a moment. Let that sink in. Potentially 620 million fruitful believers in local ministries "scattering" outward in *Level One, Level Two and Level Three Scattering*. If around 20 percent of these 620 million fruitful believers globally become activated in *Level Two and Level Three Scattering* as proposed, there could be 124 million fruitful message bearers engaged in ministry among near and distant culture unreached peoples. Just imagine the impact.

While Jesus may not have meant the breakdown of the four seed categories literally, I believe He did mean it as an illustration of what the Church would look like throughout this age, with a majority of professing believers not being fruitful. I would say that 25 percent of the professing body of Christ globally is a conservative (and likely fairly accurate) estimate of fruitful believers in the Kingdom. However, if there are more fruitful believers that only bolsters the point of how many more fruitful believers should be scattered to the nations in response to the Great Commission. Compare the potential number of 124 million fruitful message bearers in level one and two scattering with the current number of missionary workers in the world—430,000.[23] By faith, this is where the Lord is taking His Church.

Yet we know that such a number of fruitful believers across the global Church have not yet been activated in their calling as "scattered" for Jesus' glory. The vast majority are not aware that Jesus has purposed their lives for great glory among unreached peoples. Yet, according to our study, it is Jesus' foretold purpose that one fourth of believers are fruitful believers "scattered" into the world for His glory. They need to be mobilized through Mission Mobilization Movements scattering them from local ministries. This requires new paradigms, new ways of thinking, embracing the changes the Lord is seeking to bring among us.

WHO ARE BEING SCATTERED?

Who are these 620 million fruitful believers scattered from local ministries with the gospel of the Kingdom? They are everyday disciples of Jesus, mostly lay people. They are materially poor and wealthy alike. As seen, access or not to finance is not to be a hindrance of the Spirit's compelling. Scattered fruitful believers are educated and uneducated alike as intellectual education is nowhere found in the Bible as a qualification of bearing His message. They are from high and low classes and castes alike, not allowing religious and societal measuring sticks to define and keep them from obeying the compulsion of Christ. No measuring stick of the world can define them. They are known by the King because they are choosing to align with His heart in this hour.

God is searching for those valuing growing intimacy with Jesus, trustworthy with the secrets of His heart. They embrace a life of faith and dependence on Him. The Spirit is pursuing those ignoring what others say while living according to Jesus' standards. He beckons those disillusioned with the status quo, dreaming with God about what could be. He looks for those using time, money, gifts, abilities, and influence to advance His kingdom. They are not spiritual babes, having Christ formed within. They have gone through trial and difficulties, finding Jesus' victory sufficient for them. This has produced perseverance and spiritual strength. Importantly, they overcome the onslaught of the evil one to get the people of God to quit serving Him. The enemy is a liar and deceiver. It is essential that scattered believers learn to identify his schemes, resisting them, standing strong in who Jesus has called them to be. They are embracing core spiritual keys necessary for ongoing faithfulness in mission among the unreached.[24]

Scattered like "Lambs Among Wolves"

Jesus has perfect understanding of how history will progress. He is aware of the growing challenges in the earth and every factor behind them. Jesus guides His global Church to be aware, not naïve about the conflict between the Kingdom of God and powers and principalities. In Luke 10:3, while "scattering" the 72 disciples, Jesus counseled them, "Behold, I send you out as lambs among wolves." An increased number (maybe 620 million) of lay leaders and lay people "scattered" in *Level One, Level Two, and Level Three Scattering* to their local environments as well as near and distant culture unreached peoples, will stir up the spiritual hornet's nest. We are not to fear this reality but be wise in the midst of it. Every human being has real fears. Fear is a normal human emotion. We will never not fear. The consistent biblical exhortation, "Do not fear!" (used over two hundred times in Scripture) refers to not allowing natural fear to hold us back from what God has set before us. We overcome it to progress in all God has called us, never being paralyzed or hindered by fear, as is so common.

What is Jesus counseling by the phrase, "I send you out as lambs among wolves?" As we are "scattered," we are to be aware of the enemy's schemes, asking the Lord to reveal entrapments, snares, and pitfalls set for us. There is a growing betrayal culture globally that will only increase as Jesus revealed in Matthew 24:9–10. The enemy will seek to use this to devour believers' finances, property, and organizations through litigation in hostile environments. Slander will increase. How do we respond to these attacks? Jesus gives the answer—as a lamb among wolves! A lamb represents gentleness and total dependence on another. We are aware of hostility in "scattering," yet face it with courage and dependence as a lamb, with wisdom and shrewdness, not blindness and naivete.

Training for Message Bearer Teams

A crucial aspect of "scattering" is the needed training of message bearer teams, particularly in *Level Two and Level Three Scattering*. A few years ago, while seeking direction about where things were heading in cross-cultural mission, the Lord provided some insights. These were in context of two natural events that spoke of the potential closing of a global mission era. The first was the selling of the historic campus of the US Center for World Mission (now Frontier Ventures) in Pasadena, California, and the second was the merger of Fuller Seminary's School of Theology and School of Intercultural Studies into one, no longer providing a distinct (and globally leading) seminary emphasis in frontier, global mission to the unreached.

The US Center for World Mission, founded by Ralph Winter, symbolized cutting-edge missiology reaching the frontier peoples of the world, from the 1970s to present. As did Fuller's School of Intercultural Studies, with its lineup of top missiology professors and international students from 1965 until 2015. Both institutions represented the highest caliber training of missiologists and strategic practitioners in mission.

These two events seemed to reveal the end of an era in the mission movement dominated by US-based academic mission understanding.[25] They spoke of the passing of a torch from an American education base to a growing global mission movement from every nation. I believe the USA will continue to greatly serve the mission movement. But something has shifted as epicenters of global mission are changing. The mission force will increase from traditional mission receiving nations in Africa, South America, and Asia. It is not difficult to foresee these becoming significant global mission centers in time. This is a major reason my family was led to be based outside of North America since 2007—first in Turkey and now in Chiang Mai, Thailand, a significant mission hub. Additionally, it appears the previous hyperacademic leaning of mission training is giving way to practical, hands-on, experiential training, depending on God and His power. This shift is part of God "changing the face of global mission."

Obviously, mission training will continue to include intellectual understanding of core elements needed as message bearers, yet be increasingly adapted to the global south, experiential learning styles. Effective, adequate training is essential, where the battle in global mission is won or lost, yet is not meant to be overly focused on institutions of higher learning. These have generally reflected the "professional missionary" model instead of the widespread "scattering" model of large numbers of lay leaders and lay people as message bearer teams. Instead, mission training should be accessible to all believers at the local ministry level in *Level One, Two, and Three Scattering*.

Training and mission education will increasingly take place through a growing number of informal and nonformal specialized schools and courses as well as the myriad of expanding online opportunities. In today's interconnected world, almost everyone globally has online access to such training. These will become more available in the mother tongue languages of those being scattered as English becomes eclipsed as the lingua franca of mission.

***

The Lord is bringing change to the global Church's traditional ideas of "sending missionaries." God seems to have a widespread plan of "scattering," using one-fourth of all believers globally (good seeds), who are producing fruit, in *Level One, Level Two, and Level Scattering*—potentially 620 million people. Of these 620 million globally, might the Spirit compel 20 percent into *Level Two and Level Three Scattering*—124 million believers, as message bearers among near and distant culture unreached peoples. But what are these faithful, fruitful message bearers doing among the unreached? Does God have a specific ministry strategy to bring about the greatest measure of fruit possible? The answer is a resounding yes! Let's look at this in detail in the next chapter.

17

Cultivating Church Planting Movements

In part 4, we have already seen the Holy Spirit's strategy of fulfilling the Great Commission begins with local ministries becoming ablaze as Mission Mobilization Movements, aligning with their core identity as God's multiplying, missionary people. Local ministries and larger structures are mobilized to implement core principles within. In time this produces a significant scattering effect among members, where disciples are compelled outward by the Spirit at various levels. Some 20 percent of local ministry members are potentially crossing cultural barriers to unreached peoples (either near or distant) in *Level Two and Level Three Scattering*. But what exactly is their goal? What is their strategy among the unreached? Clearly teaching local ministries this crucial strategy of the Spirit is an important aspect of mission mobilization.

This one issue has a great deal to do with whether the global Church is successful in global, cross-cultural mission or not. It is often assumed the kind of ministry done in cross-cultural mission doesn't matter. Yet the biblical model Paul used in church planting was specific, purposeful. He didn't merely do random ministry, hoping for the best. Paul had a strategic plan, given by the Holy Spirit, and is the same plan we have today.[1]

THE PRIMARY TASK OF CROSS-CULTURAL MISSION

It is common for message bearers to see evangelism as the goal of mission, a few people from a subculture of an unreached people group coming to Jesus. While evangelism is a necessary component of the process, our task is broader. Seeing simple churches multiplied to the extent there is a spiritually vital, Bible-believing church within a 15-minute walk of every unreached person on the planet is the task. To accomplish this grand plan, we come back to the New Testament. Taking our cues from the Spirit-led plan laid out in Scripture.

We suggest in this chapter that multiplying church planting movements among unreached peoples is the primary task of cross-cultural mission.[2] Ralph Winter states, "It has become steadily clearer to me that the most important activity of all is the implanting of churches."[3] Multiplying church planting movements is not the primary goal, yet they provide the means to accomplish the goal itself. If people movements to Christ across all subcultures of all unreached ethnic people groups is the goal (we consider this in detail in the next chapter), then cultivating church planting movements is the means to that goal.

Potentially millions of message bearer teams[4] scattered to near or distant cultures take up the primary task of seeing church planting movements developed across their target unreached subculture. An often-used description for the same concept is disciple making movements. We prefer calling them church planting movements, as we've established the global Church, made up of millions of individual local churches, is God's vehicle for the Great Commission. Thus, churches multiplying churches is at the core of God's mission strategy. Obviously, churches are made up of disciples making disciples, but the vehicle is reproducing churches, representing the one universal, global Church. Multiplying churches speaks of community, while multiplying disciples speaks of individuality. The means God has apparently set up to "disciple all ethnic peoples" are simple, culturally relevant, Spirit-filled, reproducing churches.

It could be said ministry activities ought to be measured by whether they contribute to planting churches in neighborhoods, office buildings, apartment high rises, across a town or city. If evangelism, the purpose is gathering people into simple churches. If teaching English, the goal is gathering them into simple churches. If hospital work, gathering these into simple churches. If anti-trafficking, those worked with brought into contact with simple churches. There are many potential ministry activities within a targeted subculture. They are not ends in themselves, but means for simple churches being developed village to village, neighborhood by neighborhood, apartment high rise by apartment high rise in a systematic way.

A criticism of the church planting emphasis is Jesus Himself didn't plant churches, so why should we? This overlooks Jesus' purpose during His three years of ministry. Jesus came to inaugurate the Kingdom of God, bringing it near, for all to experience. His ministry mainly trained the disciples who would become apostles, empowered to change the world after His ascension. Jesus focused primarily on Israel, the Jews, while following His ascension and the coming of the Spirit, the door was thrown open to the Gentiles, the nations. Following Pentecost, church planting is seen as the primary ministry method. This pattern has not ceased today.

Planting Simple, Culturally Relevant Churches Everywhere

In chapter 15 we looked at Bobby Clinton's five commitments of movements. The fourth commitment is essential as we consider church planting movements. A "commitment to participate in a non-bureaucratic, cell-group organization."[5] Church planting movements don't reproduce a denominational brand or church network format. Instead they multiply simple, cell-group type fellowships of believers culturally relevant to the target subculture which reproduce within the subculture. The structure continues, even after a potential whole village or neighborhood has been baptized. David Lim asserts, "It is this small group, intimate dynamic that anchors believers in quality discipleship through family style devotions, prayer and spiritual interaction on a daily basis."[6]

Each simple church is developed in a culturally relevant way to the specific subculture targeted—religious worldview, social class, socioeconomic status, education level, and more. These fellowships do not look identical to one another or a home "church." Multiplied in adaptive ways, meeting the cultural situation of the people, relevant in appearance, worship style and music, expression, and communication style to the people's subculture. Disciple making trainer, David Watson, confirms they lay down particular forms of worship, prayer, preaching, service schedules, forms of church government, sense of time, culturally ethnic taboos the Bible is silent on and anything not a nonnegotiable element of church.[7] A mistake in mission history has been the tendency to plant churches appearing foreign to the local people, wondering why indigenous people don't seem interested.

A common excuse in global mission is little fruitfulness is the result of the resistance of the people. While this plays a role amid certain people groups globally, it may serve the global Church better to ask if our ministry methods, particularly in church planting, have some fatal flaw within a people group. Though 2,000 years removed from the apostolic method of the New Testament, it is necessary to apply its principles to all our modern mission efforts. Let's consider the apostolic church planting model for today.

The Acts 19 Phenomenon

Acts 19:8–10 is a startling passage, providing results of Paul's apostolic church planting model. We introduced it in the last chapter. Paul was in Ephesus, where he spent three years. It was the longest he spent in any city during his entire ministry. He began teaching about the Kingdom of God in a synagogue according to his usual custom when coming to a new city. But when some of the Jews turned against him, he departed. Tradition holds Tyrannus was a wealthy believer in Ephesus who offered a building he owned to Paul to use for ministry training among the various house churches spread across Ephesus. "Reasoning together daily" (v. 9) meant teaching, training, casting vision, rooting them in God's Word and ways of the Kingdom. The last statement of the passage (v. 10) is the startling piece: "And this continued for two years, so that all who dwelt in Asia heard the word of the Lord Jesus, both Jews and Greeks."

How did Paul's training of believers in Ephesus result in Luke confidently stating all who dwelled across Asia Minor (modern day Turkey, Greece, Syria, Israel, and Palestine) heard the word of the Lord in two short years? This was a significant miracle based on apostolic principles. Only making sense if we understand Paul's training in Ephesus being focused on church planting. Apparently, Paul's ministry base was the first church planting training school, scattering message bearer teams from the church at Ephesus all over Asia Minor, multiplying church planting movements. Most believers today assume Paul himself did the church planting. This is not supported by Scripture. Paul was not superhuman. Instead he trained message bearers in church planting principles, and they implemented them everywhere they went. Disciples scattered from the church at Ephesus multiplying churches.

We know from Paul's epistles, and the book of Revelation, many of the churches across Asia Minor were never visited by Paul. He didn't start them and never physically visited them himself. The gospel exploded across Asia Minor through deliberate church planting teams scattered from the church at Ephesus who learned the apostolic method from Paul. Through their efforts the gospel was accelerated across Asia Minor, reaching all the unreached of that day in that region. A staggering feat!

Part of our difficulty is understanding planting churches through modern lenses. The modern understanding of "church" limits our ability to cooperate with the Holy Spirit's strategy. Some have even said the modern model of "church" could be the greatest stumbling block to the fulfillment of the Great Commission. It looks impossible to plant a church among the unreached like what many of us are familiar with in our home countries.

A Definition of Church Planting Movements

What, then, is a church planting movement? David Garrison, author of the seminal work on church planting movements, defines it as a rapid reproduction of culturally relevant, simple churches which reproduce themselves over and over within a subculture of an overarching unreached ethnic people group.[8] In other words, they are disciple making movements where obedient disciples make obedient disciples within the context of reproducing churches reproducing churches. They make Jesus known in the heart language of the local people, making Him real among their cultural worldview and understanding, transforming lives, relationships, and communities. As one church planting trainer says, "Our goal is not only the multiplication of churches or numbers of believers, our goal is to see transformation!"[9]

Such movements keep in mind planting many churches within a particular subculture of an ethnic people, not one single church. For example, working toward one hundred churches will progress a message bearer team toward this even if not necessarily reaching the goal.[10] The planting of one church may have as its goal to grow to be a large megachurch. This is not the apostolic model. Instead one church within a subculture grows to fifty or one hundred people, then multiplies with several families scattered to another part of town, neighborhood or apartment building where there are no churches. The reproduction of churches is constantly in mind. The goal is never a megachurch but the multiplying of small, mobile, simple, local churches across a people group. This was the New Testament model and how churches spread so widely in the first century. They are not reliant on buildings, paid leaders or other elaborate elements added to a "church."

The Holy Spirit is inspiring the implementation of this apostolic model all over the world. For example, in the Muslim nation of Indonesia 1,200 small, simple, reproducible churches were planted using this model. In a particular unreached ethnic people group within a nation in the Horn of Africa there were six known believers. Within a seven-year time period 2,500 small churches were planted having an average of 30 believers each.[11]

What Church Planting Is Not: Denominational Reproduction

Church planting movements are not denominational reproduction or developing a church branch. Denominational ministry structures ought to think differently, suspending traditional church planting concepts. Church planting movements are not easily multiplied by ministry structures having significant bureaucracy in decision making, wanting the new churches to be the exact image of the denominational churches back home. They need to give way to local church elders making decisions necessary to multiply and reproduce on the ground. A reason for slow progression among unreached people groups is decisions made by head quartered leaders knowing little of a local church situation. Ministry structures lay down preconceived ideas of "church," allowing the grassroots process to take root. The new churches can be connected to the ministry structure, while not controlled by them.

Church Planting Movements in Hostile Circumstances

Church planting movements often emerge in hostile, difficult, persecuted situations. Not unlike the early Church in the New Testament under the oppressive Roman Empire and jealous Jewish leaders, despising the new faith. Difficult governmental or religious systems among unreached peoples is not a reason to believe church planting movements cannot take place. God loves to work His greatest miracles in such circumstances. It is God's will to break open all presently hostile unreached peoples through the multiplication of rapid reproduction church planting movements, just as He did across the Roman Empire of the first century. In fact, some of the most spiritually healthy church planting movements happen in these environments because persecution weeds out the uncommitted and those with ulterior motives. Oppressive situations purify the churches, serving their rapid reproduction in an ongoing way.

Because multiplying church planting movements is a key strategy of the Spirit in fulfilling the Great Commission, it is not surprising the enemy's greatest attacks surround such efforts. Message bearer teams and new local churches are experientially engaged in spiritual warfare. Standing against evil through the victory of Christ. This is not a secondary issue. The enemy seeks to hold his ground among unreached people groups. When the body of Christ obeys Jesus, scattering message bearer teams to near and distant unreached peoples multiplying church planting movements, the hornet's nest is stirred up. We must know the schemes of Satan (2 Corinthians 2:11), spiritually resisting him in every meddling way. An aspect of multiplying church planting movements must be preparing believers for persecution, standing strong in faith against those who do not love the Kingdom of God.[12]

MULTIPLYING CHURCH PLANTING MOVEMENTS— A DELIBERATE PROCESS

Church planting movements have a deliberate process. Ministry doesn't happen by itself, without deliberate plans. We sometimes forget Paul used practical plans, given by the Spirit, recorded in the New Testament for our benefit. We cannot do better than the model provided us by the Spirit, though we rely on His leading applying the principles in different contexts. The apostolic model is not a formula, producing certain results. By implementing principles commended by the apostles, under the same Spirit's guidance, we see breakthroughs among unreached peoples.

It is possible to use the process of Jesus sending out the 12 and 72 in Matthew 10 and Luke 10 as a loose framework for church planting.[13] Many principles here were later used by the apostles in church planting efforts. A major difference being Jesus' admonition to the 12 and 72 to only go to the Jews. Whereas following His resurrection, Jesus' commission (still binding on us today) was to all the ethnic peoples of the world.

A scattered message bearer team initially targets a particular unreached people group, prayerfully considering what subculture, within that larger group, to focus on. Ethnic peoples are obviously diverse. Identify a subculture sharing age, values, interests, experiences and traditions. For example, a skater community in Yangon, Myanmar; a community of prostitutes in Kolkata, India; a particular caste of an ethnic people in Colombo, Sri Lanka; a certain academic department at a university in Bangkok, Thailand; a Somali community in Toronto, Canada; internet technology workers in Delhi, India; a high-rise apartment block in Istanbul, Turkey. As David Garrison encourages, look for responsiveness within the subculture where evidence has already shown the people are receptive to spiritual things.[14]

1. Begun and Sustained through Committed Intercessory Prayer

Once an above subculture within an overarching unreached people group is identified, bathe that subculture in prayer.[15] Pray for responsiveness, softening to the gospel, light to shine, darkness to flee, and more. Spirit-led Intercession continues throughout the entire process of church planting. Every message bearer team should be committed to daily corporate intercession for the target subculture. Some teams spend elongated time every day just in worship and intercession. In addition, consider one or two people on the team to take up the primary role of intercession. While the whole team is engaged in daily intercessory prayer, these see their primary role in the church planting effort as strategic intercession. Consider developing a prayer room onsite focused on seeking God's face day and night for the particular subculture.

2. Meeting Felt Needs—Platform Issues

Second, a message bearer team looks for felt needs among the targeted subculture community. The team should strive to be a practical blessing to the local community in some tangible way. This helps overcome barriers of mistrust toward perceived outsiders. It can also produce income for the message bearer team among the community. Maybe a small business tailoring to some specific need. The point is getting the team in contact with local people through natural relationships. This puts them in culturally understood categories to the locals. Without such contacts the team is often misunderstood, remaining on the outside of a culture.

Pray for specific felt needs coming to the surface through relationships and conversations. For example, a physical problem, a husband losing a job, a wayward son, concerns about the harvest that year, problems with a relative, being tormented by a spirit or many other felt needs. Prayer in the name of Jesus links that prayer with a potential answer. Such miracles open doors among unreached peoples as suggested by church planting trainer Jerry Trousdale.[16] These natural relationships and connections within the community lead to the third element of the deliberate process.

3. Widespread Sowing of the Gospel

A third process of the church planting movement includes sowing the gospel, through acts of love, in the target subculture. David Garrison reveals, "We have yet to see a church planting movement emerge where evangelism is rare or absent."[17] As the message bearer team seeks to meet felt needs while praying for felt needs, they also seek every opportunity for mass evangelism (when the opportunity allows for it) and personal evangelism where testimonies of the life changing power of Christ to save, heal and deliver are proclaimed and demonstrated. This is not done haphazardly, but with focus. Message bearers look for responsiveness in particular people and groups. For example, a Bible correspondence course in Turkey. Muslim Turks anonymously request a free Bible be sent to them with background teaching, showing interest, receptivity. Message bearers follow up the person, building on their receptivity. In time teams potentially even settle within their village, neighborhood, apartment block, implementing principles of church planting movements. Every oppor-

236

tunity is taken toward personal, friendship evangelism within the cultural framework. This is best done through natural relationships along relational lines in a widespread way. These are the web of people's own family relationships, drawing new believers into the community of faith. Because of this it is helpful to focus evangelism on heads of households. These are influencers among families, workplace, and more.

4. Persons of Peace

Throughout the process the team is asking God for a "person of peace." This term comes from Luke 10:6 where Jesus instructed the 72, sent out two by two. "Persons of peace" are usually key figures in the community, a crucial tool in seeing whole family conversions to Christ. They may be a prominent businessman or community elder and show signs of being hungry for spiritual things. Through building relationships, the team discerns their receptivity to the gospel. They are not a believer yet, but are exhibiting desire to learn about Jesus, open to spiritual discussions. "Persons of peace" are the initial extension of the message bearer team into the community. The Spirit's plan is always for message bearers to work through "persons of peace" because they are part of the subculture community. The message bearer team are outsiders, from a near or distant culture. Working through the "person of peace" enables the gospel to take root within that community, not as a foreign entity. The vision is constant throughout. Wanting to see family conversions (web of relatives connected to the head of household) through the person of peace over time. This is the basic step to village and tribal conversions through contextual evangelism. The person of peace in time is the best evangelist to share their faith (from house to house) with their community as insiders (and not as outcasts).

5. Studying the Bible Together

As the relationship deepens, the "person of peace" is invited to study the Bible one on one with one of the team members. They are still not followers of Jesus. If possible, invite one or two of their close friends (also showing receptivity to spiritual discussions) to join you. Through periodic meetings, take them through phases one and two of the gospel of the Kingdom.[18] Opening the Bible and reading verses, discussing the key ideas and concepts, lays the foundation to grasp the gospel, what it is, why it is necessary and how to respond to it. As Jerry Trousdale asserts, the key is inviting obedience to what is understood.[19] Depending on the individual, this process could take significant time. Message bearers are now "discipling" "persons of peace" before they come to faith in Jesus by making the gospel relevant to their worldview, helping change their paradigm.[20]

While "discipling" this person or small group, invite a wider circle of their relationships to study the Bible. The "person of peace" invites close, personal relationships.[21] Research reveals a majority of people come to Jesus along lines of personal, trusted relationships. We will consider this more in the next chapter. A "person of peace" is influential in the community, particularly among their family, neighborhood, or village. They host a small group in their home interested in studying the Bible, learning what it says and how to obey it. Most unbelievers (even unreached peoples) assume they know what the Bible says, but actually have never considered it or had it read to them. Providing opportunity to meet in a safe, comfortable environment of their own is often a key in their coming to salvation. Together, work through the author's *Proclaiming the Kingdom* book or another suitable, foundation providing series of Bible studies.[22] Through these methods unbelievers are gathering together, studying the Bible and then coming to Jesus over time. This step by step process typically is reversed in ministry. We prematurely seek to win them to Jesus, before laying necessary groundwork overcoming generations of biased worldview against faith in Christ, and then invite them to gather. It is no wonder it rarely works.

6. Discipling before They Are Born Again

Maybe by this time a "person of peace" has come to Jesus, but not necessarily so. The process is a journey together, regularly considering what the Bible actually says, grasping foundational information and encouraging obedience. People from a Hindu, Muslim, Buddhist background have a completely different worldview. Much time must be spent overturning false outlooks, understandings, ways of thinking, showing the relevance of Jesus and how the gospel is superior to their worldviews. This is not done through argument, but through their own seeing of Scripture, discussing it together. The Holy Spirit thrusts His Word into the hearts and minds of human beings.

At each meeting the opportunity is given for each person to respond to Jesus by believing in Him, providing some detail of what this means. This is what *Phase Two* of the gospel of the Kingdom details.[23] Adequate time is given to helping each person understand the "new birth" and what it entails. This small group Bible study in time begins to have people becoming believers, choosing to follow Jesus. They are shown they are not changing religions but making Jesus Lord of their lives. By this time hopefully the "person of peace" has done so. Potentially the whole group together chooses to follow Jesus. These are "people movements to Christ."[24]

7. Becoming a Small, Simple Church

Once several Bible study participants are becoming believers, that small group is ready to become a simple church. Often the group is made up of the "persons of peace" family and relatives, co-workers in their company or fellow students at university. The message bearer team teaches about baptism as soon as possible following a declaration of faith. It should not be delayed.[25] Baptism is best done in groups coming to Jesus together. The majority of churches related to church planting movements are small churches of five to thirty people, often meeting in a home.[26] They are committed to regular, even daily, family devotions, influencing one another with truths from Scripture (Deuteronomy 6:5–9) as the most basic root of spiritual growth and discipleship. Each newly developed simple church should be self-propagated by the locals (not merely by the message bearer team) and is usually quite informal. They are the best leaders of the new local ministry. When led indefinitely by outsiders, the church planting movement easily becomes stagnant.

8. Emerging Local Leadership

Local leadership of the new church emerges from the local community. The "person of peace" is usually a respected, credible leader in the community. The message bearer team, from the beginning of the initial Bible study, has asked God to raise up leaders for the coming church, looking for natural leaders within the community, having a good reputation and credibility.

The message bearer team is aware of the biblical qualifications of leaders, focused on inner life, character issues and secondarily giftedness.[27] The new leaders follow the elder and deacon model of the New Testament churches. Most unreached people groups have communal cultures, preferring to lead by group and committee, instead of one individual pastor. It is common in church planting movements to appoint an elder committee for a new simple church, even up to seven leaders.[28]

The emerging leaders have come to Jesus, watching the message bearer facilitate the Bible studies. Along the way the message bearer team stops coming to the meetings themselves, mentoring the elders in the background. During regular times of mentoring, the emerging leader and message bearer go over the Bible portions the church will discuss at the next meeting. Message bearers share insights about the passage, empowering the emerging leader to guide the discussion with the new church group. It is helpful to guide the new elders with a mapped out, systematic approach to teaching the foundations of faith to the new church. The new leaders are not seminary trained. They need equipping resources to guide the new local church while always looking to God, trusting in Him as they grow in hearing His voice and receiving revelation. These resources may take the form of predeveloped Bible studies or laid out truths of the Christian faith.[29] It is common to have online training along this line available in their heart languages. Paul's letters to the churches helped the new elders as the new churches relied on oral telling of the gospel, before it was available in written form.

It is necessary for the message bearer team to affirm local leadership as the church's authority, remaining in the background themselves. This enables a local church to become truly indigenous from the outset. This is what Paul did with the New Testament churches. On average he spent five or so months helping root them in foundations of their faith and appointing qualified local leaders to oversee the churches. He then left them to develop and grow through their own experiences. Paul remained in close contact via letters yet allowed churches to grow into maturity through their own development, not doing the work for them.

The emerging leader(s) are not paid by the church. That may come later but most church planting movements globally are led by bivocational lay leaders with a level of respect within the subculture community.[30] The leaders identify with the local community because they are one of them. This is essential for reproduction of the new church across the subculture.

9. Next Steps

The question inevitably rises if the new church should look like other traditional churches within the subculture, people group or country. Most often, traditional churches have been influenced heavily by the West, failing to be enculturated. The final outcome of church planting movements is usually a different expression of Christian faith among the local people. The churches look less like the churches where the message bearer teams are sent from and more like the socioreligious culture they are planted in.

Other churches have a worship team, should we as well? Others line up their chairs in rows, should we? Others pray in a particular way, should we teach our members to look like that when they pray too? Ideally, these questions are answered by the new church elders and leaders, not the message bearer team.[31] By searching Scripture related to core elements of biblical churches they come to biblical, Spirit-led conclusions.

A big question is where the new church should meet? Again, this is a question for the new group to answer, while not bringing economic difficulty to the new church. From the beginning, the new church should be aware of their ability to sustain itself. They should also be thinking of the future when they multiply new churches. How will their example impact the future, multiplied churches? If a new church rents a building, the reproduced churches will think this is the standard way to reproduce, pressured to rent a building as well. There is obviously nothing wrong with renting a building, but when doing so hinders the multiplication of a church planting movement, a major problem has arisen. Church planting movement churches typically meet in a member's home, a meeting room of an apartment high rise, a meeting room of an office building where a member works, in a common space connected to a particular neighborhood or the like.

Believers in the new church are immediately encouraged to reach out along their web of relationships, sowing seeds of the gospel, by declaring what Jesus has done for them.[32] They may not yet be rooted in Scripture, but are sharing whatever they know and have experienced. Particularly how God has directly impacted their lives, showing He is real. They invite inquirers and seekers to start small Bible studies just as was done initially among them.

It is good practice to immediately get the new church giving tithes and offerings. Not primarily for the new church having funds, but each family learning to trust God, stewarding what God has given, filled with gratitude. How believers handle money speaks volumes of their discipleship. The funds can be initially budgeted in a simple way consisting of four categories: (1) global mission (2) church planting (3) giving to the poor (4) church-related needs. These funds allow the new church to discern how to use them according to the Spirit's leading in their local setting.[33] The elders teaching God's Word can be given special gifts from the "church-related needs" category (Galatians 6:6). This should not be seen as a salary as the most effective model is emerging leadership remaining bivocational.

10. Local Churches Reproducing

From the beginning of the church being planted, they are looking to reproduce. This should be considered in another neighborhood, apartment high rise or area of town of the same subculture community of the unreached people group. As well as geographically further away, potentially among a different subculture of the same unreached ethnic people. The same process of a Mission Mobilization Movement (see chapter 10) should be happening among this new church. The gospel includes teaching this core theme in Scripture and new churches need to be rooted in that DNA. All church members consider their web of relationships for direct evangelism, while 15 percent in time sense God leading them outward to near cultures, while an additional 5 percent to further distant cultures. A spiritually healthy church, unencumbered by outside, controlling authority, will be producing church members, disciples, compelled by the Spirit in this fashion.

This is different from street witnessing and other non-community-based evangelism. These approaches do not allow the gospel to spread naturally along relational lines of family, friends, co-workers, or university classmates. When rapid reproduction does not happen, it is often because church members do not feel freedom to share on their own, thinking they need the message bearer or other outsider, who is more knowledgeable, to do the work for them. The initial local church members must believe multiplication is natural, not requiring outside aids to start new churches. They are empowered to reach the lost, naturally drawing them to new churches.

The elders of the initial church appoint and train new elders and deacons just as they had been empowered themselves. They themselves are able to do this, not relying on an external body to do it for them. The freedom of reproduction within the unreached community is the key to ongoing multiplication movements of new churches. Newly identified and appointed leaders participate in on-the-job training, learning from the elders by doing. They are not taken away to Bible school elsewhere but get the hands-on training necessary by staying within their new leadership situation. With the development of online Bible schools and programs of late, this has become more realistic than ever before.

***

The big picture goal is a spiritually vital, vibrant, Bible believing local church within a 15-minute walk of every person on the planet. Across major cities, there are simple churches within every high-rise apartment building, neighborhood, office building, and more. Within smaller towns, there is a local ministry for every 300 or so people. This is a huge undertaking and where the Holy Spirit is leading the global Church.

In addition, a growing percentage within subcultures of ethnic people groups are coming to Jesus, becoming believers. Growing from less than 2 percent of believers within the unreached ethnic group's population, to upward of 15–20 percent of that population believing and obeying Jesus. Though hindered by spiritual powers of darkness, God desires to reveal Jesus to all Hindu, Muslim, and Buddhist peoples, bringing transformation. Through His global Church, God seeks to banish darkness, releasing exceedingly light in the midst of unreached peoples. This is where the Spirit is taking His Church. Mobilizing and equipping local ministries to multiply church planting movements is a key purpose of mission mobilization.

18

Igniting People Movements to Christ

We saw in the last chapter the primary task of global, cross-cultural mission—multiplying church planting movements. Now we consider details of the overarching goal of church planting movements—igniting people movements to Christ. Church planting movements are the task of global mission, while multitudes of people movements to Christ among every subculture of every unreached ethnic people are the goal of mission. All "global mission" activities ought to be evaluated by whether or not they propel us toward these two ends. In addition, mission mobilization should empower God's people to see people movements to Christ ignited among unreached peoples.

THE ROLE OF CULTURE

The concept of people movements to Christ[1] is new to many followers of Jesus. It can be inferred around two-thirds of those coming to Christ historically in Africa, Asia and Latin America did so through various forms of people movements. Without the influence of people movements, the masses of believers on these continents would likely look different and be considerably weaker.

They did not come into the Kingdom in isolation, one here another there, but by communities. Robert Recker suggests, "God has been discipling the peoples. For every one out of a new people brought to Christian faith from his group, God has converted hundreds in chains of families. He has used the People Movement. This is the normal way by which the Christian churches have grown."[2]

The global Church has become overly familiar with the Western influence of individualism concerning people coming to faith in Jesus. Westerners tend to act for themselves, apart from consulting neighbors or families. Resulting in habits of independent decision-making.[3] Western church culture historically reinforced this streak of independence through evangelism focusing on individual decisions. This has been taken so far as to assume individual decisions to follow Christ are more sincere if going against family and other relational ties. This is a highly problematic presupposition, not based in Scripture or most cultures of the world. The non-Western, majority worldview possesses a group orientation. An individual is not an independent unit, but part of a group. Decisions are made communally, influenced by what the family chooses, not merely the individual. As highly social beings, humans were created for community life.[4]

Message bearer teams multiplying church planting movements among Hindu, Buddhist, and Muslim peoples, incarnate this core life perspective of those they are reaching. This includes cultural recognition that individual decisions are often seen as betrayal. In communal cultures, only a rebel would decide something alone, apart from discussing with family and friends. As Paul Hiebert asserts "business choices, who to marry, personal problems are settled within the group. The vast majority of the world lives with this engrained cultural worldview."[5]

Several years ago, I was in Kolkata, India, teaching seminars among Indian church and mission leaders. Out for dinner one evening, I had a sobering yet insightful conversation with a key Indian mission leader. He shared his concern over the difficulty of reaching India for Christ, suggesting traditional evangelism alone would not be enough. He told me how his Indian mission organization had targeted several villages for evangelism. They did weekend crusades, door-to-door preaching, and more. Months went by, and he planned some renovation work on his house. Surprisingly, day workers showed up who were from a village where the evangelism had taken place. Yet none of the young men had any recollection of the message the organizational teams had brought. They certainly recalled the team itself and the events. But the message had had no impact whatsoever. This left the leader visibly discouraged, even distraught. He then lifted his eyes to me, suggesting, "You know what I think the only solution for India is? People movements to Christ among entire families, villages, neighborhoods, places of work and many other subcultures sharing interests, socioeconomic level, age, and common life experiences."[6] I have come to wholeheartedly agree with his conviction. Not only for India, but for all unreached peoples.

GOD USES CULTURE

Utilizing this innate part of human makeup, the Holy Spirit often draws people to Jesus in communities, not one by one. Yet as S. D. Ponraj affirms from his early missionary experience in rural India, "We had not been instructed (in missionary training) how to handle group conversion movements to Christ, though we had several experiences like these."[7] Seeing unreached peoples reached means breaking up the larger group into subcultural units of people sharing age, likes, traditions, customs, and language. Then targeting each individual subculture through church planting movements, providing opportunity for the community to come to Jesus in small groups. Repeating this process across the subcultures of the unreached people group, results in reaching many more people than through an individualistic approach.

Subcultures of unreached peoples often come to Jesus through a chain reaction of group decisions where church planting movements are being initiated as documented among several Muslim communities in Jerry Trousdale's inspiring book *Miraculous Movements*.[8] People movements to Christ move through the web of relationships (often blood lines) where small groups (sometimes nuclear families) decide to follow Jesus. The process is most effective when a respected person from the community becomes a follower of Jesus, with a transformation visible to all, sharing how this change took place. The witness of those within their own community who have been powerfully impacted is often a trigger of a people movement. Believers (even spiritually immature ones) within the subculture are a powerful force in bringing others to decide together for Christ. The fact that they are like them in background, education, age, and perspective is a motivating tool for a group deciding for Christ.[9]

In individualistic societies, people have freedom to make choices other members of the group don't want to make. In non-Western, communal cultures, this is more difficult. When evangelism has an individualistic bent within these cultures, it typically means only the marginalized respond to the gospel. A common conclusion is the people are resistant to the gospel. Though potentially true, it is more likely the approach didn't resonate with their cultural worldview. Global mission is riddled with this problem, with few questioning the approach.

WHAT ARE PEOPLE MOVEMENTS?

First let's define what is meant by "people." In this context people means a tribe, caste, or specific ethnic group, a tightly knit segment of any society. The people may be extended family, a clan, or a tight knit village sharing ethnic background and culture. "Movement" means these "people" are moving into the body of Christ, becoming followers of Jesus. According to the "father of the Church Growth movement," Donald McGavran, "a people movement results from the joint decision of a number of individuals all from the same people group, enabling them to become Christians without social dislocation, while remaining in full contact with their non-Christian relatives, thus enabling other segments of their people group, across the years, after suitable instruction, to come to similar decisions, joining churches made up of members of the same subculture of people."[10] In simpler terms, McGavran says people movements are "a mass transfer of loyalties" to Jesus.[11] Robert Recker explains, "We are speaking of a multiple shift of people from one religious allegiance to another, and that this transfer of loyalties takes place not one by one, but in concert."[12]

This appears to be the most natural way subcultures of ethnic peoples come to Christ within most communal culture unreached peoples, finding it difficult to do so any other way.[13] People movements are not necessarily significant numbers becoming Christians. They are not mass movements. It is common among people movements for small groups in sequence to come to faith in Jesus, being instructed and baptized together. Sometimes this occurs quickly and sometimes not. One small group this week, another next month, and so on. McGavran ventures to say that "the figure of 50% or more rate of growth per decade is indicative of the presence of a people movement."[14]

People movements are typically the result of an extensive process of hearing of the gospel over a period of time. They don't tend to spring up in a vacuum. This is why we can have great faith for a massive harvest among today's unreached people groups. Many have had the gospel communicated in various ways over decades and even centuries. They have heard teaching and preaching about Jesus, seen books, tracts, or clips of YouTube videos. Maybe even opened and read a bit from a Bible. Yet with little immediate fruit. However, a tipping point may be coming, needing the right circumstances and environment for those who have heard, yet not yet believed, to become ripe to now believe in faith, through people movements to Christ among them.

Internet, social media, satellite TV, and other tools of the globalized world are also providing unreached peoples examples of what followers of Jesus are like, what a church is and seeing testimonies of how Jesus transforms lives. These messages are all accessible now in private (in the confines of a home), where no one hostile will see them searching for content about what it means to know Jesus. Though generally these bits of information are not enough to bring people to saving faith in Christ, they are used to whet their appetite, preparing unreached peoples to come to Jesus given the right circumstances. Coming into contact with message bearer teams multiplying church planting movements, as we saw in the last chapter, is often where focused understanding of Christ is experienced. In a trusted relationship context, questions can be asked and clear, biblically based answers offered. People movements to Christ most often take place in the context of a targeted church planting movement dynamically connected to proclaiming the gospel of the Kingdom.[15]

It is necessary to remember unreached people groups are so for a reason. They are often steeped in a religious worldview passed down by multitudes of generations. It often takes time during the discipling phase to help groups move along the road of putting off the old way of thinking and behaving and coming under the authority of Jesus. As McGavran taught, "in the discipling phase they may not yet be believers, but hearing the message and grasping what that reorientation might look like."[16] They are often counting the cost as a group of what such a decision will look like. Their lives showing evidence of the change is not the goal of the discipling phase. Instead, the goal is helping them understand the message, open their hearts, and begin making the switch of loyalties to Christ and to the Bible, preparing to cross over to the Kingdom of God. Spiritual and ethical change and growth takes place during the teaching phase once they are a follower of Jesus in the Kingdom of God.

A COMMON CONCERN

Resistance to the people movement concept surrounds it being interpreted to mean individuals within the group do not have saving faith leading to salvation. In reality, it is necessary for every individual within the group to personally believe in Jesus to become a believer. They are truly becoming a follower of Jesus, not merely changing external or religious affiliation. God is not interested in more religious Christian adherents, but multitudes of true disciples of Christ. The influence of people movements to Christ depends on true experience with Jesus of becoming a believer across the movement itself.

People movements are not "group conversion" of which there really is no such thing. Individuals have a mind, soul, and spirit with which to make choices. Yet individuals make up groups, which together do make decisions. Each individual within the group must come face to face with Jesus, believing in Him as God made flesh, taking their sin upon Himself, being regenerated, turning away from the old life and embracing Jesus' Kingdom ways.

Yet they do so together as a family unit, a village, a subculture of skaters in Yangon, Myanmar, or a group of IT workers in Bangalore, India. They each individually hear the gospel over and over, talk about it as a group, mull it within their hearts, deciding whether they should proceed with following Jesus as a way of life. They do this in intimate relationship with each other, taking the step in connection with others doing so as well. Because of the relationships involved, the decision to follow Jesus is at times deferred to wait for other family members or close-knit relations moving in the direction, but not there yet. When done together, decisions to follow Christ are strengthened and enhanced.

This is the testimony of a present church planting movement in central Thailand that has produced a people movement to Christ among Thai people, being called "the fastest growing church in Thailand's history."[17] "The Free in

Jesus Christ Church Association (FJCCA) was a relatively small network of churches until the pivotal movement during Christmas in 2016. Due to the passing of the King of Thailand, the large Christmas event which had been planned had to be cancelled. So instead of having a big Christmas gathering in the main town, they decided to go to the surrounding villages to hold smaller evangelism events in 17 villages. "As a result, more than 5,000 people heard the gospel and 700 people became believers and 17 house churches were started."[18] "In a country where church growth has been slow over the last 200 years there have been 7,100 new believers in the past year alone." They have seen explosive growth "in a manner similar to the early church in Acts."[19]

In a people movement, members of the close-knit group encourage those they love with what they have found in Christ. This influence is contagious and is the natural response of the human heart finding its home in Jesus. In communal cultures, this contagious aspect of the gospel running swiftly (2 Thessalonians 3:1) along relationship lines is central to people movements. To see groups brought to faith in Jesus together, it is necessary not to take individual believers out of the community. This common practice produces unnecessary antagonism as onlookers observe Christians appearing to influence their people to follow a foreign God. It creates barriers to the wider reception of the gospel among the community. Communities come to Jesus when a movement toward Christ occurs across the society.

PEOPLE MOVEMENTS IN SCRIPTURE

Anchoring the concept of people movements to Christ among unreached peoples, it is necessary to consider it from Scripture. Donald McGavran affirms the New Testament reveals how large subcultures of one ethnic people, Jews, chose to follow Jesus. He tells how that new community of Jesus followers produced subgroups of Jesus followers among other, often very different people groups.[20] These biblical accounts are thrilling to all who care about the gospel crossing cultures as well as caring how subcultures become followers of Jesus. The majority of New Testament churches were planted similar to the church planting movement method of the previous chapter, producing people movements to Christ among the culture and society. Thus,

250

the New Testament model is supremely instructive in cross-cultural mission today.

A People Movement among the Jews (Acts 2–7)

The birth of the Church on the day of Pentecost was a powerful people movement to Christ. While there were people from many ethnic backgrounds in Jerusalem at Pentecost—Parthians, Medes, Elamites, Mesopotamia, etc. (Acts 2:9–11)—they were all devout Jews (Acts 2:5), grafted into Judaism through circumcision. Though not representative of one ethnic people group, they were representative of one "people"—the Jews, possessing significant group identity as the "chosen people." The Holy Spirit took that group identity, using it as the foundation to launch the Church and world Christian movement. The three thousand coming to faith on the day of Pentecost were all Jews. For a few years (the time period between Acts 2–7) the Jerusalem church was made up of one like-minded people—Jews.

Let's consider the progression among the Jews, seeing the people movement to Christ.[21] In the upper room there were about 120 believers (Acts 1:15). To this group were added 3,000 men (with their wives and children this group was closer to 8,000) (Acts 2:41) on the day of Pentecost itself (one day). These 3,000 Jews, from so many ethnic backgrounds, would have taken word back to their hometowns, proclaiming the strange yet wonderful things happening in Jerusalem. Later in the New Testament we find churches in the towns and regions represented in Jerusalem at Pentecost. Yet Peter, Paul, nor any other apostle ever visited those places. What happened? People movements to Christ, among relatives and communities, initiated by the 3,000 new believers from so many diverse ethnic backgrounds. In the entire Mediterranean region, the interconnected web of relationships was such that in almost every Jewish synagogue, family members affirmed they had relatives who were Jewish followers of Jesus (the New Way).

In Acts 5:14, following the Ananias and Sapphira incident, we read, "And believers were increasingly added to the Lord, multitudes of both men and women." Acts 6:7 records, "The number of the disciples multiplied greatly in Jerusalem, and a great many of the priests were obedient to the faith." Most scholars agree that about four years (AD 30–34) transpired between the day of Pentecost in Acts 2 and the martyrdom of Stephen in Acts 7.[22] The Jerusalem church, all Jewish people, experienced an impressive people movement to Christ during that four-year timeframe, eventually bursting beyond the confines of Jerusalem itself.

People Movements in Judea, Galilee, and Samaria (Acts 8–12)

Starting in Acts 8, the church in Jerusalem was forced outward from Jerusalem by the persecution of Saul. This event was orchestrated by God to push the now comfortable Jerusalem churches to recall Jesus' final words to scatter outward (Acts 1:8).[23] God often uses pain and adversity to waken His people to the focal point of the Kingdom and His own purposes in their generation. In Acts 8 the people movement among the Jews now spread to initiate a people movement among the Samaritans. Acts 8:5 tells us Philip went to Samaria (a Jewish subculture who were despised because they were half Jewish while involved in paganism) where "the multitudes with one accord heeded the things spoken by Philip, hearing and seeing the miracles he did" (Acts 8:6). Luke specifies in Acts 8:12, "both men and women were baptized." This was significant as it was the first such people movement outside Jerusalem, particularly among an ostracized Jewish people.

The clear implication is many families came into the Kingdom together in Samaria. Empowering a people movement to Christ within that particular subculture of the overarching Jewish ethnic people group. Before coming to Jesus, they were related individuals, with close family and relative ties, living in community. They decided for Jesus together. This is a primary principle of people movements—they spread most rapidly among family members.[24] In most societies and cultures life revolves around family relationships. This has always been true. It should not be surprising that through this web of trust and closeness, the gospel can run freely, particularly in majority world, communal cultures.

A secondary stream of people movements is close friends and like-minded colleagues. It was rare in the New Testament, and the exception in the modern world today, that people came to faith through a random witness of a stranger. It does happen, yet the general rule is people come to Jesus through others they know, trust, and respect at some level. Working along lines of webs of family and close friend relationships is a necessary way to see people movements to Christ among subcultures of unreached people groups. This is how churches can be planted in every village, neighborhood, apartment building, and town. Bridging connections from one city we find relatives and trusted friends of those new believers in a nearby location, building on them as a foundation—our "persons of peace." It is helpful to remember this is the natural compulsion among born-again, new creation people, possessing the inexhaustible person of the Holy Spirit compelling them outward.

When larger numbers of people come to Jesus together it is more difficult for the majority people to ostracize them. When one or two marginalized, fringe people come to the Lord, it is easier for family members, and society at large, to treat them with contempt, cutting them off and boycotting their business. Yet when a group decides to follow Jesus together, they act as a protection from certain persecutions. The best answer to ostracism and mistreatment is groups of people coming into the Kingdom together.

This doesn't mean there is no need to count the cost and sometimes bear the reproach of breaking with family ties. Many in the Jewish people movement faced father or mother standing against those following the Way. But apart from the people movement spreading wildly, it would not have been possible for that individual to stand. They could appeal to other relatives, friends, and community members following Jesus, making the sacrifice that much easier overall. In addition, such groups coming to Jesus are unusual, producing a positive effect. When "multitudes" come into the Kingdom together others wonder what this is about. What have they seen and heard? Should I be following Jesus too?

The book of Acts records whole villages and family groups coming to Jesus at once. In Acts 9:31 churches in all parts of Judea, Galilee, and Samaria multiplied as they grew in the "fear of the Lord" and "the comfort of the Holy Spirit." During this time Peter was traveling throughout these regions and visited a little church of Jewish believers in Lydda. Peter was used to heal Aeneas in Lydda, where the result was, "All who dwelt in Lydda and Sharon saw him (Aeneas healed and walking around) and turned to the Lord" (Acts 9:35). All in these two villages came to Jesus that day—a significant people movement to Christ. They maintained their village social, leadership and relationship structures. They heard the stories about Jesus over the last years of His ministry, heard about His teaching and doing good through hearsay from others. They had some information to build upon, particularly for those with any Jewish background. Seeing the power of Christ in this instance, together with the pieces they had previously heard, created the conducive environment to believe in Him. Now they needed in-depth teaching of the Kingdom, which they would get, due to the emergence of a church planting movement in their region.

People Movements among the Gentiles

Through the book of Acts the Holy Spirit has given the global Church an incredible representation of people movements to Christ. Not only within the Jewish cluster but crossing into the Gentiles (non-Jews) as well. Peter was led by the Spirit in Acts 10 to interact with the Italian Roman Centurion, Cornelius, breaking down the staunchly held stigma of Jews relating with Gentiles. Cornelius invited his relatives and close friends to hear Peter (v. 24), evidently a considerable crowd as verse 27 states, "He went in and found many who had come together." In verse 44 the Holy Spirit fell upon all gathered in Cornelius' home—the implication being they chose to follow Jesus together, experiencing the Holy Spirit in practical ways. They were then baptized in water together. Cornelius' decision to follow Jesus, with relatives and close friends, might have launched a people movement among the Italian Romans through the web of family and natural relationships. Scripture does not reveal what happened following this extraordinary event. Small groups coming to faith together like this are the basis of people movements to Christ.

We have the first large scale account of a people movement among Gentile peoples in Acts 13 in Antioch.[25] Scripture does not reveal how the Gentile church in Antioch was started. It was evidently not started by Paul as he was in Tarsus at its inception. It was likely one of the Proselyte believers (Gentiles who became Jews by circumcision and took the Law) who was scattered from Jerusalem in Acts 8:1–4 (maybe Nicolas of Antioch who was one of the seven deacons in Acts 6:5) had family members and friends who believed in Jesus. They then spread the message of the Way to their Gentile friends and connections, making its way to Antioch. The international make-up of this Gentile church is significant (Acts 13:1).

254

Barnabas went to Tarsus to get Paul and brought him to Antioch, where they stayed for about a year teaching the church (Acts 11:25–26). During that year a large community of Gentiles came to Jesus in Antioch in a short time (vv. 21, 24), initiating a people movement among the Greeks. It is important to note the Gentile people movement at Antioch was not planned. It was spontaneous, ignited by believers spreading the word among their web of trusted relationships. For one year Paul was part of it, observing the grace of God at work (v. 26). Seeing the Gentile people movement at Antioch had a profound impact on Paul's understanding of his ministry calling, and eventual strategy, among the Gentiles—church planting movements igniting people movements to Christ across Asia Minor.

From the Antioch church in Acts 13, we see the first organized, planned cross-cultural mission outreach of the New Testament. The Spirit-led sending of Paul, Barnabas, and John Mark as the first ever cross-cultural mission team. The Holy Spirit had already called Paul in Galatians 1:16 and Acts 26:17, clarifying his destiny of preaching the gospel to the Gentiles. The Spirit's guidance in Acts 13 was not Paul's commissioning to ministry. But a further expression of the broad calling he already possessed.

Through Paul's experiencing unplanned people movements in Antioch, he recognized church planting principles could be used among Gentiles, in turn igniting people movements to Christ among them. It is worth noting Paul never planted churches among the Gentiles, or even saw a single Gentile convert, until after his time in Antioch. After experiencing a people movement to Christ among a Gentile (Greek) people during that year, he saw multitudes of Gentile peoples coming to Jesus in groups (Acts 13–28) as a result of his laboring and training others in church planting movement principles. During that year in Antioch, Paul developed a clear-cut, Spirit-led ministry strategy among unreached peoples that he used for years to come. His year in Antioch was pivotal.

People Movements in Mission History

Beyond the New Testament itself the concept of igniting people movements to Christ is rife throughout mission history. As Robert Recker recounts,

Stephen Neill calls attention to the first Protestant mass movement in India between 1795 and 1805 in the midst of the illiterate Nadar (Shanar) community. J. Waskom Pickett places the significant year as 1818 when three thousand Nadars were gathered in. Between 1875 and 1879 nearly 9,000 Nadar persons became Christians. There also was the Chuhra movement of the Sialkot District, the Anglican-Lutheran movements of Chota Nagpur and Assam (1860), the movement of the Madigas and other in the Telugu country (1860s), the sweeper movement in the united provinces, the Andhra Desa movement which has jumped several caste lines, the movement among the Ooriya Gras, the Santals and others. Looking farther afield we think of the Karens (1792), the Bataks (1862), and movement in Korea (1884), the movement among the mountain tribes of Taiwan where between 1929 to 1960 about 50% of the eleven different groups of Malayo-Polynesian peoples became Protestant Christians, the early growth under persecution in Madagascar (1869), the wildfire growth in Ethiopia, movements among the Ibo, Yoruba and Tiv in Nigeria, movements in Brazil, Chile and Colombia and the Naranjo people movement in Argentina, movements in Chiapas-Oaxaca, Mexico and many more. Where does one begin?[26]

All of these historical movements were people movements to Christ across a particular ethnic people group or subculture within, most of them in the 1800s.

Emulating Paul

Paul is a biblical figure every believer is meant to emulate. We see in him a focused life purpose of two priorities—knowing Jesus in ever increasing ways (Philippians 3:10) and bringing others (primarily in the Gentile world) into the redeemed family of God through church planting movements igniting people movements to Christ.

First, Paul consistently pressed into God, growing in experiential understanding, revelation and knowledge of Jesus and His ways, fascinated by His beauty. Paul's face set toward "laying hold of that for which Christ Jesus has laid hold of me" (Philippians 3:12). Drawing near to the Lord, fellowshiping with the Holy Spirit, led by Jesus into certain situations and out of others. Paul allowed Jesus' power to be demonstrated through him among the Gentiles. Effective message bearers seek the heights of wholehearted, surrendered, dead to self, relationship with Christ.

Yet spiritual quality and vitality was not enough. Second, Paul, led by the Spirit, had a clear plan of how to go about His ministry. His constant fellowship with the abiding Christ, along with a practical understanding of how subcultures of ethnic peoples were brought to faith in Christ, inspired him. Paul was a great intellect, constantly observing and drawing understanding from what he saw—the consummate learner of how people come to faith in Jesus. He put those principles into practice, under the Spirit's leadership in each circumstance, among every Gentile city and town that he went. The Holy Spirit is inviting His global Church to emulate Paul in the biblical, apostolic model in cross-cultural mission.

✦✦✦

I trust we have clearly seen the progressive four-point strategy of the Holy Spirit in fulfilling Jesus' Great Commission. Answering the question, "What do we mobilize the global Church to do?" It is a progression from millions of individual local ministries as Mission Mobilization Movements equipping the global Church to embrace her core identity, scattering at least 20 percent of church members to near and distant subcultures and unreached peoples, multiplying church planting movements so a thriving local ministry is within a 15-minute walk of every person on the planet, resulting in millions of people coming to saving faith through people movements to Christ across family lines, co-workers, and university relationships.

In this way, God's promise in Luke 5:4, "Launch out into the deep and let down your nets for a catch," will be realized through the corporate, global Church. Let us set our hearts to faithfully align with and pursue this inspiring big-picture strategy on the Lord's heart, mobilizing local ministries to prioritize these strategies.

Glossary

Because some of the words, phrases or concepts used in the book may not be known and understood by all in the same way, we've sought to clarify particular meaning to help the reader. We've marked the first time each is used in the writing with italics and a reference to see the glossary here.

Mission Movement: We define the mission movement as the widespread, comprehensive, global advance of followers of Jesus and churches, empowered by the Holy Spirit, taking the good news across every kind of barrier to every ethnic people group, until in each one there are adequate numbers of believers who worship, obey, and serve Jesus to spread the gospel among their own ethnic people.[1] This same definition is used in this book for cross-cultural mission and global mission.

Mission Mobilization: We spend considerable time in chapter 2 defining mission mobilization. At a macro level mission mobilization is the strategic process through which the global body of Christ is empowered by the Spirit of God to emphasize the message, vision and strategies of the Great Commission, within local ministries in every nation, activating every member in their assigned roles, widespread scattering of members to cross cultural barriers both near and distant, proclaiming and demonstrating the gospel to peoples outside of relevant access to it. At a grassroots, or micro level, it is the strategic process of an individual community of believers moving along the journey of being educated, inspired and activated in the Great Commission, every disciple engaged and fulfilling their assigned roles in the Great Commission.

Abandoned Devotion for Jesus: Abandoned devotion for Jesus is defined as wholehearted love for Christ born out of experiencing God's love for us in increasing measures. Because of gratitude and thankfulness believers abandon themselves unto the Lordship of Jesus, not holding anything back from Him, choosing to obey Him. Abandoned devotion is characterized by growing in the fear of the Lord, love of God's Word, walking in His ways, prayer, worship, obedience to God and serving Him as the overflow of that love. Abandoned devotion is active and fluid, meant to be consistently growing within disciples. Abandoned devotion is the spiritual foundation from which zeal for the Great Commission proceeds.

Global Mission Mobilization Movement: The international thrust God is preparing the global Church for related to widespread, comprehensive mission mobilization, growing as a separate but dynamically connected part of the mission movement. The growing number of ministries, organizations, national associations, courses, and conferences devoted to mission mobilization reveal this growing trend. Together, the Spirit is bringing about a movement toward deliberate and direct mobilization being implemented across His body, orchestrated by His own hand.

Local Ministries: Refers to both individual churches and individual non-church, ministry fellowships interchangeably. When used it is always in the context of one individual local ministry, not a larger church network, denomination, or organizational structure, unless specified.

Core Identity: What is the global Church's core identity? We are sons and daughters of the most high God: bought with His blood for His glory and purposes. We are God's 'missionary people,' His channel for multiplying biblical, Spirit-led, spiritually vibrant churches among all least reached peoples, seeing the Kingdom of God rooted among them, diffusing His righteousness and justice among the nations. This identity must influence all aspects of church life, motivating us to prioritize mission mobilization across our local ministries.

Mission Mobilizers: Individual leaders across the body of Christ who understand a portion of their calling as enabling and empowering disciples, particularly within individual local ministries and ministry structures, as well as entire local ministries, to be educated, inspired and activated in their purpose and journey in the Great Commission.

Mission Mobilization Movements: Any entity (whether a local ministry, denominational, organizational or church network structure or national evangelical or mission association) where the Spirit of God is emphasizing the message, vision and strategies of the Great Commission, as a natural overflow of wholehearted, abandonment to Jesus, activating members in their assigned Great Commission roles, spreading mission mobilization in a contagious way to other local ministries.

Unreached Ethnic Peoples: Roughly one-third of the world's population is still in the category of unreached people groups, having too small of an indigenous church to adequately reach their own people. Usually where 2 percent or less of the ethnic group population are follower of Jesus.[2]

Message Bearers: Message bearers are an alternative term for missionary, alleviating the cultural and historical baggage associated with the term "missionary." It means those who cross some form of ethnic barrier with the intent to develop church planting movements igniting people movements to Christ, whether among near or distant culture peoples, whether crossing a city or crossing continents to do so.

Great Commission: The Great Commission (Matthew 28:18–20; Mark 16:15–20; Luke 24:45–49; John 20:21–23; Acts 1:8) is Jesus' last command given to the global Church just prior to His ascension to the right hand of the Father. It is Jesus' binding purpose of His global Church between the time periods of His first and second comings. It is meant to be our core identity as the people of God.

Near Culture Peoples: Those ethnic people groups who are similar to our own, sharing same language, country of citizenship, cultural traditions and yet are from a different ethnic people group. An example is the ethnic Karen people group in Thailand. A "near culture people" to them is the Akha ethnic people in Thailand. They all share the overarching Thai language and traditions and yet are two distinct ethnic peoples. While still cross barriers to reach out to them, those barriers are minimal.

Distant Culture Peoples: Those ethnic groups who are very different to our own, not sharing language, citizenship, cultural traditions or much of anything. An example is the tribal Chewa people group in Malawi, Zambia, and Mozambique. A "distant culture people" to them is the Sudanese Arabs in Sudan as the Chewa and Sudanese Arabs do not share language, traditions nor culture. Crossing these tribal and ethnic barriers requires many more steps, training, preparation and understanding.

Church Planting Movements: A church planting movement is a rapid reproduction of culturally relevant, simple churches which reproduce themselves over and over within a subculture of an overarching unreached ethnic people group.[3] In other words, they are disciple making movements where obedient disciples make obedient disciples within the context of reproducing churches reproducing churches. They make Jesus known in the heart language of the local people, making Him real among their cultural worldview and understanding, transforming lives, relationships, and communities.

People Movements to Christ: According to the father of Church Growth movement, Donald McGavran, "a people movement results from the joint decision of a number of individuals all from the same people group, enabling them to become Christians without social dislocation, while remaining in full contact with their non-Christian relatives, thus enabling other segments of their people group, across the years, after suitable instruction, to come to similar decisions, joining churches made up of members of the same subculture of people."[4] To simplify, he has said people movements are, "a mass transfer of loyalties" to Jesus.[5] Robert Recker explains, "we are speaking of a multiple shift of people from one religious allegiance to another, and that this transfer of loyalties takes place not one by one, but in concert."[6]

Scattering of Message Bearer Teams: Scattering is an alternative term for "sending" message bearer teams, though not only in the traditionally understood form of sending missionaries. Scattering happens when followers of Jesus move out from the walls of their local ministry and deliberately engage their workplace, university, families, neighborhoods with the gospel. It proceeds to consider near culture peoples in a city, province, state, or nation that are unreached, finding ways to relocate and go to them. It also includes relocating families as teams to distant culture peoples potentially geographically far away. Jesus as Sower is the One who scatters His people into the world to bring forth a great harvest.

Level One Scattering: The moving outward of believers from their local ministry to their direct relationships with the gospel of the Kingdom. A natural example is workplace evangelism, where conversations about God become a part of normal daily interactions within an office, work or campus setting. Every believer is meant to be involved in this level of scattering.

Level Two Scattering: When a team of believers (lay leaders and lay people) from a local ministry, previously faithful to Level One Scattering, respond to the Spirit leading them to a near culture unreached people within a 50 to 200-mile vicinity of the local ministry. They identify a section of a city, neighborhood, apartment complex, or company that comprises a subculture of an unreached people. They are there to live and work, while incarnating the gospel, seeking to plant a simple church.

Level Three Scattering: This is the more traditional approach of mission sending. Level Three Scattering is when a team of believers (lay leaders and lay people) from the local ministry embraces God's leading to a distant culture unreached people. These may be within the same geopolitical nation where they are, in a neighboring country or even farther away, crossing continents. Similar to above, they identify a subculture of an unreached people group the Spirit is leading them to. That group is quite different from their own cultural background. They do not share the same language, basic customs, or world-view. There is a much larger learning curve to enculturate the gospel within that particular cultural understanding.

Bibliography

Adams, Wes and Hughey, Rhonda. *Revival: Its Present Relevance and Coming Role at the End of the Age*. Grandview: Fusion Ministries, 2010.

Allen, Roland. *Missionary Methods: St. Paul's Or Ours?* Grand Rapids: Eerdmans Publishing Co, 1962.

----------. *The Spontaneous Expansion of the Church*. Grand Rapids: Eerdmans Publishing Co, 1962.

Banks, Robert J. *Paul's Idea of Community: The Early Church Houses In Their Historical Setting*. Grand Rapids: Eerdmans, 1980.

Barclay, William. *The Parables of Jesus*. Louisville: Westminster John Knox Press, 1970.

----------. *The Letters to the Galatians and Ephesians*. Louisville: Westminster John Knox Press, 1976.

Bickle, Mike. *After God's Own Heart*. Lake Mary: Charisma House, 2009.

----------. *Growing in Prayer: A Real-Life Guide to Talking With God*. Lake Mary: Charisma House, 2014.

Blauw, Johannes. T*he Missionary Nature of the Church: A Survey of the Biblical Theology of Mission*. Grand Rapids: Eerdmans Publishing Co, 1974.

Bolger, Ryan K. Ed. *The Gospel After Christendom*. Grand Rapids: Baker Academic, 2012.Bonhoeffer, Deitrich. *The Cost of Discipleship*. New York: The MacMillan Co. 1963.

Bosch, David J. *Transforming Mission*. Maryknoll: Orbis Books, 1991

Bounds, E.M. *The Complete Works of E.M. Bounds on Prayer.* Grand Rapids: Baker Book House, 1990.

Bruce, F.F. *The Spreading Flame: Advance of Christianity, Volume 1: AD 1–800.* Grand Rapids: Eerdmans Publishing Co, 1958.

Bush, Luis & Beverly Pegues. *The Move of the Holy Spirit in the 10/40 Window.* Seattle: YWAM Publishing, 1999.

Chadwick, Owen. *The Reformation.* New York: Penguin Books, 1964

Chan, Francis. *Multiply: Disciples Making Disciples.* Colorado Springs: David. C. Cook, 2012.

Clinton, J. Robert. *The Making of a Leader: Recognizing the Lessons and Stages of Leadership Development.* Colorado Springs: NavPress, 1988.

Clinton, J. Robert and Stanley, Paul D. *Connecting: The Mentoring Relationships You Need to Succeed in Life.* Colorado Springs: NavPress, 1992.

----------. *The Bible and Leadership Values: A Book By Book Analysis.* Pasadena: Barnabas Publishers, 1993.

----------. *Clinton's Biblical Leadership Commentary – Leadership Insights from Eight Important Bible Books.* Pasadena: Barnabas Publishers, 1999.

----------. *Clinton's Biblical Leadership Commentary Series: Titus – Apostolic Leadership.* Pasadena: Barnabas Publishers, 2001.

Conn, Harvie M. Ed. *Theological Perspectives on Church Growth.* Philipsburg: Presbyterian and Reformed Publishing, 1976.

Duewel, Wesley. *Mighty Prevailing Prayer.* Grand Rapids: Zondervan, 1990.

----------. *Revival Fire.* Grand Rapids: Zondervan, 1995.

Dyrness, William A. & Engel, James F. *Changing the Mind of Missions: Where Have We Gone Wrong?* Downers Grove: InterVarsity Press, 2000.

Eastman, Dick. *Change the World School of Prayer Manual.* Every Home For Christ International, 1991.

Edwards, Jonathan. *The Life and Diary of David Brainerd.* Chicago: Moody Press, 1957.

Ekstrom, Bertil, Ed. *Church In Mission: Foundations and Global Case Studies.* Pasadena: William Carey Library, 2016.

Friedman, Thomas L. *The Lexus and the Olive Tree: Understanding Globalization.* New York: Anchor Books, 2000.

----------. *The World Is Flat: A Brief History of the Twenty-First Century.* New York: Farrar, Straus and Giroux, 2005

----------. *Thank You For Being Late: Version 2.0.* New York: Picador, 2016.

Gallagher, Robert and Paul Hertig, eds. *Missions in the Book of Acts: Ancient Narratives in Contemporary Context.* Maryknoll: Orbis Books, 2004.

Garrison, David. *Church Planting Movements: How God Is Redeeming a Lost World.* Midlothian: Wigtake Resources, 2004.

----------. *A Wind In The House of Islam: How God Is Drawing Muslims Around the World To Faith in Jesus Christ.* Midlothian: WigTake Resources, 2014.

George, David C. *Layman's Bible Book Commentary: 2 Corinthians, Galatians, Ephesians.* Nashville: Broadman Press, 1979.

Gilliland, Dean S. *Pauline Theology and Mission Practice.* Eugene: Wipf and Stock Publishers, 1998.

Gibbs, Eddie. *I Believe In Church Growth.* London: Hodder and Stoughton, 1981.

Glasser, Arthur F. *Announcing the Kingdom: The Story of God's Mission in the Bible.* Grand Rapids: Baker Book House, 2003.

Global Mission Mobilization Initiative (GMMI). *Handbook For Great Commission Ministries: Effective Tools To Mobilize and Equip Local Ministries For Cross-Cultural Mission.* Armstrong: IGNITE Media, 2016.

Global Mission Mobilization Initiative (GMMI). *Multiplying Mission Mobilization Movements Facilitation Manual.* Armstrong: IGNITE Media, 2019.

Greenway, Roger, John Kyle, Donald McGavran. *Missions Now: This Generation.* Grand Rapids: Baker Book House, 1990.

Guthrie, Stan. *Missions In the Third Millennium: 21 Key Trends for the 21st Century*. Colorado Springs: Paternoster Press, 2000.

Hedlund, Roger E. *Evangelization and Church Growth: Issues From The Asian Context*. Madras: McGavran Institute, 1992.

Hession, Roy. *The Calvary Road*. Fort Washington: CLC Publications, 1950.

Hiebert, Paul G. *Anthropological Insights for Missionaries*. Grand Rapids: Baker Books, 1985.

Howard, David. *Student Power in World Evangelism*. Downers Grove; Inter-Varsity Press, 1970.

Huntington, Samuel P. *The Clash of Civilizations and the Remaking of World Order*. New York: Simon and Schuster, 1996.

Jenkins, Philip. *The New Faces of Christianity: Believing the Bible in the Global South*. New York: Oxford University Press, 2006.

----------. *The Next Christendom: The Coming of Global Christianity*. Oxford: Oxford University Press, 2002.

Johnson, Todd M. and Ross, Kenneth R. Eds. *Atlas of Global Christianity*. Edinburgh: Edinburgh University Press, 2009.

Johnson, Todd M. and Zurlo, Gina A. *World Christian Encyclopedia: Third Edition*. Edinburgh: Edinburgh University Press, 2019.

Johnstone, Patrick. *The Future of the Global Church: History, Trends and Possibilities*. Colorado Springs: Biblica Press, 2011.

----------. *The Church Is Bigger than You Think*. Rosshire: Christian Focus, 1998.

Joyner, Rick. *The Harvest: 20 Year Anniversary Edition*. Fort Mill: Morningstar Publications, 2007.

Kane, J. Herbert. *A Concise History of the Christian World Mission*. Grand Rapids: Baker Book House, 1978.

Ladd, George E. *The Gospel of the Kingdom: Scriptural Studies in the Kingdom of God*. Grand Rapids: Eerdmans Publishing Company, 1959.

----------. *The Young Church: Acts of the Apostles*. New York: Abingdon Press, 1964.

----------. *A Commentary on the Revelation of John*. Grand Rapids: Eerdmans Publishing Company, 1972.

Latourette, Kenneth Scott. *A History of the Expansion of Christianity Volume 5: The Great Century*. New York: Harper and Brothers, 1943.

----------. *A History of Christianity*. New York: Harper and Row, 1953.

Lingenfelter, Sherwood G. and Mayers, Marvin K. *Ministering Cross-Culturally*. Grand Rapids: Baker Book House, 1986.

----------. *Leading Cross-Culturally: Covenant Relationships for Effective Christian Leadership*. Grand Rapids: Baker Academic, 2008.

Livingstone, Greg. *Planting Churches in Muslim Cities: A Team Approach*. Grand Rapids: Baker Book House, 1993.

Mandryk, Jason. *Operation World: 7th Edition*. Colorado Springs: Biblica Publishing, 2010.

Matenga, Jay and Gold, Malcolm. *Mission in Motion: Speaking Frankly of Mobilization*. Pasadena: William Carey Library, 2016.

McClung, Floyd. *You See Bones, I See An Army: Changing The Way We Do Church*. Seattle: YWAM Publishing, 2008.

McGavran, Donald A. *The Bridges of God: A Study in the Strategy of Missions*. New York: Friendship Press, 1955.

----------. *Understanding Church Growth*. Grand Rapids: Eerdmans Publishing Co, 1990.

Mears, Henrietta C. *What the Bible Is All About*. Wheaton: Tyndale House Publishers, 1987.

Mellis, Charles. *Committed Communities: Fresh Streams for World Missions*, Pasadena: William Carey Library, 2013

Morgan, G. Campbell. *The Missionary Manifesto: The Fourfold Commission*. New York: Revell Company, 1909.

----------. *The Acts of the Apostles.* Old Tappan: Revell Company, 1924.

----------. *The Analyzed Bible: The Prophecy of Isaiah: Volume II.* New York: Revell Company, 1910.

----------. *The Gospel According to Matthew.* New York: Revell Company, 1911.

----------. *The Gospel According to John.* New York: Revell Company, 1933

----------. *Handbook for Bible Teachers and Preachers.* New York: Revell Company, 1912

----------. *Life Applications from Every Chapter of the Bible.* Grand Rapids: Revell Books, 1926.

----------. *The Parables and Metaphors of Our Lord.* Old Tappan: Revell Company, 1943

----------. *The Birth of the Church: An Exposition of the Second Chapter of Acts.* Old Tappan: Revell Company, 1968.

----------. *The Teaching of Christ.* London: Pickering and Inglis, 1913

----------. *Parables of the Kingdom.* New York: Revell Company, 1997.

Motyer, J. Alec. *Isaiah: An Introduction and Commentary.* Downers Grove: IVP Academic, 1999.

Murray, Andrew. *The Key to the Missionary Problem.* Fort Washington: CLC Publications, 1979.

Neill, Stephen. *A History of Christian Missions.* New York: Penguin Books, 1990.

Newbigin, Lesslie. *The Household of God: Lectures on the Nature of the Church.* New York: Friendship Press, 1954

Newell, Marvin. *Crossing Cultures in Scripture.* Downers Grove: InterVarsity Press, 2016

Norton, Wilbert. *To Stir the Church.* Madison: Student Foreign Missionary Fellowship (SFMF), 1986.

Orr, J. Edwin. *The Second Evangelical Awakening in Britain*. London: Marshall, Morgan and Scott, LTD, 1949

----------. *The Light of the Nations: Evangelical Renewal and Advance in the Nineteenth Century*. Grand Rapids: Eerdmans Publishing Co, 1965.

----------. *The Flaming Tongue: The Impact of 20th Century Revivals*. Chicago: Moody Press, 1973.

----------. *Campus Aflame: A History of Evangelical Awakenings in Collegiate Communities*. Wheaton: International Awakening Press, 1994.

Pawson, David. *Come With Me Through Isaiah*. Traveler's Rest: True Potential Publishers, 2010.

Pickett, J. Waskom. *Christian Mass Movements in India: A Study With Recommendations*. New York: Abingdon Press, 1933.

Pierson, Paul E. *Themes From Acts*. Ventura: Regal Books, 1982.

----------. *The Dynamics of Christian Mission: History Through A Missiological Perspective*. Pasadena: WCIU Press, 2009.

Pink, Arthur W. *An Exposition of the Sermon on the Mount*. Grand Rapids: Baker Book House, 1950.

----------. *The Prophetic Parables of Jesus*. Memphis: Bottom of the Hill Publications, 2011.

Piper, John. *Let The Nations Be Glad: The Supremacy of God in Missions*. Grand Rapids: Baker Book House, 1993

Piper, John and David Matthis. *Finish the Mission: Bringing the Gospel to the Unreached and Unengaged*. Wheaton: Crossway, 2012.

Ponraj, S.D. *Church Planting Approach To Mission*. Madhupur: Indian Institute of Multi- Cultural Studies, 1987.

Pratney, Winkey. *Revival – Its Principles and Personalities: Twenty Centuries of Vision and Visitation*. Lafayette: Huntington House Publishers, 1994.

Riss, Richard M. *A Survey of 20th Century Revival Movements In North America*. Peabody: Hendrickson Publishers, 1988.

‒‒‒‒‒‒‒‒‒. *Images of Revival: Another Wave Rolls In.* Shippensburg: Revival Press, 1997.

Shaw, Ryan. *Waking the Giant: The Resurging Student Mission Movement.* Pasadena: William Carey Library, 2006.

‒‒‒‒‒‒‒‒‒. *Engaging the Holy Spirit: Understanding His Dynamics Among Believers.* Armstrong: IGNITE Media, 2012.

‒‒‒‒‒‒‒‒‒. *Studies in the Book of Colossians: A Call To Behold the Supremacy of Jesus.* Armstrong: IGNITE Media, 2012.

‒‒‒‒‒‒‒‒‒. *Spiritual Equipping for Mission: Thriving As God's Message Bearers.* Downers Grove: InterVarsity Press, 2014.

‒‒‒‒‒‒‒‒‒. *Proclaiming the Kingdom: A Roadmap For Bearing God's Message Among All Peoples.* Armstrong: IGNITE Media, 2018.

‒‒‒‒‒‒‒‒‒. *Studies in the Sermon on the Mount: A Call to Kingdom Life As True Disciples.* Armstrong: IGNITE Media, 2017.

‒‒‒‒‒‒‒‒‒. *Studies in Matthew 13: Jesus' Parables of the Kingdom.* Armstrong: IGNITE Media, 2018.

‒‒‒‒‒‒‒‒‒. *Studies in Matthew 24–25: Jesus' End-Times Discourse.* Armstrong: IGNITE Media. 2021.

Sheets, Dutch. *Intercessory Prayer.* Ventura: Regal Books, 1996.

Shenk, Wilbert R. *Changing Frontiers of Mission.* Maryknoll: Orbis Books, 1999.

Simson, Wolfgang. *Houses That Change the World: The Return of the House Churches.* Waynesboro: Authentic, 2001.

Smith, Alex G. *Siamese Gold: The Church in Thailand.* Bangkok: OMF Publishers, 1999.

‒‒‒‒‒‒‒‒‒. *A Strategy to Multiply Rural Churches.* Bangkok: OMF Publishers, 1977

Spitters, Denny and Matthew Ellison. *When Everything Is Missions.* Orlando: Bottom Line Media, 2017.

Stephenson, Paul. *Constantine: Unconquered Emperor, Christian Victor.* London: Quercus, 2009.

Stewart, John. *The Nestorian Missionary Enterprise: A Church on Fire.* Edinburgh: Clarke Publishers, 1923.

Stott, John R.W. *The Message of the Sermon on The Mount.* Downers Grove: InterVarsity Press, 1978.

----------. *The Message of Acts.* Downers Grove: InterVarsity Press, 1990.

----------. *The Message of Ephesians.* Downers Grove: InterVarsity Press, 1979.

----------. *One People.* Downer's Grove: InterVarsity Press, 1971.

Swartley, Keith, ed. *Encountering the World of Islam: Second Edition.* Littleton: Bottom line Media, 2014.

Taylor, Hudson, A Retrospect: T*he Story Behind My Zeal For Missions.* Independently Published, 2018.

Taylor, William D. Antonia van der Meer, Reg Reimer. *Sorrow and Blood: Christian Mission in Contexts of Suffering, Persecution and Martyrdom.* Pasadena: William Carey Library, 2012.

Tozer, A.W. *The Knowledge of the Holy.* New York: Harper and Row, 1961.

Trousdale, Jerry. *Miraculous Movements.* Nashville: Thomas Nelson, 2012.

Tucker, Ruth A. *From Jerusalem To Irian Jaya: A Biographical History of Christian Missions.* Grand Rapids: Zondervan Academie, 1983.

Van Engen, Charles. *Mission on The Way: Issues in Mission Theology.* Grand Rapids: Baker Book House, 1996.

----------. *God's Missionary People: Rethinking the Purpose of the Local Church.* Grand Rapids: Baker Book House, 1991.

----------. The State of Missiology Today: Global Innovations in Christian Witness. Downer's Grove: IVP Academic, 2016.Wagner, C. Peter. *The Acts of the Holy Spirit.* Ventura: Regal Books, 1994.

Walls, Andrew F. *The Missionary Movement In Christian History.* Maryknoll: Orbis Books, 2000.

----------. *Mission In the 21st Century: Exploring the Five Marks of Global Mission.* Maryknoll: Orbis Books, 2008

Wallstrom, Timothy. *The Creation of a Student Movement to Evangelize the World.* Pasadena: WCIU Press, 1980.

Walvoord, John. *Matthew: Thy Kingdom Come.* Chicago: Moody Press, 1974.

Watson, David L. and Paul D. *Contagious Disciple Making: Leading Others on a Journey of Discovery.* Nashville: Thomas Nelson, 2014.

Weinlick, John R. Count Zinzendorf: *The Story of His Life and Leadership In the Renewed Moravian Church.* Bethlehem: The Moravian Church In America, 1984.

Winter, Ralph D. and Hawthorne, Steven C. *Perspectives on The World Christian Movement: Fourth Edition: A Reader.* Pasadena: William Carey Library, 2009.

Winter, Ralph D. *Four Men, Three Eras. Article from Perspectives on the World Christian Movement.* Pasadena: William Carey Library, 2009.

Wilson, David and Lorene. *Pipeline: Engaging the Church In Missionary Mobilization.* Littleton: William Carey Library, 2018.

Wright, Christopher J.H. *The Mission of God: Unlocking the Bible's Grand Narrative.* Downers Grove. IVP Academic, 2006.

----------. *The Mission of God's People: A Biblical Theology of the Church's Mission.* Grand Rapids: Zondervan, 2010.

Wu, Jackson. *One Gospel for All Nations.* Pasadena: William Carey Library, 2015.

NOTES

Introduction

1. The concept of God bringing changes in mission has been the subject of many important books over the last few decades including *Missions in the Third Millennium* by Stan Guthrie; *Changing the Mind of Missions* by Willian Dyrness; *Transforming Mission* by David J. Bosch; *Changing Frontiers of Mission* by Wilbert R. Shenk; *Mission in the 21st Century* by Andrew Walls; *The New Faces of Christianity* by Philip Jenkins, *World Christian Encyclopedia* by Todd Johnson and Gina Zurlo.
2. Paul Pierson, *The Dynamics of Christian Mission*: History Through A Missiological Perspective (Pasadena: WCIU Press, 2009), 135.

Chapter 1: Why Mission Mobilization?

1. In chapter 15 we look at the difference between *"mobilization from the outside"* and the much more effective *"mobilization from the inside,"* referring to mobilization happening from within a local ministry instead of a believer going outside their local ministry to be mobilized through a mission education course, mission conference or the like.
2. Reuben Kachala, Missio Nexus On Mission Virtual Conference 2021, https://missionexus.org/onmission2021kachala/.
3. See details of what Mission Mobilization Movements are in chapter 15.
4. Mahesh De Mel, personal interview recorded in my personal journal, February 2018.
5. David Howard, *Student Power in World Evangelism* (Downers Grove: InterVarsity Press, 1970), 97.
6. Kenneth Scott Latourette, *A History of the Expansion of Christianity Volume 5: The Great Century* (New York: Harper and Brothers, 1943), 21.
7. Wikipedia authors, "Christianity by Country" *Wikipedia*, https://en.wikipedia.org/wiki/Christianity_by_country.
8. J. Edwin Orr, *The Flaming Tongue* (Chicago: Moody Press, 1973), 48.
9. J. Robert Clinton has defined Life Purpose as "a burden like calling, a task or driving force or achievement, which motivates a leader to fulfill something or to see something done." J. Robert Clinton, *Clinton's Biblical Leadership Commentary* (Pasadena, CA: Barnabas Publishers, 1999), 515.
10. J. Robert Clinton, A four-section mission statement detailing how we believe God wanted our lives together to be spent for His glory on earth.

11. For an Example see this article: *Finish the Task: When Mottos Hijack the Mission*, https://www.imb.org/2018/12/27/finish-task/.

12. Archived website for AD2000, http://www.ad2000.org/re70528.htm.

13. G. Campbell Morgan, *The Gospel According to John* (New York: Revell Company, 1933), 231.

14. Morgan, *John*, 78.

15. We spend a whole chapter in chapter 7 looking intently into the subject of what it Biblically means to fulfill the Great Commission.

16. Patrick Johnstone, *The Future of the Global Church: History, Trends and Possibilities* (Downers Grove: InterVarsity Press, 2011). See chapter one on Demography: Nine Global Challenges.

17. G. Campbell Morgan, *Handbook for Bible Teachers and Preachers* (Grand Rapids: Baker Book House, 1982), 19.

18. We will look in detail at this truth in chapters 8 and 9.

19. Mike Adegbile, unpublished paper, "The Great Commission as the Core Task of the Church."

20. "Status of World Evangelization 2021," Joshua Project, https://joshuaproject.net/assets/media/handouts/status-of-world-evangelization.pdf.

21. "Unreached People Groups," Joshua Project, https://joshuaproject.net/help/definitions.

22. Steve Shadrach, "Mobilization: The Fourth (and Final?) Era of the Modern Mission Movement" *EMQ*, Volume 54, Issue 3.

23. Todd M. Johnson, Gina Zurlo, Peter Crossing, "World Christianity and Mission 2020: Ongoing Shift to the Global South", *International Journal of Missionary Research*, https://journals.sagepub.com/doi/full/10.1177/2396939319880074.

24. Donald McGavran, *Understanding Church Growth* (Grand Rapids: Eerdmans, 1990), xvi (preface to the first edition).

25. Message bearer is an alternative term for the traditional concept of "missionary." I tell the story in chapter 2 of where this phrase came from. Yet these look different today, with many sent and funded differently (see chapter 16), focusing on different mission activities (see chapter 17), expecting different results (see chapter 18).

26. *What is Personal Identity? Definition, Philosophy and Development*, article, https://study.com/academy/lesson/what-is-personal-identity-definition-philosophy-development.html

27. Mike Adegbile, unpublished paper, "The Great Commission as the Core Task of the Church."

28. Christopher J. H. Wright, *The Mission of God's People: A Biblical Theology of the Church's Mission* (Grand Rapids: Zondervan, 2010), 78.

29. G. Campbell Morgan, *The Birth of the Church: An Exposition of the Second Chapter of Acts* (New York: Revell Company, 1968), 11.

30. Wright, *The Mission of God's People*, 38.

31. David J. Bosch, *Transforming Mission* (Maryknoll: Orbis Books, 1991), 389–390.

32. Charles Van Engen, *The State of Missiology Today: Global Innovations in Christian Witness* (Downers Grove: IVP Academic, 2016), 4.

33. Wright, *The Mission of God's People*, 63.

34. G. Campbell Morgan, *The Teaching of Christ* (London: Pickering and Inglis, 1913), 176.

35. Some of these include Let's Mobilize His Church (Latin America), Mission Campaign Network (Kenya), Global Mobilization Network (International), Center for Missionary Mobilization and Retention (USA), Global Cast Resources (International) and many more. While many more have been around longer than a decade and continue to gain clarity and focus in mobilization. Some of these include Center for Mission Mobilization, Simply Mobilizing, Perspectives, GMMI and more. In addition, almost all of the major global mission networks like the Lausanne Committee (international), COMIBAM (Latin America), MANI (Africa), WEA Mission Commission (international) and more now have

mobilization tracks and departments which they did not have before.
36.   Johnstone, *The Future of the Global Church*, 57.
37.   Johnstone, *The Future of the Global Church*, 94.
38.   Paul Bendor-Samuel, "COVID-19, Trends in Global Mission and Participation in Faithful Witness," *Transformation: An International Journal of Holistic Mission Studies*, November 2, 2020, https://journals.sagepub.com/doi/full/10.1177/0265378820970225.
39.   Bendor-Samuel, "COVID-19."

Chapter 2: What is Mission Mobilization?

1.   Sherwood Lingenfelter, *Ministering Cross-Culturally* (Grand Rapids: Baker Book House, 1986), 19.
2.   Max Chismon, Email Correspondence, September 13, 2021.
3.   Bevin Ginder, "An Outstanding Definition of Missions Mobilization," *Global Cast Resources*, https://globalcastresources.com/2017/12/31/video-mobilization-mobilizer-defined/
4.   Larry Reesor, "A Fresh Perspective On Mobilizing the Church," *Mission Frontiers Magazine* (January-February, 2000), http://www.missionfrontiers.org/issue/article/a-freshperspective-on-mobilizing-the-church.
5.   Shadrach, "Mobilization: The Fourth (and Final?) Era of the Modern Mission Movement," *EMQ*.
6.   Steve Shadrach, "The Key to World Evangelization," *The Traveling Team* -http://www.thetravelingteam.org/articles/mobilization.
7.   Steve Hawthorne, "Mobilizing God's People for God's Mission," *Self-published article*, May 8, 2015.
8.   Hawthorne, ""Mobilizing God's People."
9.   Wright, *The Mission of God's People*, 23.
10.   Shadrach, "The Key to World Evangelization," http://www.thetravelingteam.org/articles/mobilization
11.   We will consider Mission Mobilization Movements in detail in chapter 15.
12.   Adapted from the author's study guide, Studies in the Sermon on the Mount: A Call to Kingdom Life as True Disciples (Armstrong: IGNITE Media).
13.   https://medium.com/backyard-theology/nine-common-christian-words-that-never-appear-in-the-bible-742232aff566
14.   Dean Gilliland, *Pauline Theology and Mission Practice* (Eugene: Wipf & Stock Publishers, 1998), 50.
15.   Dean Gilliland, *Pauline Theology and Mission Practice* (Eugene: Wipf & Stock Publishers, 1998), 50.
16.   Glasser, *Announcing the Kingdom*, 214.
17.   Greg Parsons, "Why Stay Here? Mobilizing the Home Front," *Mission Frontiers*, January–February (1995), http://missionsfrontiers.org.
18.   Shadrach, "Mobilization: The Fourth (and Final?) Era of the Modern Mission Movement," *EMQ*.
19.   Shadrach, "Mobilization," 51.
20.   Shadrach, "Mobilization," 56.
21.   For historic details see part 3.
22.   Barna Research Group, https://www.barna.com/research/half-churchgoers-not-heard-great-commission/.
23.   We will consider this in detail in chapter 16 when we discuss the biblical concept of "scattering."
24.   Todd Johnson and Gina Zurlo, "Status of Global Christianity 2015," *International Bulletin of Missionary Research*, https://www.researchgate.net/publication/308361629_Status_of_Global_Christianity_2015_in_the_Context_of_1900-2050.

25. Todd Johnson and Sandra Lee, *From Western Christendom to Global Christianity*, Article in Perspectives Reader Fourth Edition (Pasadena: William Carey Library, 2013), 387.

Chapter 3: Core Aspects of Mission Mobilization

1. Learn more about 10 keys to spiritual effectiveness in mission through the author's book on this crucial subject, *Spiritual Equipping For Mission: Thriving As God's Message Bearers*, (Downer's Grove: InterVarsity Press, 2014).
2. Find a comprehensive breakdown of the Gospel of the Kingdom in the author's book, *Proclaiming the Kingdom: A Roadmap For Bearing God's Message Among All Peoples*, (Armstrong: IGNITE Media, 2018) available through IGNITE Media.
3. Justin Dillehay, "Bible Literacy Crisis: And What You Can Do About It In 2020," *The Gospel Coalition*, January 14, 2020, https://www.thegospelcoalition.org/article/bible-literacy-crisis/.
4. John R. W. Stott, *The Bible In World Evangelization*, Article in Perspectives Reader Fourth Edition, 21.
5. There are two portions of such a plan. First is a daily devotional plan, and second is a book-by-book plan for in-depth study. Make a plan to devotionally read two Psalms, a Proverb and a chapter in the Gospels daily. As you read, commit to "prayer-reading." Don't merely read the words but interact with God using the truths line by line in the verses. Additionally, commit to in-depth study of the Bible. Invite the Spirit to lead you to particular Bible books each year to study in depth.
6. See the author's study guide, *Studies in the Book of Colossians* (Armstrong, IGNITE Media, 2012), available through IGNITE Media.
7. Wikipedia authors, "Salvation history," *Wikipedia*, https://en.wikipedia.org/wiki/Salvation_history.
8. A. W. Tozer, *The Knowledge of the Holy* (New York, NY: Harper Collins, 2009).
9. Denny Spitters and Matthew Ellison, *When Everything Is Missions* (Orlando: Bottom Line Media, 2017).
10. Alex Smith, *Siamese Gold: The Church in Thailand* (Bangkok: OMF Publishers, 1999), 36–40. Though these examples are particularly about Thailand, they were also common in missions universally from 1850 to 1950.
11. "Definitions," Joshua Project, https://joshuaproject.net/help/definitions.
12. "Missions Stats: The Current State of the World," The Traveling Team, http://www.thetravelingteam.org/stats.
13. Alex Smith, *A Strategy to Multiply Rural Churches* (Bangkok: OMF Publishers, 1977), 204–208.
14. McGavran, *Understanding Church Growth*, 20–30.
15. Ralph Winter, Bruce Koch, "Finishing the Task: The Unreached Peoples Challenge," *International Journal of Frontier Mission* 19, no. 4 (winter 2002), https://www.ijfm.org/PDFs_IJFM/19_4_PDFs/winter_koch_task.pdf.
16. Winter and Koch, "Finishing the Task."
17. GMMI, *Handbook for Great Commission Ministries* (Armstrong: IGNITE Media, 2016), 115–121.

Chapter 4: Types of Mission Mobilizers

1. We consider this concept further in chapter 15 comparing "mobilization from the outside" with "mobilization from the inside."
2. John Stott, *The Message of Ephesians* (Leicester: IVP, 1989), 166.
3. Stott, *The Message of Ephesians*, 167.

4.   J. Robert Clinton and Paul D. Stanley, *Connecting: The Mentoring Relationships You Need to Succeed in Life* (Colorado Springs: NavPress, 1992) I am indebted to my professor, Dr. J. Robert Clinton, for the various categories of "mobilizer" found in this section. In his extensive studies on leadership he has identified nine types of "mentors." Though not exactly the same, the noted types of "mobilizers" are similar to his types of mentors. His findings inspired my thinking and applying the idea of many "mobilizer" types.

Chapter 5: Mission Mobilizer: Rebuilding Ancient Ruins

1.   Henrietta Mears, *What the Bible Is All About* (Wheaton: Tyndale House Publishers, 1987), 144–145.
2.   Gina Zurlo, Todd M. Johnson and Peter Crossing, "Status of Global Christianity 2020," *Center for the Study of Global Christianity*, https://www.gordonconwell.edu/center-for-global-christianity/wp-content/uploads/sites/13/202
3.   Pierson, *The Dynamics of Christian Mission*, 26.

Chapter 6: Jesus' Fourfold Commission

1.   These Four Great Commission passages studies are part of a Bible study guide called Great Commission Bible Studies - https://www.globalmmi.net/product/great-commission-bible-studies-small-groups-encountering-gods-mission-heart-in-the-bible, by the author, published by IGNITE Media. I am indebted to G. Campbell Morgan's "The Missionary Manifesto" and other Bible expositors related to insights into these four commission passages.

Chapter 7: Biblical Basis of Fulfilling the Great Commision

1.   In this portion on various passages in Isaiah I am indebted to the writings of J. Alec Motyer's *Isaiah*, G. Campbell Morgan's *The Prophecy of Isaiah* - Volume II and David Pawson's *Come with Me Through Isaiah*.
2.   Motyer, J. Alec. *Isaiah: An Introduction and Commentary* (Downers Grove: IVP Academic, 1999), 349.
3.   Motyer, 352.
4.   G. Campbell Morgan, *The Parables and Metaphors of our Lord* (Old Tappan: Revell Books, 1956), 134.
5.   Webpage of Global Population - https://www.worldometers.info/.
6.   Ladd, George E. *The Gospel of the Kingdom: Scriptural Studies in the Kingdom of God* (Grand Rapids: Eerdmans Publishing Company, 1959), 123; 130.
7.   Ladd, Gospel of the Kingdom, 126.
8.   Ryan Shaw, *Studies in Matthew 24-25: Jesus' End-Times Discourse* (Armstrong: IGNITE Media, 2020). See this book for an in-depth study on Jesus' End-Times Discourse in Matthew 24-25.
9.   Good Reads Quotes of CS Lewis - https://www.goodreads.com/work/quotes/2976220-the-problem-of-pain.
10.   Tweet of Mike Bickle - https://twitter.com/mikebickle/status/951533157316202496?lang=en.
11.   Rick Warren, "Finishing the Task: Bibles, Believers and Bodies of Christ In Every Nation," Article, National Christian Foundation - https://www.ncfgiving.com/stories/finishing-the-task-bibles-believers-and-bodies-of-christ-in-every-people-group/.
12.   These are adapted from Warren's items and added to from a variety of other sources.
13.   This portion has been adapted from the author's in-depth *Studies in Matthew 24-25: Jesus'*

End-Times Discourse pgs. 45-53 (Armstrong, IGNITE Media, 2020), available through IGNITE Media.

14. See Chapter 18 for a complete overview of People Movements to Christ.
15. See Chapter 17 for a complete overview of Church Planting Movements.
16. These trends are adapted from a teaching series by Mike Bickle titled Positive Spiritual Sign Trends In the Church - https://mikebickle.org/watch/2016_02_19_1800_MB_FCF.
17. Plan All Nations - https://www.planpte.org/.
18. Joshua Project - https://joshuaproject.net/resources/articles/how_many_people_groups_are_there.
19. Joshua Project - https://joshuaproject.net/resources/articles/how_many_people_groups_are_there.
20. Joshua Project - https://joshuaproject.net/people_groups/statistics.

Chapter 8: God's Macro Plan: The Global Church's Core Identity

1. G. Campbell Morgan, *The Birth of the Church – An Exposition of the Second Chapter of Acts* (Old Tappan: Revell Books, 1968), 12.
2. Ryan Shaw, *Engaging the Holy Spirit: Understanding His Dynamics Among Believers* (Armstrong: IGNITE Media, 2012), 52.
3. Morgan, *The Birth of the Church*, 13.
4. Shaw, *Engaging the Holy Spirit*, 51.
5. Shaw, 5.
6. Quoted in Charles Van Engen's book, *God's Missionary People: Rethinking the Purpose of the Local Church*, (Grand Rapids; Baker Book House, 1991), 27.
7. Van Engen, 27.
8. Van Engen, 28.
9. Van Engen, 28.
10. Van Engen, 28.
11. Lesslie Newbigin, *The Household of God: Lectures on the Nature of the Church* (New York: Friendship Press, 1954), 164-65.
12. Blauw, Johannes. *The Missionary Nature of the Church: A Survey of the Biblical Theology of Mission* (Grand Rapids: Eerdmans Publishing Co, 1974), 121.
13. John R. W. Stott, *One People* (Downers Grove: InterVarsity Press, 1971), 17.
14. Newbigin, *Household of God*, 169-170.
15. Van Engen, *God's Missionary People*, 47.
16. William Barclay, *The Letters to the Galatians and Ephesians*, (London: Westminster John Knox Press, 1976) p 61.17. Mears, What the Bible Is All About, 431.
18. Mears, 431.
19. Morgan, *Handbook for Bible Teachers and Preachers*, 224.
20. David George, *Laymans' Bible Book Commentary – 2 Corinthians, Galatians, Ephesians* (Nashville: Broadman Press, 1979), 95.
21. Howard A. Snyder, "The Church in God's Plan," Article in *Perspectives* Reader Fourth Edition, p. 154.
22. Mears, *What the Bible Is All About*, 437.
23. Snyder, "The Church in God's Plan," 155.
24. Barclay, *The Letters to the Galatians and Ephesians*, 67.
25. Dr. J. Robert Clinton, *The Bible and Leadership Values: A Book by Book Analysis* (Pasadena: Barnabas Publishers, 1993), 260.
26. G. Campbell Morgan, *Life Applications From Every Chapter of the Bible* (Grand Rapids: Revell Books, 1995) 349.
27. Morgan, *Handbook for Bible Teachers and Preachers*, 225.
28. Charles Van Engen, *God's Missionary People*, 52.

29. Wright, *The Mission of God's People*, 23.
30. Wright, 73.

Chapter 9: God's Micro Plan: A Local Church's Characteristics

1. George Ladd, The Young Church: Acts of the Apostles (New York: Abingdon Press, 1964), 64.
2. Everett Ferguson, "Why and When Did Christians Start Constructing Special Buildings for Worship?" Christianity Today, November, 2008 - https://www.christianitytoday.com/history/2008/november/why-and-when-did- christians-start-constructing-special.html.
3. Definition of local church quoted by Wendell Evans in Greg Livingstone's Planting Churches in Muslim Cities: A Team Approach (Grand Rapids: Baker Book House, 1993), 170.
4. Morgan, *The Birth of the Church*, 159; Ladd, The Young Church, 65.
5. See part 4 and the Spirit's Four-Point Strategy for Fulfilling the Great Commission.
6. Morgan, *The Birth of the Church*, 165.
7. Morgan, *The Birth of the Church*, 159.
8. Ladd, *The Young Church*, 65.
9. Morgan, *The Birth of the Church*, 160.
10. See the author's book *Proclaiming the Kingdom: A Roadmap For Bearing God's Message Among All Peoples* (Armstrong, IGNITE Media, 2018).
11. Paul E. Pierson, Themes From Acts (Ventura: Regal Books, 1982), 43.
12. Ladd, *The Young Church*, 66
13. Ladd, *The Young Church*, 66.
14. Pierson, *Themes From Acts*, 44.
15. Morgan, *The Birth of the Church*, 165.
16. Adapted from Van Engen's book *God's Missionary People: Rethinking the Purpose of the Local Church*, 90-97.
17. Reuben Kachala, "The Acts 1:8 Challenge." Abandoned Times Articles, February 2020 - https://www.globalmmi.net/the-acts-18-challenge.

Chapter 10: Historical Eras # 1–2: AD 30 – 1500

1. I am indebted in part 3 to the Church, mission, revival history writings of Dr. Paul Pierson, Dr. Ruth Tucker, Dr. Ralph Winter, Dr. J. Edwin Orr, Dr. Kenneth Scott Latourette, Dr. Andrew Walls, Dr. Wes Adams, Winkey Pratney and Wesley Duewel.
2. Wes Adams, *Revival: Its Present Relevance & Coming Role at the End of the Age* (Grandview: Fusion Ministries, 2010), 85.
3. Adams, 86.
4. I am indebted to the careful research of Wes Adams as he laid out the 500-year epochs of Biblical and Church history, 87.
5. J. Herbert Kane, A Concise History of the Christian World Mission (Grand Rapids: Baker Book House, 1982), 7.
6. Tucker, From Jerusalem to Irian Jaya, 31.
7. https://historica.fandom.com/wiki/Christianity_in_the_Roman_Empire.
8. Tucker, From Jerusalem To Irian Jaya, 57.
9. Tucker, 35.
10. Pierson, The Dynamics of Christian Mission, 71.
11. Tucker, From Jerusalem to Irian Jaya, 40.
12. Pierson, The Dynamics of Christian Mission, 74.
13. Tucker, From Jerusalem To Irian Jaya, 44.

14. Tucker, 44.
15. John Stewart, *The Nestorian Missionary Enterprise: A Church on Fire* (Edinburgh, Scotland: Clarke, 1923), 198.
16. Pierson, *The Dynamics of Christian Mission*, 86.
17. Pierson, 85.
18. Pierson, 102.
19. Pierson, 126.

Chapter 11: Historical Era # 3: 1500s To Present: Sub-Eras 1–2

1.   Pierson, *The Dynamics of Christian Mission*, 135.
2.   Adams, *Revival*, 25.
3.   Adams, 147.
4.   Tucker, *From Jerusalem to Irian Jaya*, 70.
5.   Pierson, *The Dynamics of Christian Mission*, 190.
6.   Pierson, 230.
7.   Tucker, *From Jerusalem to Irian Jaya*, 69.
8.   Pierson, *The Dynamics of Christian Mission*, 190.
9.   Pierson, 191.
10. Tucker, *From Jerusalem to Irian Jaya*, 69.
11. Tucker, 192.
12. Adams, *Revival*, 98.
13. Adams, 199.
14. Stephen Neill, *A History of Christian Missions* (London: Penguin Books, 1964), 243.
15. Kenneth Scott Latourette, *A History of Christianity*, 1081.
16. Ralph Winter, "Four Men, Three Eras," *Frontier Mission Fellowship*, 4 - http://frontiermissionfellowship.org/uploads/documents/Fourpercent20Menpercent20Threepercent-20Eras.pdf.
17. Jonathon Edwards, *The Life and Diary of David Brainerd* (Chicago: Moody Press, 1957).
18. Pierson, *The Dynamics of Christian Mission*, 201.
19. Tucker, *From Jerusalem to Irian Jaya*, 115.
20. Tucker, 202.
21. Pierson, *The Dynamics of Christian Mission*, 204.

Chapter 12: Historical Era # 3: 1500s To Present: Sub-Eras 3–4

1.   Adams, *Revival*, 101.
2.   Ralph Winter, "Four Men, Three Eras," 4.
3.   Tucker, *From Jerusalem to Irian Jaya*, 175.
4.   Pierson, *The Dynamics of Christian Mission*, 248.
5.   Kenneth Scott Latourette, *A History of Christianity*, 1081.
6.   Adams, *Revival*, 104.
7.   Adams, 104.
8.   Wesley Duewel, *Revival Fire* (Grand Rapids, MI: Zondervan, 1995), 206.
9.   Adams, *Revival*, 57.
10. Orr, *The Flaming Tongue*, 11.
11. Orr, 105.
12. Orr, 104.
13. Marjorie Lee Chandler, "Fuller Seminary Cancels Course on Signs and Wonders," *Christianity Today*, February 21, 1986, https://www.christianitytoday.com/ct/1986/february-21/fuller-seminary-cancels-course-on-signs-and-wonders.html.

14. On a personal note, this organization is dear to my heart. My parents, Dan and Karen Shaw, served the Samo tribe in the western highlands of Papua New Guinea (where I was born) with Wycliffe Bible Translators, from 1969 – 1982, still members to this day. "Uncle Cam" Townsend rocked my oldest brother on his knee as a baby.
15. Ralph Winter, "Four Men, Three Eras," 9.
16. Wikipedia page, Donald McGavran - https://en.wikipedia.org/wiki/Donald_McGavran.
17. McGavran, *Understanding Church Growth*, 47.
18. Wikipedia page, Ralph D. Winter - https://en.wikipedia.org/wiki/Ralph_D._Winter.
19. Ralph Winter, "Four Men, Three Eras," 11.
20. Joshua Project Definitions, https://joshuaproject.net/help/definitions - Unreached People Group.
21. Pierson, *The Dynamics of Christian Mission*, 249.
22. Perspectives of the World Christian Movement website - https://www.perspectives.org/About#/HTML/our_history_and_ministry_vision.htm.
23. Kairos Course webpage - https://www.kairoscourse.org/about-kairos.

Chapter 13: Global Systems as Great Commission Platforms

1. Tucker, *From Jerusalem to Irian Jaya*, 111.
2. Johnstone, *The Future of the Global Church*, 60.
3. Johnstone, 111.
4. Wikipedia Definitions - https://en.wikipedia.org/wiki/Pax_Romana
5. Thomas Freidman, *Thank You For Being Late: An Optimists Guide For Thriving In the Age of Accelerations* (New York: Picador, 2016), 3.
6. Freidman, 4.
7. Dan Bricklin, "Thomas Friedman's View of Globalization," http://www.bricklin.com/albums/fpawlf2000/friedman.htm#:~:text=Thepercent20simplepercent20definitionperce nt20ofpercent20globalization,cheaperpercent20thanpercent20everpercent20beforepercen t2Cpercent20and.
8. History of the iPhone - https://en.wikipedia.org/wiki/History_of_the_iPhone.
9. Bricklin, "Thomas Friedman's View of Globalization,".
10. Bricklin, "Thomas Friedman's View of Globalization,".
11. Bricklin, "Thomas Friedman's View of Globalization,".
12. Friedman, *Thank You For Being Late*, 33.

Chapter 14: Where Are We Now: A New Era

1. World City Populations 2021 - https://worldpopulationreview.com/world-cities
2. Steve Shadrach, "On Mission Virtual Conference 2020," Missio Nexus, https://missio-exus.org/onmission2020stephen-2/.
3. Shadrach, "Mobilization: The Fourth (and Final?) Era of the Modern Mission Movement," EMQ.
4. Shadrach, EMQ.
5. Adams, *Revival*, 130.

Chapter 15: Multiplying Mission Mobilization Movements

1. Roland Allen, *The Spontaneous Expansion of the Church* (Eugene: Wipf and Stock Publishers, 1997), 6.
2. Research gleaned through the author's research in 2002 among campus ministry leaders, mission leaders and church leaders. This research was compiled into the author's book

Waking the Giant: The Resurging Student Mission Movement (Pasadena: William Carey Library, 2006).

3. Missionary Statistics - http://missionaryportal.webflow.io/stats.

4. https://ocresearch.info/sites/default/files/DAWNpercent202.0.pdf.

5. http://www.operationworld.org/africa/owtext.html.

6. Tshepang Basupi, "Can You Believe Me For 1 Million Missionaries From Africa" Abandoned Times Article - https://www.globalmmi.net/can-you-believe-me-for-1-million-missionaries-from-africa.

7. Clinton, *Clinton's Biblical Leadership Commentary*, 535.

8. This is the premise of Charles Mellis' landmark book, Committed Communities: Fresh Streams for World Missions, (Pasadena: William Carey Library, 2013).

9. *Handbook for Great Commission Ministries*, 23, published by IGNITE Media. This Handbook is designed to serve local ministries seeking to implement tools and principles to mobilize and equip their own members.

10. *Handbook for Great Commission Ministries*, 23, 37 ff.

11. Learn more about these six roles in the Great Commission in the GMMI *Handbook for Great Commission Ministries*, available through IGNITE Media, 115-123.

12. Learn more about a step by step strategy for multiplying mission mobilization movements utilized by GMMI through the GMMI Facilitation Manual, available through IGNITE Media.

13. Unpublished paper by Randy Mitchell titled Presentation For the Anglican Church of Nigeria.

14. Randy Mitchell Unpublished Paper.

15. Jason Mandryk. *Operation World: 7th Edition* (Colorado Springs: Biblica Publishing, 2010), 610.

16. Operation World Webpage – South Sudan - https://operationworld.org/locations/south-sudan/.

17. Arabic is the sixth hardest language to learn for English speakers according to this article - https://www.jumpspeak.com/blog/hardest-languages-to-learn.

18. In GMMI circles, we call these Mobilization Coordinators. They serve to mobilize their ministry structures with a vision for global mission using a proven step by step strategy. For more info on these leaders and how GMMI serves them, please click here - https://www.globalmmi.net/movements/mobilization-coordinators.

19. Much of this prayer section has been adapted from the GMMI *Handbook for Great Commission Ministries* found here - https://www.globalmmi.net/product/handbook-for-great-commission-ministries, published by IGNITE Media.

20. Find a comprehensive listing of apostolic prayers in the *Handbook for Great Commission Ministries*, 89-93, available through IGNITE Media.

21. GMMI provides a mobilization tool along this line for local ministries called Great Commission Bible Studies. Learn more here – GlobalMMI.Net.

22. Jason Mandryk, *Operation World: The Definitive Prayer Guide To Every Nation*. Biblica, 2010.

23. Joshua Project Website - https://joshuaproject.net/.

Chapter 16: Scattering Message Bearer Teams to the Unreached

1. We use the term "scattering" in this context in the most positive sense, understanding it is often a term used to refer to something negative. This is explained later in the chapter. Please note a definition in the glossary.

2. Allen, *Spontaneous Expansion*, 9.

3. Allen, 10.

4. Ralph Winter, in his breakthrough presentation at Lausanne 1974, labeled three types of

evangelism to three different groups – E-1 is evangelism from one person of the same culture to another; E-2 evangelism is from one culture to a near culture to their own; E-3 evangelism goes from one culture to a distant culture. These three levels of scattering are based on this E-Scale. *Perspectives* Reader, Ralph Winter, William Carey Library, 347-360.

5. This is the well documented concept of influencing the Seven Pillars of Society with the Gospel.

6. Please see the author's book, *Proclaiming the Kingdom*, for a five-phase user-friendly guide to bear the message of Christ.

7. Dave Ramsey, "Dave's Advice on Tithing and Giving," *Ramsey Solutions*, https://www.ramseysolutions.com/budgeting/daves-advice-on-tithing-and-giving.

8. Weinlick, John R. *Count Zinzendorf: The Story of His Life and Leadership In the Renewed Moravian Church* (Bethlehem: The Moravian Church In America, 1984), 100.

9. Tucker, Ruth A. *From Jerusalem To Irian Jaya: A Biographical History of Christian Missions* (Grand Rapids: Zondervan Academie, 1983), 69.

10. Pierson, *The Dynamics of Christian Mission*, 190.

11. Email correspondence with Dr. David Lim about this historically connected interpretation.

12. Adapted from the author's study guide *Studies in the Sermon on the Mount*, available through IGNITE Media.

13. J. Hudson Taylor, *A Retrospect: The Story Behind My Zeal For Missions* (Aneko, 2015), 41.

14. Paul E. Pierson, *Themes From Acts*, 12-13.

15. I am indebted to the writings of G. Campbell Morgan, Arthur W. Pink and William Barclay on this parable.

16. Ryan Shaw, Studies in *Jesus' Parables of the Kingdom* (USA: IGNITE Media, 2018) p. 19-29, available through IGNITE Media.

17. G. Campbell Morgan, *Parables of the Kingdom*, 59.

18. Morgan, *Parables*, 56.

19. Morgan, *Parables*, 57.

20. The Holy Bible, American Standard Version (ASV), (Thomas Nelson, Inc. 1901).

21. Morgan, *Parables*, 54.

22. Status of Global Christianity, 2021, In the Context of 1900 – 2050. https://www.gordon-conwell.edu/center-for-global-christianity/wp-content/uploads/sites/13/2020/12/Status-of-Global-Christianity-2021.pdf.

23. Missionary Statistics - http://missionaryportal.webflow.io/stats.

24. See the author's book *Spiritual Equipping For Mission: Thriving As God's Message Bearers* (Downer's Grove: InterVarsity Press, 2014).

25. See part 3 (and chapters 11, 12, 13 in particular) for more about the mission eras of history and where we are now.

Chapter 17: Cultivating Church Planting Movements

1. I am indebted to the writings about Church Planting Movements of David Garrison (Church Planting Movements), Greg Livingstone (Planting Churches in Muslim Cities) and David Watson (Contagious Disciple-Making) in this chapter.

2. McGavran, *Understanding Church Growth*, 31.

3. Ralph D. Winter, "Gimmickitis," *Church Growth Bulletin*, January 1966.

4. Using the suggested numbers in the previous chapter, we can guesstimate the number of message bearer teams the Lord intends to scatter. Of 620 million believers globally who are fruitful Christians, 20 percent engage in Level Two and Level Three Scattering as message bearers = 124 million. If we average a message bearer team as 10 believers, dividing 124 million believers by 10, we get 12.4 million message bearer teams scattered among near and distant culture unreached peoples.

5. Clinton, *Clinton's Biblical Leadership Commentary*, 535

6. Personal email correspondence with Dr. David Lim, April 2021.
7. David Watson, *Contagious Disciple Making*, 13.
8. David Garrison, *Church Planting Movements* (Richmond: IMB, 2000), 7.
9. Jerry Trousdale, *Miraculous Movements*, 111.
10. David Garrison, *Booklet on Church Planting Movements*, 41.
11. Reports on Church Planting Movements at Ethne Conference in Seoul, South Korea, December 2012.
12. David Garrison, *Booklet on Church Planting Movements*, 43.
13. Unpublished Booklet on Igniting Church Planting Movements; How to Run the Race God's Way by Tom Adleta, 12.
14. Garrison, *Church Planting Movements*, 42.
15. Garrison, Booklet titled *Church Planting Movements*, 33.
16. Trousdale, *Miraculous Movements*, 127 -141.
17. Garrison, Booklet on *Church Planting Movements*, 33.
18. The author's book *Proclaiming the Kingdom* has been designed with the purpose of pre-conversion discipleship in mind. There are many other resources available meeting this same purpose, including Discovery Bible Studies.
19. Trousdale, *Miraculous Movements*, 106-107.
20. Watson, Contagious Disciple Making, 143.
21. Article titled How Are People Actually Coming to Faith Today - https://www.biola.edu/blogs/biola-magazine/2016/how-are-people-actually-coming-to-faith-today.
22. Discovery Bible Studies like Creation to Christ are popular.
23. Ryan Shaw, *Proclaiming the Kingdom: A Roadmap For Bearing God's Message Among All Peoples*. Armstrong: IGNITE Media, 2018.
24. We consider this end goal of cross-cultural mission in detail in chapter 18.
25. Garrison, *Church Planting Movements*, 38.
26. Trousdale, *Miraculous Movements*, 117.
27. Garrison, *Church Planting Movements*, 35.
28. Trousdale, *Miraculous Movements*, 117.
29. See the author's book *Proclaiming the Kingdom*, available through IGNITE Media.
30. Garrison, *Church Planting Movements*, 35.
31. Watson, *Contagious Disciple Making*, 170.
32. Garrison, booklet on *Church Planting Movements*, 38.
33. Garrison, 37.

Chapter 18: Igniting People Movements to Christ

1. This is a term popularized by Donald McGavran in the 1950s. It is a crucial concept few in the mission movement discuss today. It needs resurrecting as it holds keys to seeing ministry breakthrough's among unreached people groups. I am indebted to McGavran as much of this chapter is adapted from McGavran's crucial insights and contributions as very few scholars have written much on the concept of "People Movements to Christ."
2. Robert Recker, Chapter on "What Are People Movements" in Harvie Conn's *Theological Perspectives on Church Growth*, 80.
3. Donald McGavran, *The Bridges of God: A Study in the Strategy of Missions* (London: World Dominion Press, 1955), 9.
4. *Perspectives on the World Christian Movement* Fourth Edition, Chapter 106 titled "Evangelization of Whole Families" by Wee Hian Chua, 654.
5. Hiebert, Paul G. *Anthropological Insights for Missionaries* (Grand Rapids: Baker Books, 1985), 51.
6. Notes recorded in my personal journal following this exchange in August 2018.
7. S. D. Ponraj, *Church Planting Approach to Mission*, 6.

8. Jerry Trousdale, *Miraculous Movements*, 111-126.
9. Hedlund, Roger E. *Evangelization and Church Growth: Issues From The Asian Context* (Madras: McGavran Institute, 1992), 93-94.
10. Donald McGavran's precise definition of "People Movements," *Understanding Church Growth*, 223.
11. Robert Recker, Chapter on "What Are People Movements" in Harvie Conn's *Theological Perspectives on Church Growth*, 79
12. Recker, 80.
13. Waskom Pickett, *Christian Mass Movements In India* (Lucknow: Lucknow Publishing House, 1933), 330
14. Recker, *What Are People Movements*, 80.
15. See the author's book *Proclaiming the Kingdom: A Roadmap For Bearing God's Message Among All Peoples.*
16. McGavran, *Understanding Church Growth*, 123.
17. Rich and Lisa Cho, "The Fastest Growing Church In Thailand's History," OMF Thailand - https://omf.org/thailand/2018/08/29/the-fastest-growing-church-in-thailands-history/.
18. Dwight Martin, *Free in Jesus Christ Church Association Church Planting Movement in Central Thailand*, Unpublished Booklet, 2.
19. Katie Bracy, "They Made CT's Cover and Now They Are Using Their Voices To Redefine Global Missions," *Christianity Today*, https://www.christianitytoday.org/stories/what-people-are-saying/2020/they-made-cts-cover-now-theyre-using-their-voices-to-redefi.html.
20. McGavran, *The Bridges of God*, 9.
21. McGavran, 17- 23.
22. Webpage - http://www.generationword.com/bible_school_notes/Timelinepercent20of-percent20Acts.htm.
23. McGavran, 19.
24. McGavran, 21.
25. McGavran, 23.
26. Recker, *What Are People Movements*, 85-86.

GLOSSARY

1. Paul Pierson, *Themes From Acts*, 11.
2. Joshua Project - https://joshuaproject.net/help/definitions - Unreached People Groups.
3. Garrison, *Church Planting Movements*, 7.
4. Donald McGavran's precise definition of "People Movements," *Understanding Church Growth*, 223.
5. Robert Recker, Chapter on "What Are People Movements" in Harvie Conn's *Theological Perspectives on Church Growth*, 79.
6. Recker, 80.

About the Author

Ryan Shaw has been personally involved in mission mobilization across the global Church for twenty years, traveling to over 65 nations in a mobilization capacity, primarily in the global south. The last fifteen years have included direct involvement in training ministry leaders in mission mobilization. He, his wife Kelly and their two children, Noah and Emma, have lived outside their home country (USA) for the last seventeen years, three and half in Canada, four in Turkey and the last ten years in Chiang Mai, Thailand. This has been strategically purposeful as the epicenter of missions and mobilization is shifting from the West. He has observed firsthand the global Church's limited outlook on mission mobilization while conversely seeing the transformation possible when local ministries prioritize mission mobilization within the life of their fellowships.

Ryan is a fourth-generation message bearer (alternative term for missionary). His great-grandparents and grandparents served in south India and then the Philippines from the late 1930's to 1950's. Ryan's parents did Bible translation with Wycliffe Bible Translators in the western highlands of Papua New Guinea from 1969–1982, where he spent his first seven years. Ryan has a Bachelor's degree in Christian Ministries (1997) from Azusa Pacific University (Azusa, CA) and a Master's degree in Intercultural Studies (2001) from Fuller Theological Seminary's School of Intercultural Studies (Pasadena, CA).

Ryan serves as President/International Lead Facilitator of an international mission mobilization resourcing ministry called *Global Mission Mobilization Initiative (GMMI)*, formerly called Student Volunteer Movement 2 (SVM2), which he helped found in late 2002. GMMI changed the name in 2019 as the ministry's emphasis in mobilization widened from predominantly focused on the student generation to the wider body of Christ. GMMI has its international headquarters in Chiang Mai, Thailand along with its *Global Mobilization Institute,* providing specialized training for mission mobilizers, pastors, ministry leaders and message bearers from diverse nations, organizations, ministries, and denominations across the body of Christ.

Ryan is the author of twelve mission, mobilization and Bible study related books and study guides. He speaks internationally for conferences, seminars, and churches and can be reached at <u>rshaw@globalmmi.net</u>.

GlobalMMI.net

GMMI serves the global Church as a resourcing ministry for the growing mission mobilization movement through:

- *Mobilizing* tools, strategies, prayer initiatives, conferences
- *Equipping* trainings, internships, teachings, materials

Core Objectives:

- Multiplying mission mobilization movements (within national associations, church/ denomination/ organization networks, local ministries) using proven strategies
- Empowering mission mobilizers who mobilize, coach, and equip ministry structures
- Producing high quality, strategic, mobilizing, and equipping tools, materials and resources serving the global Church
- Discerning and emphasizing biblical, Spirit-led models and core messages of mission mobilization through teaching resources, training schools and courses
- Cultivating a spiritual community in Chiang Mai, Thailand, of interns, staff and students strengthening the mission mobilization movement globally
- Spiritually contending (through prayer, worship, as a voice, training, perseverance) for all God wants to release through mission mobilization in the global Church

IGNITE Media is the media arm of GMMI providing high quality tools and materials (books, booklets, bible studies, blog) as well as a podcast, teaching library and other resources serving local ministries in the growing mission mobilization movement. Check out our selection of resources at **www.globalmmi.net/ignite-resource-store** or contact **ignitemedia@globalmmi.net**. You can find all of Ryan Shaw's books and studies at IGNITE Media.

CONNECT WITH US

Connect with Ryan:

- FACEBOOK – facebook.com/Ryan.Shaw0809/
- EMAIL – RSHAW@GLOBALMMI.NET

Learn More About GMMI:

- WEBSITE – GLOBALMMI.NET
- FACEBOOK – facebook.com/GMMIOnline
- EMAIL – INFO@GLOBALMMI.NET

Learn More About Rethinking Global Mobilization and Other IGNITE Media Resources:

- WEBSITE – RETHINKINGMOBILIZATION.COM
- WEBSITE – globalmmi.net/ignite-resource-store
- EMAIL – IGNITEMEDIA@GLOBALMMI.NET

Printed in Great Britain
by Amazon

22178600R00175